1) relationships are essential to a successful college experience.

2)

How
College
WORKS

How College **WORKS**

Daniel F. Chambliss

Christopher G. Takacs

Harvard University Press
Cambridge, Massachusetts
London, England

First Harvard University Press paperback edition, 2018
Second Printing

Library of Congress Cataloging-in-Publication Data
Chambliss, Daniel F., 1953–
How college works / Daniel F. Chambliss, Christopher G. Takacs.
pages cm
Includes bibliographical references and index.
ISBN 978-0-674-04902-4 (cloth : alk.paper)
ISBN 978-0-674-97980-2 (pbk.)
1. College students.   I. Takacs, Christopher G.   II. Title.
LA229.C43 2013
378—dc23   2013018548

For my teachers, Penny Rosel and Kai Erikson.
—*Dan*

For my parents, William and Donna.
—*Chris*

Contents

How
College
WORKS

1

The Search for a Solution

In an era of fixed or even shrinking resources, can the quality of collegiate education be improved at no additional cost? Can students get more out of college without spending more money? We believe the answer is yes. We believe that there are methods—simultaneously reliable, powerful, available, and cheap—for improving what students gain from college. Such methods consistently work well, handsomely repay whatever effort goes into them, can be used by almost anyone, and require not much time and almost no additional money. When one knows where to look, these methods are available both to formally designated higher education leaders—deans, presidents, department chairs, and program heads—and also in varying degrees to individual professors, to parents, and even to students themselves. With a basic understanding of how college works, we suggest, almost anyone ready to act can noticeably improve what students get out of college. This book, then, describes the crucial experiences of a good undergraduate education, and formulates some effective interventions—methods for improvement—usable by leaders who want to make a difference.

To learn how college works, we began by trying to understand students' own lives in college; after all, that is ultimately what leaders would like to influence. For ten years we followed a random sample of nearly one hundred students at our own institution (we'll call it "the college"; the research and institution are more fully described below), trying to spot those decisive moments that changed the direction or intensity of their experience.

We quickly realized that students' perspective is often significantly, and consequentially, different from that of administrators, teachers, and adults in general. They just see things differently. Consider incoming students' view of their academic responsibilities. Freshman year happens long, long before senior year; it can be an overwhelming experience whose immediacy drowns out much longer-term planning. Academics are logistically important, but they are not necessarily the central activity in college.[1] Students don't automatically assume that academic work is worthwhile; unfamiliar disciplines in particular need to be legitimated in their eyes. When students choose their courses, they give less attention to official "advisors" than to friends, dormmates, parents, and—when actually sitting at a computer and registering for courses—the online class schedule, which tells them what is open and fits their schedule. In making these choices, students base their registration decisions on the limited information that is easily available to them, irrespective of what may be "in the catalog," on websites, or in the emails sent by academic advisors. Once enrolled, students are affected only by courses they actually take—all others are irrelevant, however good, or interesting, or rigorous, they may be for their own enrollees. (A seemingly obvious point, yes, but with huge implications.) When it's all done, then, any one student is touched by only a few courses and a small percentage of professors; even among those few teachers, only one or two might really have a lasting impact. From an administrator's perspective, then, students' lived worlds can seem quite limited, their lines of sight rather short and their angle of vision rather narrow.

So while it's important to understand and respect students' experience— that is, after all, what leaders are trying to influence—one can't assume that the students' own prescriptions for improving college will be correct. Freshmen don't realize, for instance, that the dorms they may least prefer (long institutional hallways, shared bathrooms, multiple roommates) may in fact be the most helpful in their own search for friends on campus. They don't realize that in calling for "smaller classes" they are in fact calling for limits to their own chances of getting into those classes. In opting for double majors, they may not see that later options will thus become closed to them. In Richard Light's groundbreaking book about education at Harvard, *Making the Most of College*, students said that some of their most valuable courses were in foreign languages, but it doesn't follow that colleges should just require that students take more language courses. Instead, scholars need to discover why such classes are valuable—they must discover how college works—and then see whether that understanding can be applied more broadly.

The Beginnings of an Answer

Students in college face a roughly chronological sequence of predictable major challenges, named in our chapter titles. First, they must successfully enter the social world of college, most importantly by finding friends. Failing that, little else matters. Then they must make academic choices—what courses to take, what major to declare, and which professors to study with, ask advice of, and get help from. A bit later, after settling in with a group of friends, students gain from establishing broader networks that connect them to the opportunities available in the college community generally. Throughout those years, they try to master the various academic learning tasks in their program. Finally, they consolidate whatever gains they've made in their college years, and prepare to move on. In the following chapters we describe how students handle these challenges and how the college's own practices help or hinder them.

More striking to us, though, was one particular detail of how students mastered these challenges—one detail, we might say, of how college actually works in helping students succeed. Time after time, in descriptions of a wide variety of situations, students told us of how encounters with the right person could make a decisive difference in their college careers. At orientation, Maudie, who planned to major in psychology, happened to meet a nice professor in the Chinese Department; within two years Maudie was living and studying full time in Beijing. When George arrived, he was assigned to a "quad" with three roommates—who became three of his best friends. In his freshman dorm Dan met a nice young woman, a tutor in the college's Writing Center, who taught him the basics of good composition, which he had never learned in high school. John was a football player, but when he joined an *a cappella* group, it opened new networks and then new opportunities in musical theatre. Hannah met a helpful philosophy professor who became acquainted with her interests, and then directed her to yet another professor in anthropology, where she found a wonderful academic home. When Claire almost accidentally stumbled into an art history class with Professor Swanson, she "was hooked" and quickly shifted her scheduling and her major. Time and again, a single dinner at a professor's home, or a single focused conversation with a professor about the student's work, seemed to have an outsized impact on the student's success—for very little effort by the professor. Human contact, especially face to face, seems to have an unusual influence on what students choose to do, on the directions their careers take, and on their experience of college.[2] It has leverage, producing positive results far beyond the effort put into it.

More generally, person-to-person relationships are fundamental at every stage—before, during, and after the core learning activities of college:

1. Satisfactory personal relationships are a *prerequisite* for learning. Only by having friends will students "buy into" the college experience at all, and devote the time and effort to learning. Students who fail to find friends, or at least workable substitutes, are likely to drop out of college, if not officially then at least emotionally. As Vincent Tinto has argued, student persistence in college "entails the incorporation, that is integration, of the individual as a competent member in the social and intellectual (academic) communities of the college."[3]

2. Personal connections are often the *central mechanism and daily motivators* of the student experience. A respected teacher who invites students into her home can become a role model for intellectual life; friends who study seriously increase one's own time studying; intense arguments with dormmates often provide the most salient moral education. When their friends go abroad, students are more likely to do so; when a professor sits down for a one-on-one writing conference, the student will concentrate more on her writing.[4] Faculty-student interactions both inside and outside the classroom have dramatic effects on student learning.[5] Students' motivation is dramatically variable, even within a single course,[6] and that motivation often depends on connections to other people. (Of course, "peer effects" are not always positive: peers can increase binge drinking,[7] and some evidence suggests that participating in Greek-letter organizations can hurt academic work.)[8] Especially at crucial turning points, we found, face-to-face interactions can be decisive, for good or ill. Peers seem to especially matter when they coalesce into what we call "microcommunities," organized around their own values, meeting regularly, and providing networks to other friends and acquaintances.

3. Finally, for countless students, long-lasting friendships with fellow students and sometimes teachers are a *major result* of the college experience. Alumni frequently told us that friendships were the most valuable result of their undergraduate years, overshadowing even

treasured academic gains. It's well known, too, that college can be a fabulous marriage market.[9] A closeness to others unmatched in later life; relationships that last a lifetime; a network of friends called on in time of need, as well as the extended network of alumni helpful in job searches—all of these can infuse the undergraduate experience with emotional significance and depth, beyond even the acquisition of important technical skills.

This pervasive influence of relationships suggests that a college—at least insofar as it offers real benefits—is less a collection of *programs* than a gathering of *people*. Programs matter, to be sure. Certainly, to learn physics properly one must at some point study electricity and magnetism, and every university needs departments of literature and mathematics. At colleges like St. John's, Columbia, and the University of Chicago, well-designed core curricula that are supported by the senior faculty reliably offer serious undergraduate educations. Excellent curricula and imaginative programs can attract better students and professors—that is, the right people. And some programs are so central to a specific institution that they are arguably inseparable from the faculty itself. Some programs at the college worked quite well indeed: a nationally recognized college-wide writing program; a wildly popular preorientation outdoor leadership program; and a perennially strong choral music program, for instance. All had strong and committed leadership, all easily meshed with the long-standing culture of the college, and all brought people together in time and space in ways that tapped, and then cultivated, already-existing student motivation. Regardless, all such curricula are difficult to design, organize, and maintain; their results are often uncertain; and in every case, they depend for success on the quality of the personnel committed to them. Curriculum is nice, but may not be fundamental for a good college. But good people, brought together in the right ways, we suspect are both necessary and perhaps even sufficient to create a good college.

The *people* (friends, acquaintances, teachers, staff) whom a student encounters matter more than the *programs* because the people are alive—or more precisely, because they can instantaneously adjust to the shifting needs and interests of their fellow creatures, the students. Most college students are not relentlessly focused on a single goal, nor is a good college a single-purpose factory that churns out one clearly defined product. More like a church or even a family, a college serves multiple interests which are constantly shifting, even for those individual students. Thoughtful teachers and administrators know that. Yes, the students we studied gained academic skills (see Chapter 6) such as writing, speaking, data analysis, and critical thinking, as well as the specialized knowledge and techniques of various disciplines. But they also realized other gains, which they often considered more important: finding friends, mentors, or life partners; dramatically improving their confidence in facing challenges; even gaining an eagerness to try new things and to enter adult life with optimism. For some students, the four years' experience in itself, even apart from any later payoffs, was worth the time and expense. Therefore, getting the right people together at the right time is the single best thing that leaders can do. In our research, students who were somewhat opportunistic in their goals, who shifted their efforts according to what they found available (better teachers, more engaged fellow students, new activities) were regularly more satisfied overall, and at least in that sense more successful in college. Having helpful people (teachers, friends) readily available makes all these gains possible.

Criteria for Recommendations

So how might that be achieved? Leaders at all levels who want to help students are stopped by a host of obstacles and shortages: political opposition, competing priorities, lack of money or personnel, or just a shortage of their own energy. What they need are workable solutions, not utopian visions, expensive new initiatives, piles of additional work, or huge fights with the faculty. Throughout this book we try to develop recommendations, presented in full in Chapter 8, on which leaders can readily act with a good chance of success. Because our goal is to realistically maximize those odds—that is, for improvements that might actually come about—we used four criteria in developing recommended actions:

1. They should be *effective*, as shown by research; they should demonstrably and reliably produce substantial benefits, so that effort spent in pursuing them is not wasted.
2. They should be highly *leveraged*, so a small effort produces disproportionately positive results; payoffs should be quick, so as to reinforce the parties involved. That way, at least ideally, efforts become self-sustaining and don't require ongoing work.

3. They should be at least close to *resource neutral*, not requiring major new infusions of money, time, or people. Few institutions these days have extra resources just lying around.
4. They should be widely *available*, so that the full range of leaders can use at least some of them. No one should have to wait on a president's approval, or a vote of the faculty, or the completion of new buildings, to start acting.

These criteria are rigorous. They quickly exclude a host of popular and potentially good ideas whose value seems well established. Student research or senior projects, for instance, which we agree provide major benefits, are at the same time quite expensive, especially in terms of faculty time. Freshman seminars as well entail both obvious and hidden costs that may not be justified by the gains (see Chapter 4). Calls for reconfiguring the entire professoriate to "be more student friendly," or to adopt new pedagogical methods, or to absorb the latest research in the neuroscience of learning, sound good, but are unlikely to bear fruit because they would require dramatic changes in the work habits of many people. Curricular reform and strategic planning, perennial fillers of faculty calendars, require huge time investments, often with too little to show in positive results. Online courses obviously increase access to some version of college, but the corresponding loss of face-to-face contact could prove damaging to students' motivation. Finally, at the national level, the universal adoption, under federal and accreditor duress, of sweeping assessment reforms over the past decade has entailed tremendous labor costs with little actual evidence of improvement to collegiate education. All such efforts have their partisans, but few reliably deliver benefits to students.

Reforms are often praised precisely for being big and dramatic rather than for being small and effective. After all, it's more fun to talk about Big Solutions. In this book, by contrast, we want to find the smallest possible solutions yielding the greatest possible impact. We think the power of personal contact may be the key element in such solutions.

The College

In our research we closely studied students at a single institution—Hamilton College in Clinton, New York. We are fully aware of the advantages and drawbacks of such "case study" research. One advantage is obvious: Hamilton is our own college, so we know it intimately. Dan has taught there since 1981 and Chris was an undergraduate between 2001 and 2005. Located at roughly the geographic center of New York State, Clinton is rural, bucolic, somewhat isolated, and—importantly for campus life—in the center of New York's "snow belt"; the area averages about 100 inches of snowfall each year. Chartered in 1812, in many respects Hamilton (we'll call it "the college") is a stereotypical New England liberal arts college. Just over 1,800 students are enrolled, 53 percent women and 47 percent men. Set in a beautiful 1,350-acre campus atop a wooded hill, the college is expensive (over $53,000 in comprehensive fees in 2011–2012), with lavish facilities. A well-paid faculty of over 180 full-time professors, plus part-timers and adjuncts, gives it a nine-to-one student-faculty ratio. Its endowment in the early 2000s stood near three-quarters of a billion dollars, and the percentage of its 20,000 alumni donating in a given year put it in the top 1 percent of all higher education institutions in the country. In the years of our research the acceptance rate ranged closely around 30 percent, while around 50 percent of students received financial aid, including grants, loans, or work. SAT score submission was optional, but at a minimum, one-third of each entering class had scores between 650 and 740. (In other words, the students aren't in the nation's very top tier, but they're close.) Around one-fifth of enrolled students were multicultural.

Overall, then, the college is small, rich, and selective. It's also secular, undergraduate only, teaching-centered, and—unusual even for small liberal arts colleges—lacking the standard distribution requirements. Its students are not typical American college students. We recognize that. In a host of ways, upper-income students such as those so numerous at the college have advantages at every stage of education. They come from stronger secondary schools (often with "feeder" links to elite colleges) where they had higher test scores, more extracurricular activities, more documented "talents," and even better athletic abilities than their less-fortunate peers. They have far more access to good counseling, expensive tutoring, AP courses, high-rank teaching, and the best admission counseling, and their parents are more likely to understand the college admission game (and the college experience itself), since they're more likely themselves to have attended selective colleges.[10] Once in college, they are more likely than their less-fortunate peers to successfully integrate both socially and academically.

So the disadvantage of studying the college is clear: it is not like most of American higher education. It's neither a large public research nor a regional university, nor an urban community college, nor a conservative religious college, although we hope to offer those schools some useful ideas. We can't even try to be relevant to the recent expansions of higher education into the for-profit sector, online universities, MOOCs, and the like. These new models have changed the very meaning of words like "campus," "classes," "college," and even "university." They may offer valuable programs, but they are neither what college has traditionally been nor what we are talking about: a physical gathering of young adults where personal growth is conjoined with intellectual development. The college certainly fits the older definition, and is an almost classic model of an American college, but we are fully aware that it's not typical.

Still, in studying students at a single institution, close up, we hoped to learn how college actually works in students' daily lives. Both within and between colleges, there are huge variations in how much students progress,[11] and we see those variations play out even within the college. Well-prepared students sometimes do poorly; students "at risk" often do quite well, graduating at higher rates than their peers at less selective institutions; and students in between learn a great deal or fall apart. Our goal here is first to discover the mechanisms—the social processes—that lead students down or away from certain pathways,[12] and second to determine how these processes might be leveraged to improve college education. We wanted to know why such variations happen, in order to identify institutional mechanisms that might help any student at any institution.[13]

The case study of students at one institution also allowed us to see how institutional policies actually affect students. We were able to follow a sizable number of individual students, over time; gather additional data on specific issues as they arose; watch, at close range, the effect of modified policies and new initiatives (for instance, the rise and fall of a mandatory sophomore seminar, and the dropping of distribution requirements); retrace our steps when our earlier methods proved inadequate; and in the end, pull together findings that do justice to how specific policies and programs work together (or compete), rather than artificially isolating universal "best practices" whose effectiveness may easily depend on context. We could get beneath statistical correlations and discover, for instance, the path-dependent mechanisms by which students choose courses and majors; the importance of peers and professors in sustaining student motivation; and the dynamics through which some extracurriculars expand, but others drastically limit, students' access to peers.

Given our pragmatic aims, some major topics in higher education must be set aside for now. Social class, most importantly, is a crucial predictor of students' educational success, and is central to debates in sociology regarding whether higher education is an engine of social mobility (helping people move up) or instead a reproducer of inequality. These are critically important scientific and policy questions, but they cannot be ours. Yes, social class is vital, but the fact is, it's not yet clear what leaders within particular institutions—our audience—are supposed to do about it. Lifting all children in America out of poverty would dramatically improve the country's educational results. But no dean or president, however influential, can just change her current students' history or background. It's a bit like the argument we heard once at a higher education conference where a state governor, describing how important high school preparation is to college success, said, "Our first step must be to improve high schools, by raising standards and requirements." The college leaders filling this large room were left baffled and muttering; why was he telling *them* this? We want to know, instead, what people working in colleges can actually do.

The Research

Beginning in 1999, and continuing until the end of June 2010, supported by a series of major grants from the Andrew W. Mellon Foundation, Hamilton College undertook a longitudinal, multimethod, comprehensive effort at "assessment of liberal arts education and student outcomes at a residential college." Our work was to consider the very broad array of outcomes available to students in college, from job skills and disciplinary information to personal development, ethical growth, and the fostering of friendships. The challenge was to conduct a single-institution case study that might be helpful not only to other small colleges, but also to the vast range of higher education institutions.

Our research was applied social science, using all the methods of our discipline in pursuit of practical, not theoretical, knowledge. Dan Chambliss is a sociologist with thirty years' experience in researching the social psychology of organizations. He has served as director of the Mellon Assessment Project since its inception. In 2004, Chris Takacs, a former student assistant, joined Chambliss in leading the Project; since 2007, he has been a graduate student in the sociology PhD program at the University of Chicago. We have been supported over the years by a Faculty Working Group, an administrative assistant, scores of student assistants, and a number of professional research consultants.

During the Project's first year (1999–2000), the Faculty Working Group developed three guiding principles. First, we would start from the student experience, not the college's efforts (initiatives, courses, majors, activities). We cared about what students could gain from going through college. Heeding warnings from the literature, we didn't assume that such gains necessarily occurred through courses, or teachers, or curricula.[14] Too often, assessment—mistakenly, we think—measures the success of courses, professors, pedagogies, and departments. The problem with that approach is that professors can get good evaluations by teaching seminars filled with groupies. Entire departments can be outstanding taken on their own, but still be irrelevant to most students. A college can have thirty-five excellent academic departments (as measured by the standard department review) out of forty, and still be producing poor student outcomes—if most students are in the remaining five departments. A college's proper goal isn't to have a pile of good programs or departments; it's to have well-educated students. So we tracked students to see how their college careers progressed. In social science parlance, the student experience was our "unit of analysis."

Second, to accurately represent the range of student experience at the college, we relied on scientific sampling of the student body. One needn't evaluate every individual in a population to learn what's happening, but the selection of representatives should be careful. We used a statistically random sample for our central "panel" study of one hundred; a "census" of all students for transcript, Senior Survey, and course-evaluation studies; and more deliberately chosen groups for several focus group studies—for example, Dean's List students, returnees from study abroad, and science majors.

Finally, our work was to be multimethod, using all of the available tools of social science, to offset the intrinsic weaknesses of particular research methods. We rely heavily on face-to-face interviews with students, but students' comments about class sizes and availability were cross-checked against actual enrollment and registration data. To validate interesting but potentially misleading anecdotes from interviews, we used a number of large-scale standardized surveys, carefully sampled and quantitatively evaluated. Student progress in writing was assessed using (1) students' own papers, blind-evaluated by outsiders; (2) interviews with the students themselves about their (self-perceived) progress; and (3) questionnaire surveys of entire graduating classes, cross-referencing the results to understand what factors seem in fact to be most important. Focus groups revealed the vigorous emotional reaction of Dean's List students to various financial aid policies; routine course evaluations uncovered weaknesses in a required seminar program. Finally, we employed student research assistants who themselves were living their college lives. In numerous debriefing sessions, they corrected our oversights and possible misunderstandings of answers and context. In general, we tried to work as careful social scientists, balancing belief in our findings with a healthy dose of skepticism, and working in conformity with regular professional standards.[15]

These principles (the student as unit of analysis, careful sampling, multiple research methods) were applied in a range of studies:[16]

1. *The Alumni Interviews.*   We began by sketching the big picture. In 1999, with a one-year planning grant from the Mellon Foundation, we conducted a simple interview study of alumni, telephoning a random sample of one hundred graduates either five or ten years after their leaving the college—long enough for them to have understood some of the real results of their education, but short enough for the college to have remained basically unchanged since their attendance. We successfully interviewed seventy-eight of these graduates, asking half a dozen open-ended questions: "Overall, how would you characterize your time at the college?" "What were the best and worst aspects of your experience . . . ?" and so on.

In our eleven years of student outcomes assessment, this study was probably the most effective tool we found; we recommend it highly. At little cost, in a short time, we learned valuable information that was easily and broadly applicable. For instance: (1) a handful of professors had vastly disproportionate impact; (2) some of the most valuable outcomes were social, not academic; and (3) faculty aspirations about changing students' view on life were—well, a bit inflated. Some alums, in fact, were baffled by a question we asked about "crucial experiences" and the major life changes resulting from college, indicating they had little interest in such transformative outcomes. It was a huge disappointment to our faculty interviewers! (However, at the same time, alums who had gone abroad did say that doing so probably was a transformative experience.) Other findings—the importance of good introductory classes—were more immediately useful, and the results were reported to the faculty at regularly scheduled meetings.

2. *The Panel Study.*   Alumni interviews, though, are retrospective, and memories fade or sometimes brighten a bit too much. How do students actually achieve gains in real time? At the heart of our research lies a ten-year repeated-interview study with enrolled students. In the fall of 2001, we drew a random sample of one hundred members of the incoming class. These students would constitute what researchers call a "panel," to be followed throughout their college careers and for at least five years afterwards. For each year in college, and every two years beyond that, our student assistants conducted detailed interviews with each member of this panel, ranging from thirty minutes to an hour and a half.

As of 2011—six years after graduation, for most—eighty-four of the one hundred remained in our sample, an excellent retention rate by social science standards. At the outset, five of the selected panelists refused to talk with us; eleven others dropped out or were lost at different points along the way. In any given year, we talked with around sixty to seventy, and twenty-five participated in all six rounds of interviews between 2001 and 2009. By the end of our work, we had completed a total of 394 interviews. Panelists' own words and stories were central to our analysis and appear throughout this book as illustrations of our findings. We've given the students pseudonyms to protect their privacy. (We've also pseudonymized all dormitories and particular campus organizations for the same reason.) After much thought, we've also taken the liberty of editing their remarks for clarity. Most of our readers have never seen unedited, verbatim transcripts of contemporary college students talking informally to a peer; let's just say, it doesn't always represent the best in standard English usage. The filler word "like" can be annoyingly frequent, so we've cut many of those, for instance. In no case, we believe, has the substance of what students said been modified. Although anthropologists might argue that some cultural flavor is lost, we think that eliminating needless distractions was worth it. We also collected essays and papers the panelists wrote during college, and received from the Admission Office copies of high school papers they had submitted with their college applications. From the Registrar, we received the students' transcript information, to learn what courses they took, in what order, with what grades, and from which professors.

In total, then, a panelist's file included both self-report and objective data on that student's work and experience throughout college and for a time afterwards, seen from multiple angles. Such detailed quantitative and qualitative longitudinal data are quite expensive to obtain in terms of time, administrative labor, and the commitment of research staff. But they capture their students' experiences relatively soon after they happen, avoiding some of the pitfalls of retrospective observations. In reading through each panelist's interviews in chronological order, we could identify where students faced (apparently) minor choices that proved to be major turning points; how their early, sometimes passionate, commitments often limited their options farther down the road; and even how memories of their early years became subtly distorted with the passage of time. Only with longitudinal data, following individuals over years, could we discover the existence of the pathways that, once chosen, could easily lead students to different destinations.

3. *The Senior Survey Database.*   Interviews from our Panel Study provide rich, vivid details, but standing alone they can be misleading. Dramatic anecdotes may not actually be typical. It's also difficult to generalize from the inevitably small samples. Standardized, quantifiable surveys, by contrast, can ensure the reliability of research findings. For many years, the college has annually administered a Senior Survey to all graduating students in the week before commencement. The survey is designed and used by members of the Higher Education Data Sharing Consortium, an association of more than one hundred private colleges and universities across the United States. The eighty-plus questions on the survey cover a wide range of issues—academic, social, and personal—regarding the student's college experience. Participation rates at the college are typically very high, sometimes approaching 100 percent.

In 2007, our associate Shauna Sweet compiled the survey results covering the seven years 2000–2006, creating an integrated database that allowed her to run over-time trend and multivariate analyses on a host of topics. We were thus able, for instance, to track the rise and fall of overall student satisfaction during those years; compare the perceived "learnability" of quantitative, writing, and public speaking skills; and, controlling for a host of potentially confounding factors, examine the importance of being a guest in a faculty home to students' overall happiness with having attended the college. On those and other subjects, then, we had quantifiably verified, statistically controlled findings.

4. *The Writing Study.*   Still, even quantifiable surveys remain at heart compilations of self-reports; we also wanted objective measures of student progress. Our Writing Study, overseen by Sharon Williams, was based on 1,068 student essays collected over five years, many of them as part of the Panel Study.

Other papers were gathered from a variety of classes, using conservative sampling assumptions designed to make demonstrable improvement in a student's work relatively difficult to prove. The papers were evaluated by "blind" outside reviewers, specially trained for the purpose. We were then able to link student (objective) writing scores to student (subjective) self-reports of perceived improvements, showing for instance that on the whole, students knew when their writing improved. The Writing Study and its findings are explained in more detail in Chapter 5.

5. *Projects of Opportunity.*   Finally, over the decade of our work, members of our Faculty Working Group and research team conducted a host of smaller "projects of opportunity" including focus group studies of Dean's List and "B&B" ("best and brightest," as nominated by the Admission Office or faculty) students; of students returning from study abroad; of campus social life; and so on. We collected and evaluated 288 videotapes of sophomores and seniors giving talks to classes; conducted several quantitative analyses of student course evaluations; and ran quantitative analyses on the course transcripts both of our panel students and of the entire student body, examining topics such as course selection and breadth of course choice, trends in GPA over a student's career, and student enrollment patterns in classes of various sizes.

Our conclusions, generated from research at a single institution, have been vetted against the broader data and literature of contemporary higher education research. In addition to membership in the HEDS Consortium (organizer of the Senior Surveys), the college was from 2006 to 2010 one of forty-nine colleges and universities nationwide participating in the Wabash National Study of Liberal Arts Education, overseen by Professor Charles Blaich of Wabash College. The Wabash Study was a comprehensive, longitudinal study of critical factors affecting outcomes of liberal arts programs. While our findings are framed quite differently, we believe they are consistent with the conclusions of the Wabash Study. We have also benefitted from the research of the New England Consortium on Assessment and Student Learning, especially their work on the freshman experience. Lee Cuba of Wellesley College, one of the leaders of the NECASL project, has generously shared his knowledge and expertise with us on multiple occasions. Throughout our book we have drawn on and cited dozens of valuable studies reported in the rich literature on higher education. Lastly, from 2002 through 2008, Dan Chambliss served as a member (and Executive Committee member) of the

Middle States Commission on Higher Education, overseeing accreditation of more than five hundred colleges and universities in the Mid-Atlantic region (including New York, New Jersey, Pennsylvania, and other states). We are thus generally familiar with the entire array of higher education approaches and outcomes, and with the instruments and findings of popular assessment programs of recent years, including the National Survey of Student Engagement (NSSE), the Collegiate Learning Assessment (CLA), and others.

Our goal here is pragmatic: to help colleges get better results. So we haven't written a comprehensive ethnography of college life, as have Michael Moffatt, Cathy Small, and Mary Grigsby.[17] As those studies point out, much of college life is not really about academic education. A number of recent books have persuasively focused on the often disappointing realities of undergraduate education.[18] Any experienced student of organizations might well say, "Of course!" Employees or members of all kinds of institutions or groups have personal commitments and interests diverting them from their official duties. Businesses must constantly monitor workers to keep them "on task." Many churches are short of devout members, armies chronically need more true warriors, and even families are often not as close and loving as they're supposed to be. Why would we expect college students to be solely devoted to their studies? Colleges are obviously not always first-rate collections of thinkers, but our goal is to make them more so, not simply point out their shortcomings.

Over the pages to come, we will follow students as they face a defining set of challenges in college—entering the community, choosing what paths to follow (academically and socially), belonging to various groups on campus, learning the skills teachable by higher education, and leaving the community for what students call the "real" world. All of these challenges, we will see, are fundamentally shaped by personal relationships, which are themselves shaped by the institution in which they occur. We will trace students' paths through their years in college, identifying the choices, obstacles, successes, and failures that mark their way. Throughout the book we will uncover and describe the often-hidden forces that pave their pathways and so direct their lives. We end with conclusions and specific recommendations for how leaders of all sorts can help students get more out of their college years.

In one sentence: what really matters in college is who meets whom, and when.

2

Entering

Freshman year, it's kind of a big brawl for a couple weeks
while everyone gets to know each other. And then [later],
people settle down real quickly, and they really won't,
you know, socialize as much with other people.

(Joe, sophomore)

"Going to college" means more than enrolling in courses and pursuing a degree. For traditional-age students at a residential college, it also means entering a new community, stepping into the exhilarating but sometimes frightening world of incipient adulthood.[1] When students successfully enter this community of young adults, it can—potentially—energize and motivate them for learning, for excelling at athletics, for socializing (yes—for partying, drinking, hooking up), for giving tremendous loyalty to the institution, for pursuing careers, and sometimes even for becoming, as the cliché has it, "lifelong learners." When they don't successfully enter socially or academically, students often become lonely, demoralized, and even depressed. They may well drop out psychologically, if not physically.

Major research studies have repeatedly emphasized this point, especially as it affects students' continuing enrollment in college (retention).[2] Integration into the college community is crucial to a student's remaining in school, and thus for their physical and psychological availability for any kind of academic work. We are not saying that a student absolutely must have friends and be happy in order to do good academic work. After all, some very unhappy social isolates can perform quite well. But friendship is so strong a factor for most people as to be, for practical purposes, virtually a prerequisite for success in college.

If true, this argument has huge implications not only for student life professionals, but for academic leaders as well. Entering, as we call it, is not just an important first step; it is a necessary prerequisite (again, for most people) to a college education. It is a *sine qua non*: literally, "without which, not." If entering doesn't happen, all of the well-designed courses, the carefully planned majors, and the exciting extracurriculars won't matter at all. Those efforts will be completely wasted on students who don't find friends and find a pathway (see Chapter 3) into good courses. All of the academic excellence in the world won't matter to a student who isn't in the classroom both physically and psychologically.

The good news is that, for a few weeks at least at the beginning of school, students in fact are available and motivated, at least as much as they ever will be at college.[3] So colleges can seize that opportunity and open easy pathways for students to meet friends and join the community. Students' own efforts help in this, certainly, but institutions themselves can make integration easier, especially if they learn to help students who are less socially sophisticated and outgoing. Strangely enough, this can sometimes mean funneling students into situations—for instance, those old-fashioned, long-hallway dorms—that students themselves initially find unappealing.

First Steps

Arriving at the college, new students are often anxious, heading into unknown territory.

> I was scared. I was scared of everyone. It was kind of like high school to me again, at first, because everyone was just forming their cliques really fast and trying to get, I don't know, groups of stuff with people. (Reanna, freshman)[4]

> I was definitely really scared, didn't know what to expect. I'm from Denver, going to college in the East . . . The day I woke up to fly out to school . . . I remember waking up so early that morning, and being, like, "I wonder if there is any way I can get out of this." Because I just was, I was very afraid . . . (Ann, senior)

> My first day was a mess, you know. I cried, like, all day because I've, I've never been away from home . . . (Lydia, freshman)

Even if sometimes overly dramatized, their fear is reasonable: Will I have any friends? Will anyone talk with me, or even sit with me at lunch? Can I manage it all?

At the same time there's tremendous excitement and opportunity in this swirl, heightened by the knowledge that almost everyone around you is facing the same challenges. Students rush to meet people, get dorm rooms set up, start working out a schedule, find the dining hall, learn their way around the campus, all the while in a tumble with hundreds of other freshmen, a wave of humanity visibly eager to meet people—*any* people, at least initially. Sasha, who struggled to find her feet socially, and Russell, who found his way more easily, were both aware of the dynamics.

> In the beginning of freshman year everyone was really—all the *freshmen*— were really friendly to each other. They're all trying to find people who they feel will be, like, their good friends, or even just their "friends for now," whatever, maybe someone to eat with, you know . . . they just don't want to be doing it alone. (Sasha, sophomore)

> It would have been tough to come into a setting like this and not make any friends, especially the first couple of weeks and no one knows each other. You don't feel bad just going up to somebody and going like, "Hey, I'm Russell." Everyone's in the same boat . . . (Russell, freshman)

At the same time that they're looking for friends, students are also organizing their own newly independent lives. Many are away from home for the first time, facing all of the pleasures and challenges of living without parents (or the quasi-parental supervision of boarding schools).

> There's a ton more freedom . . . I went to a prep school, and they had check-in and you have certain study hours and everything. Here, you're free to do anything you want. You can leave and come whenever you want. You don't have to go to class if you don't want to! (James, senior)

> You're free; no restrictions; you can go to bed whenever you want; you can pick your own classes. (John, freshman)

The daily round is theirs to make up. Initially, they have only the orientation-week schedule, and an open array of classes they might take to meet the requirements, but nothing like the rigid timetables of high school.

> You're not spending your entire day in the classroom. You're like, two hours in class, and you have the rest of the time to do your work—if you wanted to do your work. It's not so much the teachers looking over your shoulder all the time, and you're held responsible for doing your own things . . . Your

parents aren't around . . . So you have to figure out how you want to work your schedule. (Harry, freshman)

No one tells them when to get up and when to go to bed, whom they can associate with, or where they must be at every hour of the day or night. Laundry will eventually have to be done, but mom isn't there to do it. Dinner is no longer "at home," but in any of several different dining halls, or in a pizza joint, or at the diner.

For children of the comfortable upper middle class, some minor conveniences have disappeared.

[Here's] the routine I had at home [in high school]: you wake up, you go to school from 8:00 to 3:00, you go to sports or whatever, you come home, you do your homework, you eat dinner, and you talk on the phone. You know, it's like a set thing . . . Dinner's on the table for you, it's nice and comfortable . . . You have your bedroom which is yours, and big enough to, like, make a mess without feeling like you have to swim to get to your bed. (Susie, freshman)

The first challenge of college is to *enter* this new world and make it sensible, to find some friends and establish a schedule. Students must manage to balance work and socializing. As Michael Moffatt says in his classic ethnography of undergraduate life, "College life, first of all, involve[s] an understanding among the students about the proper relationship between work and play in college, about the relative value of inside-the-classroom education versus extracurricular fun."[5]

For some, of course, the temptations are too much.[6]

When I got here it was like, "Oh, my gosh, college is sweet." There's beer everywhere . . . I probably tried to party almost every day, just because I sort of figured I had, like, the freedom. And my grades were not awesome first semester, and I was personally really disappointed with them . . . (George, sophomore)

Others find themselves startlingly out of place, in such a rural, relatively homogenous school.

I grew up in a [urban] Jewish community so the ratio of blondes to brunettes here was astounding. Like, I walked in and I was—I was looking to my left: there are corn fields! I'm looking to my right, lots of blond people! (Sasha, sophomore)

Even in what Joe (quoted at the head of this chapter) called the "big brawl" to find friends, then, not all brawlers stand on equal ground: some have better skills or opportunities for making friends and joining groups than others. Students at selective colleges probably have an immediate advantage, as selectivity itself improves one's odds of finding compatible peers. Elite colleges, for instance, admit wealthier and more academically prepared students than colleges in general, helping such students find each other. At the college, academically motivated peers may find more peers than in high school.

It all goes back now to people being here for a purpose. It just kind of weeds out the people that don't really want to be here. In high school . . . I went to a high school of about 1,500 kids, so I mean there are always going to be kids who are just kind of floaters, and I don't think there really are many floaters here. (Frank, freshman)

However imperfectly, all residential colleges try to admit people who show up for school, finish the basic work, can organize themselves sufficiently to live on their own, enroll for classes, and not be criminally offensive.

Admission standards, though, are just the first step in how colleges bring people together. Once in college, students are in effect guided down rather predictable paths to meeting other students[7] and, later, teachers (Chapter 3). The chaos of the first weeks of college offers perhaps the greatest opportunity for meeting numerous peers that these students will ever experience in their lives—and the institution itself plays a major role in how that unfolds.

Finding Friends

Friendship is crucial for incoming students, but having large numbers of friends is not. Most students, we found, need only a few people—*two or three good friends, and one or two great professors*—to have a rewarding, even wonderful, college experience. But where do they find them? Basically, a residential college makes finding friends easy by increasing the sheer amount of time students physically spend with specific groups of peers. As it happens, settings that may initially seem productive (orientation activities, Greek-letter societies) have real limitations, while others that appear unappealing (traditional dorms with shared bathrooms) may work best of all.

Orientation Activities: Precedence

Orientation activities are deliberately designed to help students enter the campus world. They take precedence—they happen first, before anyone is committed. During Orientation Week at the college, students encounter each other both in official activities and in the free time available during their first week on campus.

Some students enjoy the official activities.

> And it's just like a setting where they brought you in and made you completely comfortable, and you just had a lot of fun, and made awesome friends within the first few days . . . it just made everything very easy. (Anne, senior)[8]

Others, though, find general orientation activities—games, dormitory discussions, mandatory workshops on sexual harassment, drinking, diversity—to be silly and a waste of time.

> I didn't like the Orientation Week . . . It seemed like they forced us into, like, meeting people . . . a lot of the relationships weren't strong, or they weren't going to stay. I wish there was, like, more free time to just go and chill and meet people. (Katie, freshman)

More effective orientation activities seem to target selected (even if quite broadly selected) students. Nearly half of the entering class at the college participates in what we'll call "Outdoor Adventure," a weeklong camping excursion into a national park.[9] OA has prime "bonding" factors in abundance: students are physically close twenty-four hours a day; they sleep together (in tents, no less); they work together in meaningful cooperative activities. The intensity, both physical and mental, and the semblance of danger (black bears occasionally appear in camp) pull participants together. OA takes place before the official Orientation Week and so gives its participants an advantage—they begin the school year with friends already made.

I loved doing Outdoor Adventure at the beginning of the year, and I felt like I immediately formed a group of friendships right from that . . . (Sarah, sophomore)

But the advantage may only be comparative, not shared by nonparticipants.

During that first couple of weeks [of school] everyone [else] knows people from Outdoor Adventure, and it's just hard. I mean, even though a lot of kids didn't go on it, you just don't feel as connected. I think a lot of kids . . . just didn't know it was that important. I wish I had gone on it, now. (Kim, freshman)

Such presemester programs, requiring extra time in summer and often extra money, naturally favor those who can easily afford to spend the time and money.

Many institutions also offer preorientation programs for less privileged groups. The college's Higher Education Opportunity Program, for students from disadvantaged backgrounds, seems to provide its members an early network of friends. Lasting six weeks and free of charge, HEOP's activities are mandatory for participants; they run around the clock; the students live together; and they provide an early, often loose, but lasting network of acquaintances for its members—"somebody to say hi to on campus."

The only reason I met a lot of people was because I played football and because I went to that [HEOP] program . . . I got with previous students who were in the program from the other classes. Those are like my friends now. (John, sophomore)

I was in HEOP in the summer, so, like, I got to meet like twenty-eight kids already. So coming here, I already knew twenty-eight kids . . . I'm really shy. I don't tend to make friends . . . But . . . in HEOP, you just couldn't help it, you became friends because you lived next to each other for weeks. (Victoria, freshman)

In the long run, opportunity programs may somewhat isolate these students; but without such programs, there may not even be a long run.

All special orientation programs are, to some extent, competitive propositions. Participants benefit from them relative to other students, who are thus in some sense disadvantaged. Students who arrive on campus early are more likely to find a comfortable group of friends by the time exclusive cliques begin crystallizing around the end of the first semester. The gains for individual students are clear, but we don't know if such programs are a net gain for the student body as a whole.

Orientation programs enjoy one obvious advantage as a source for friends: they happen first, before anyone is committed and when everyone is available. As researchers in higher education have shown, students benefit from participating in orientation: they integrate better into college and, as a consequence, tend to stay on at higher rates.[10] On the other hand, orientation ends as school begins, so regular contact is often lost; orientation "friendships" often prove to be fleeting.

Dormitories: Proximity

At the college, where crime is very low and the campus very safe, dormitories provide a convenient venue for meeting people.[11] The combination of physical proximity to people and around-the-clock availability makes dorms an excellent setting for meeting people.

At a bare minimum, one encounters roommates.

> INTERVIEWER: How did you meet your friends?
> STUDENT: It was my dorm . . . I lived in McGinnis. It's an awesome social dorm, and I lived in a quad, and I ended up, the three other guys in my quad are like some of my, they're like my best friends here now. (George, sophomore)

When bathrooms are shared, one regularly sees other users of the bathroom. On long hallways where doors are kept open, people walk past and some say hello; when the hallway is lined with doubles or quads, residents inevitably encounter dozens of people during a single day. One student, not in such a dorm, envied his friend who "lived on a hallway, and could, like, open up his door and there were a dozen other doors with two guys or two girls in [each of] them. [The doors] were all open, and they had just kind of an interesting sense of community" (Herb, sophomore). With even modest social skills, a new student will meet people very quickly.

It would be hard not to make new friends, but especially in my dorm, I think, like, our dorm is unbelievably close . . . It's not one of the larger dorms, but it seems like most every freshman knows every other freshman [there] . . . (James, freshman)

The "built environment" of a dormitory can be decisive.[12]

The layout of the dorm is definitely important, so you know, "single pulls" [picking one's roommate], like Vernon; suite pulls [picking suitemates], like Clark and Turner, are great, you know. You get friends in. And other layouts, like Watkins and Weir, are great for your first year because you're going to be in a quad [with three roommates]. So you automatically have, like, three people that you're interacting with a lot . . . [and] all of their friends as well as all of your friends. (Mark, junior)

It's like a sleepover 24/7. And it's like you're living with your friends. [But] in McGinnis they have their own bathrooms in their room, and they keep their doors closed all the time, and they don't really, like, get out in the hall and chat with people. (Anne, freshman)

Different students prefer different dorms, each with its distinctive advantages.

Like, you know, you can choose Gould and be near everything, but you sacrifice, you know, big rooms in a big building, nice carpeted floors. Or you can live in . . . Masters, but you sacrifice location. You have to walk, you know, a half mile to get everywhere, and you're pretty much out there by yourself over there. You know, no one comes around; no one knocks on your door to say hi. (Jim, senior)

You can get like a really nice room in Wharton, but it might be a quad, you know. Or you can get, you know, like a crappy room in Turner, but it will be . . . a single, and you'll have all your friends living around you, and you'll have a kitchen. (Anne, junior)

As we've mentioned, some of the dorms least preferred by incoming students are in fact the most successful in helping to create deep, lasting friendships. Graduating seniors frequently told us that their best friends are those they met in their dormitory during their first year in college—dorms that on the first day of orientation may look "institutional," crowded, chaotic.[13] Long hallways with a dozen or more rooms, communal bathrooms where meeting others regularly is unavoidable, multistudent rooms—all of these architecturally require students to meet lots of other students.

At the same time, the architectural features that prospective college students find so appealing (single rooms, private baths, exterior doorways—"apartment-style living") can in fact quite seriously limit their own social life and happiness. Such rooms tend to isolate students; they reduce the odds of daily chance encounters with other people.

> Well, we're in [a more apartment-style dorm] even though we know practically no one [there]. My roommates and I lately have been noticing that when we go to eat dinner, like we walk around [the dining hall]—this can't be happening! We go to school with 1,800 people; we're in a big, big [dining] room; and we know nobody! . . . (Sasha, sophomore)

> There's only two of us in our [off-campus] apartment. So I make more of an effort to be on campus most of the time, and study here, and eat meals here, and it's like making dates to see people rather than just kind of hanging around. (Madeline, sophomore)

Dorms, then, have a fundamental power in producing friendships: they repeatedly (and involuntarily) bring students into close proximity.[14] This is not to say that the sheer proximity is always good. Roommate problems, for instance, are widespread in college dormitories and can be quite serious, as we'll see in Chapter 5.

Greek Life: Exclusivity

Where fraternities and sororities are prominent—at large state universities, for instance—they may be the single most-used institution for meeting other students. At the college, such "Greek-letter societies" don't have houses, and although important in campus social life they are certainly not the dominant force they are at larger schools. But they do still offer a kind of "automatic network" of friends as well as a regular social life, probably fortified by their (rather mild) exclusivity. For most potential members, not much effort is needed to be recruited, meet people, and eventually find a spot in a community where engaging with others is virtually required.

> I was impressed that [fraternities] go out and actually seek the kids they want to hang out with. And . . . especially as a freshman, just coming into a new school I was, it made me really sort of maybe want to engage the [college] social scene I guess . . . (Jay, junior)

When members live together in houses, as is common at big universities, they maximize the chances for becoming close friends with a large number of fellow members. The inescapable, twenty-four-hour contact with dozens of people, the isolation from other groups, and the inevitable pressure to conform all tend to produce very tight-knit communities.

At the college pledging takes place in the spring of freshman year, but even at that fairly early date, officially joining a "society" is often just the formalization of already-existing friendship networks—a nice example of how early contacts shape later ones.

> [I met one of my best friends] through football, and then he joined my fraternity; and another through a high school friend of mine, who then also joined my fraternity. So we really started to be friends before we all joined a fraternity. (Jay, junior)

> I joined [a sorority] last year . . . They're basically just all my friends before, and I was just kind of like yeah, why not become "officially" [a member]. I'm definitely very happy with it. (Laura, sophomore)

In these cases, Greek-letter societies just reinforce and expand already-existing same-sex networks, rather than opening new doors. Even so, broader connections with brother or sister societies provide a host of opportunities, disproportionately available to members.

Sports Teams: Time, Performance

For a variety of reasons, participation in sports teams is a wonderfully effective way to meet peers and make lasting friendships. At the college, where some 40 percent of students play on a varsity team for at least one season, sports may be the most common venue for building friendships.

> At first . . . I just knew people in my dorm, you know. But when I started playing, we started having meetings for softball . . . so I got to meet people

from here and there, and like I'm really good friends with a lot of the girls on the team. (Marie, sophomore)

I think I met my friends—let's see, through, I played rugby first semester, so that's how I, I was kind of friends with a lot of the rugby players. (Sarah, sophomore)

I swam. So I had dinner with the swim team, you know, breakfast and dinner after we had practice, and they really became . . . people who, like, I associated with because it was eat, sleep, swim, you know, study when I was in season. (Randall, sophomore)

Athletes find each other quickly. Sports programs are organized by the institution, widely publicized, and made readily available to those qualified. Some workouts begin in the middle of summer, well before fall-semester classes, providing these athletes with an immediate social advantage; right from the start, the jocks have friends. Crucially, varsity athletes spend huge amounts of time together, typically practicing at least five days a week, for three or four hours a day, often twice a day, far outpacing the time spent in a class or even in all classes combined. They travel together; they eat together; they even sleep and shower and get dressed together.

It's a lot easier to relate to those guys than just, say, some other person, because you're always around them basically, and their lifestyle is a lot like yours. You have to really kind of manage your time a lot differently than someone that doesn't have to wake up really early in the morning to go to practice . . . And then practice at night too! Your whole lifestyle kind of changes once the season comes along . . . They're going through the same things that you're going through. (Frank, sophomore)

Most of this shared time takes place in intense, performance-driven settings where teammates intimately depend on each other for help and coordination.

The college encourages sports teams more energetically than other activities, providing facilities, coaching staff, admission preferences, and equipment. Athletes at universities generally receive vastly disproportionate attention in campus newspapers, and they sometimes become campus celebrities. Students good enough to make a team are granted a nearly automatic social life, with peers who enjoy a shared interest and sometimes (but at the college, not often) a number of fans as well.[15]

The athletes' immediate social advantage may not last—in fact, as we will see, some teams become ingrown, isolating even athletes from other networks. But in the first few weeks of school, and typically afterwards, athletes have a clear advantage in meeting and making friends.

Music Groups: Numbers

Large musical ensembles, available to some students from the opening days of school, offer routine contact with a large but manageable (forty to eighty) group of peers, allowing a very efficient search for friends. It also (like a good dorm) helps students in establishing a broader network of diverse acquaintances. Later in a student's career, a small ensemble or rock band can be fun; but early on, larger groups such as the choir or the orchestra expose their members to a huge number of potential friends and acquaintances. At the college,

> you come in [freshman year] and like there's like seventy people [in choir] and you don't know anybody. And then about halfway through, you generally do a play or a musical, and everybody sort of bonds in like January, or when you get back from spring break.
>
> And since freshman year, they've just been my family. And you go on tour and I mean there's seventy people, which is a lot, a lot of people. By the end of the year, you sort of have found the particular fifteen or twenty that you see around campus all the time, that you have the same classes with; and they've sort of just been like a community. (Judy, senior)

Like sports teams, musical groups meet frequently, from once a week to every day; they call upon a shared interest; and they demand engagement.

> I sing with the choir . . . We go on tour, we do musicals, it's just fun. I sing *a cappella* with The Adirondack Singers, and all of us are in the choir. So the two [groups] sort of work together to keep improving my musical skills. That's a lot of fun. It's a lot—it's only six hours a week supposedly, but it's really a lot more time-intensive than that. I mean those are the girls who are now my friends.
>
> Everybody in the activities I do wants to be there. That's really important. When I go to rehearsal, all eleven of us . . . really want to be there. And whether we're tired or not, we're going to put in the effort and produce something. (Jane, sophomore)

Brass or string ensemble groups similarly require close coordination and mutual dependence, with attendant emotional rewards. Many musical groups are at least semimandatory, either because they offer academic credit or because they have a faculty director who expects performers to show up regularly and on time. While some musical groups are student run, many others have been organized by the college and are given generous support (supervision, facilities, time priorities in the academic schedule—only music and theatre classes have permission to meet in the evening). Like sports teams, musical groups are performance driven, in which the members and their cooperative abilities are on public display, as a regular part of their work. At the college, musical groups go on tours, sometimes to exotic locations (Italy, Scotland), and perform not only at home but also at other institutions or with other ensembles.

Extracurriculars: Shared Interests

Finally, friends can be found in a wide range of other extracurricular activities.

At many institutions, students see activities (interest clubs, publications, media) as an important source of both professional experience and career networks; they promise pathways to employment (in professional sports, or journalism, or business, or the nonprofit world). At the college, though, extracurriculars exist primarily to foster relationships among friends and acquaintances, mainly through the sheer number of contact hours between people. Extracurriculars also provide entry to campus networks.

> [Where do you meet people?] In organizations and groups, you know. That's pretty much a big place that you are to meet people, and you get to, like, talk to them more often . . . Parties? Yeah you socialize, but it's like, you tend to socialize with the people you already know. You don't really socialize with anybody else. But in organizations and in groups, you do. (Victoria, freshman)

The most engaging extracurricular organizations at the college meet on a regular schedule, have a semi-"mandatory" feel to them, have an interdependent division of labor, and often entail some public performance. The college's newspaper, for instance, is published every Friday, "employs" publicly named reporters and editors whose work is seen by perhaps two thousand readers, and requires of its staff a weekly routine of all-night Thursday sessions to "get the paper out" the following day. The routinized intensity helps to create and solidify relationships. Other groups and clubs demand less, and seem to provide less in return.

Interestingly, our panelists rarely mentioned academic settings such as classes as a place for finding friends, although this probably varies by institution.[16] Classes would seem to meet our criteria as a good place to meet people—regular encounters, mandatory attendance, and a shared topic for conversation. But in classes, attention is usually focused on the teacher. Even in seminars, the professor holds a central position. Classes are thus a good place to meet teachers and potentially find an adult mentor, but meeting fellow students is more difficult. Besides, classroom relationships have a very limited future since classes typically last only one term. Students do sometimes find friends in science lab sections, in study or project groups, on field trips, and while traveling together. But generally these occur later in the college career, after networks are already formed, and they involve very few people. In our research, only a handful of students found their best friends in academic settings.

To remain and thrive in college, students need to make friends quickly. A few major factors seem to help, with sheer physical proximity as fundamental. Beyond that, meeting people early, time spent together with a large but knowable number of people (dozens, let's say), some exclusivity, and shared interests all contribute. Interdependent public performances (team sports, music, newspaper) also seem to matter.[17] At the college, then, dormitories, sports teams, and what we might call "big music" (orchestra or choir)—that is, "high-contact" activities—are the most reliable places to make friends. Simply meeting lots of new people, as in orientation activities, isn't sufficient; only repeated, "mandatory" contact with a sizable number of others provides a sufficient pool from which to find several friends. In such settings, one needn't take initiative to meet others. For institutions, advising students to "go out and meet people!" doesn't really work. Providing well-designed opportunities does.

Even in this opportunity-rich environment, though, dormitories are special: they are available to everyone, right from the start. In some institutions, dormitories can be dangerous places where one's private space is accessible to strangers bent on theft or even assault.[18] If people are nasty to each other, dorm living can be horrible. But when safety and civility are possible, dormitories offer unrivaled communal living. Dorms are ecumenical. Living in, and benefitting from, a good dormitory requires no athletic ability, no special talent, and (importantly) almost no personal initiative. Shy, physically unattractive, socially awkward students can all benefit from dorm life, with its mandatory mingling. There's no zero-sum advantage being doled out in the construction, design, and occupancy of sociable dormitories with lots of students on shared hallways and bathrooms. Musical groups require musical ability, sports teams are for athletes, and parties require an outgoing personality, but college dorms are open to all. Encompassing a wide range of students, dorms can at least open the possibility for extending student networks to new and even unfamiliar groups.

So meeting and getting to know other students in college—a first crucial step to success—is neither an accident nor just the result of an outgoing personality. The key is routinized proximity to a large but manageable—say, thirty to one hundred—group of other available students, early on. Smaller groups don't seem to provide enough potential friends; apartment-style dorms isolate students; classes don't work unless there is a good deal of student collaborative work. Freshman seminars may help a little, but we suspect they are too small to offer sufficient opportunities, with too little student-to-student face time.

Not every college is residential, and not every college has an extensive extracurricular system, but every college (except of course online universities) has physical space in which people can meet, and some forms of routine activity that bring students together. These spaces and activities matter—they provide the necessary context in which students develop the friendships that will be vital to their persistence, satisfaction, and as we will argue, their motivation to engage academically.

Encountering Academics

At the same time they're making friends, every student must enter the academic world, however modestly.[19] Academic work gives structure to daily life, provides the institution with its official reason for being, and justifies the enormous expense in time and money that parents, the public, and donors pour into college. There are excellent institutions without intercollegiate athletics, fraternities, or dormitories, but all colleges have academic programs. If students fail to meet the (perhaps minimal) academic standards, they may have to leave college. In Chapter 3, we describe how students find courses, teachers, academic majors. But are they even prepared for the work required?

Students' initial approach to academics can be shaped by whether they actually wanted to be at their college in the first place. A fair number of our panelists said the college wasn't their first choice, a common situation among applicants to selective institutions, who often consider three, or five, or even more, possible schools.[20]

Then there is the students' own high school experience. Many at the college—not typical of most universities—attended elite private schools, and arrive with the basic tools for doing well in higher education. They can already write a decent essay; have learned math, frequently through introductory calculus; and know how to read well and how to study strategically, picking the crucial sections and, if need be, letting other parts slide.

> So far, academically it's been pretty challenging, and yet not too challenging for me. I didn't have to get used to the whole being away from home thing . . . Everything was pretty much what I was prepared for from my boarding school. They prepared me for hard work. (Sarah, freshman)

Here clearly is a "prep advantage": students such as Sarah who attended expensive private secondary schools are often better prepared academically than public school students, especially those from poor districts. "Preps" may already know, or at least know of, a fair number of other students (for instance, from sports leagues), and they often have already lived away from home, which enhances the self-confidence they exude. (This parallels the advantage, at larger universities, held by middle- and upper-middle-class students arriving in ready-made groups of friends from larger suburban high schools.) Academically grounded and already socially networked, these students make the transition to college fairly easily.

Students adapt not only to the general demands of the curriculum, but even to the specific requirements of different professors and their disciplines.

> The [writing] styles are different with philosophy. It's more of an opinion type, "analyze what they're saying." Whereas for history, you're going off on your own from something, you know, from a foundation you're taking a whole new tangent writing that way . . . one focusing on the analytical

skills, and one focusing on, you know, like a creative information-based writing style. (Ruttiger, freshman)

Professor Haber's trying to teach us how to write like historians write, instead of using lots of adjectives and pretty words . . . And Professor Quintera is trying to teach us how to, like, have graceful writing, like, like a combination of simple sentences and complex sentences, you know? (Katie, freshman)

Professors differ in the kinds of arguments they allow, the kind of logic and evidence they expect, and in the tone of the writing they encourage. Students experience these demands as "learning what professors want," adapting to new audiences.[21]

In high school I guess I was used to, for the most part, getting really good comments on writing; and here it's sort of like writing one of my first papers; a lot of improvements were needed basically. And I think it was really good that . . . you could rewrite them and stuff because you could clarify with the teachers what they wanted and to write it over. That was challenging, getting used to exactly what each professor wanted. (Sarah, freshman)

High school standouts, even valedictorians, sometimes from little public schools in modest rural districts, the winners of many prizes, widely praised for getting in the college, sometimes find they can't measure up.[22]

I was shocked, and at points, I was—I wasn't sure if I could handle it. I felt sort of like sinking. (Rick, junior)

At the mercy of arithmetic necessity, one-half of all freshmen find themselves in the bottom half of the freshman class, far lower than most of them ever thought possible. (After all, most were drawn from the top 10 percent of their high school cohorts.) They struggle, at least initially, to adapt to the competition, to the higher standards, and to a workload they didn't anticipate. Their first tests come back, and instead of an A, there's a C on the front.[23]

Kristy had been a strong student in her weak high school, but while describing her freshman year to our student interviewer she began choking up and eventually dissolved into tears.

INTERVIEWER: What would you want the college to change, if anything, about your first year?

STUDENT: I would say, "Lower the academic standards!" But that's not too likely . . . I would say that the academic standard is pretty high, you know . . . [hesitates]

INTERVIEWER: [comforting] OK, that's fine.

STUDENT: That's just a stupid answer. It's totally ignorant . . . I know I was once a really good student, and I know I've had so much, like, belief in myself. And I come in here and—like, I can't explain it. [crying—interviewer stops recording] (Kristy, sophomore)

At the end of her sophomore year, Kristy left the college.

Such failures, though, are not inevitable. As we will see, introductory-level professors can make a huge difference to these students.

Outsiders

Most students entering the college do indeed find friends, settle in, and do their work at least reasonably well. Freshman retention as reported by *U.S. News and World Report* is 95 percent, with a four-year graduation rate of 84 percent, very high indeed by national standards. Most seniors say that given the chance they would choose to attend the college again.

But some students never quite mesh with the college. Reanna didn't really want to come in the first place.

My dad did most of my college search for me . . . He brought me up here, and I applied—actually I applied, and then he brought me up here. I wanted to go out to California . . . but he wasn't too big on the idea. So he looked at the East Coast liberal arts colleges for me, and I looked at the California liberal arts colleges for me. (Reanna, freshman)

She came to the college, as her father preferred, but wasn't happy.

Still others are held back by hometown ties, perhaps a boy- or girlfriend to whom they've pledged fidelity. Honoring that pledge can become a barrier to both romantic and platonic relationships on campus.[24] Some stay in constant contact with their parents, ignoring potential adult advisors on campus. (This isn't to say that parental involvement hurts students; in fact, recent research shows that it can often help.[25]) Closely tied to people off-campus, such students may never give themselves the chance for new connections that might offer new opportunities.

In our study, as in higher education literature,[26] students of color and less wealthy students were more likely to maintain more social ties off-campus than did their white, wealthier peers. As the "social mismatch" theory of racial differences in college experience would suggest, this situation may arise because when minority students anticipate (and likely experience) some degree of social isolation in their early-college experience, they maintain strong off-campus ties as a safety net.[27] Of course, such choices can be ultimately self-perpetuating: the student spends more time in contact with friends off-campus, thereby reducing opportunities for meeting people on-campus, thus remaining isolated.

Social class can be yet another major barrier to "entering," perhaps best described in Elizabeth Armstrong and Laura Hamilton's recent book, *Paying for the Party*.[28] Many students at the college have cars and go out to dinner, but the less affluent quickly realize that they can't keep up, can't afford the dinners at expensive restaurants, can't "pick up a round" of drinks at the local bar. They don't vacation in Europe at all, much less every year. Their dorm rooms don't feature televisions, multiple computers, smartphones, and closets full of top-end clothing. The rich can meet and socialize with anyone, but poor and middle-class kids have to check their wallets, avoiding commitments (spring break trips, dinners out) they can't afford.

Finally, even for advantaged, gregarious students, the initially open doors of freshman year tend to swing shut rather quickly. Groups of friends, acquaintances, pals, and buddies can easily coalesce into cliques—tight knit, closed to outsiders, exclusive.

> When I first got to [the college], like on the weekends, you know, you could walk through campus and people would be like, "Hey we're getting together," or, "We're having a party!" . . . But as the fall progressed, all the events were very, like, exclusive: if you don't know someone, you are not on the invite list. (Cynthia, sophomore)

> Once people kind of start to find their friends, immediately all—like, all relations are cut off. Like . . . "Oh, I haven't met you yet? Well, you're probably not worth being my friend anyways . . . I already have friends." (Sasha, sophomore)

Ironically enough for a small campus, subjective feelings of exclusion, for those who suffer from them, can be exacerbated just by walking around. You see people you recognize, who ought to know you—and perhaps they do—but they may not say hello, or they walk past without a greeting or even a nod. At the college, this may be a WASPy reserve; African-American students in particular are struck by what students themselves call the "campus cool," where a simple greeting sometimes seems too much to ask. Or maybe saying hi to everyone just becomes tedious. Either way, a sense of outsiderhood can be reinforced every day in countless small actions, even while seeing others embracing or greeting each other with the most exuberant *bonhomie*. The visible friendliness all around only heightens the awareness a few students have that "I'm not part of all this, this is not my world."

Most new students, though, enter the college successfully. They meet people and make acquaintances; they find someone to eat lunch with, to sit and talk with in the common rooms. They begin to say hello on the paths across campus, and are greeted in return. They start to fit in. They loosen up, become more confident, begin to speak up in classes. All that personal contact—the hellos, the friendships, the feeling of belonging here—allows other good things to start happening. A set of basic friendships—or at least acceptance— keeps students in school.

Our panelist Dan found friends quickly in multiple settings. He went through the Outdoor Adventure course, and found his three best female friends there. He lived in Watkins, one of the more sociable dorms, where "my roommates and I were incredibly good friends," and "the guys that lived next to us" as well as "the girls that lived above us" were all good friends as well. He joined the swimming team, and several of his teammates introduced him to the fraternity he later pledged. In their sophomore year, a couple of the guys from across the hall moved to another dorm and joined a different fraternity; that "gave us different places to go, [and] helped us to meet even more people." Then through swimming teammates he "got steered into" his major, as one network led into another.

So Dan remained at the college and did well. Some relationships helped in clear ways: he "learned a lot from" his roommate, and a woman in the dorm who was a Writing Center tutor. "She helped me through a lot of my writing . . . and just taught me the basics, which I didn't get in high school," and together "these two [friends] were what really got my writing to a pretty high level."

On the other hand, his commitment to swimming prevented him from going abroad, which he later mildly regretted. His teammates also had guided him towards a major that he didn't in the end enjoy. Early relationships like Dan's, in other words, affect later choices. When their congenial roommates take certain courses, students are more likely to take those courses as well. Having met sensible student-orientation advisors, students will ask them for advice: *Do you think this would be good? Do you know about Professor Jones?* Students join extracurricular groups when friends do, and remain or leave sports teams because they like or don't like their teammates. Later on, some students will study abroad, or (like Dan) will not, depending on the preferences of their friends. In their eagerness to join the campus community, too, students adapt their academic work to those around them, trying to live up—or down—to what their peers expect.[29] For some, this means working harder; for others, it means relaxing, or hiding their aggressive study habits. Especially in residential settings, we suspect, they jump to the level of work sanctioned by their peers—for better or, often, for worse. Social life, in this broad sense, really is crucial. "At least half of college," said Michael Moffat, "was what went on outside the classroom, among the students, with no adults around."[30]

Unlike Dan, Julia couldn't really enter at all. Despite loving the campus, and finding people friendly, Julia's first few weeks at the college were rocky. She suffered from homesickness, made worse by the fact that her parents' marriage was going through difficulties. Her boyfriend, back home in New Jersey, was too far away to make regular visits. "I had two best girlfriends at home and I was calling them, like, the first few weeks from school crying all the time." She began to feel uneasy with people at the school; they felt different. She had attended a large, public, diverse high school, and now she was at a remote small college. She didn't like the college's party scene, with all the drinking and hooking up. Her mind was always elsewhere—back home. At the end of her first year, she transferred to a college closer to home.

In our sample, Julia is the best example of a student who faced the "perfect storm" of factors that would lead a student to drop out or transfer—strong ties to a community back home, weak or nonexistent ties to the college community, the feeling of social isolation or difference, family troubles, and a romantic partner who lives elsewhere.

Some higher education professionals disparage the centrality of student social life and friendships to the college experience, but may overlook their obvious necessity. At one *U.S. News* top-ten national liberal arts college we visited, a professor bemoaned students' naming of "making good friends" as a top outcome of college. Later in the same meeting, he told us that he himself joined the faculty because of the "fun" people in the department. (Other faculty in the meeting laughed at the irony.) At another small college, a colleague argued, "OK, we run a nice country club," but "we don't need to be mothering, all warm and fuzzy." Maybe "we"—the faculty—don't need to be, but someone does. Without solid peer relationships, the isolated student drops out either physically or, worse, emotionally, and the academic gains of college won't be made at all. Contrary to the image of lonely students grinding away at their schoolwork, in many cases we found in our own research that socially engaged students put more into their academic and intellectual work. Once established, solid relationships provide security and free the student from spending their time constantly looking for friends. Friendships provide the daily sustenance, the motivation needed, to engage with any academic program—indeed, the energy to do *anything*.

Successfully entering a college community, in effect, makes everything else possible.

3

Choosing

I'm not a language person. But I went [to a Chinese
table at orientation], and I met the professors. They were
so nice—really, really nice . . . And I was like, "Oh, I'll
try it out," you know? And I liked it. So I came in as a
psychology major with a minor in education, and now
I'm a Chinese major with a minor in government!
(Maudie, senior)

In an inescapable irony, college students make the freest yet most consequential decisions of their college careers when they are relatively new, that is,
when they least know what they're doing. We've already seen that incoming
freshmen face the initial challenge of successfully entering the social world
of the college. Right away they must find the cafeteria, meet some peers,
share space with roommates, pick some courses to take, join a club or two,
and—within weeks—probably wash their own clothes, perhaps for the first
time in their lives. At many schools they also find an apartment, declare a
major, pledge a sorority or fraternity, and choose their academic courses—all
decisions with lasting impact. Yet they do this knowing almost no one and
possessing no solid information about the quality of their professors, the reliability of their new friends, or the impact of the decisions they are making.

It's as if these students are wandering around in the late evening on the
edge of a crowded, moonlit forest, filled with many people and pathways,
promising excitement and adventure. They can't see very far into the distance,
certainly not into the forest itself or what's beyond it. But they do see groups of
other people and some pathways into the woods. Some people look friendlier
or more welcoming than others, some paths are broad or well lit. Heading into
the forest, a new student sees clusters of other people—a welcoming sorority;

some standoffish staff people; a popular teacher surrounded by his followers; a cliquish lunch-table crowd laughing at everyone else. She finds some smooth paths, some friendly fellow pilgrims, and she begins her journey. To a great extent—not entirely, but in important ways—she is at the mercy of her surroundings.

Although students make their own choices, they can only choose among these available options, some of which are more convenient or attractive than others. New students in particular don't know the collegiate landscape well enough to make consistently wise choices. They need the institution itself to help—for instance, to make it easy to find good courses, teachers, and advisors.

Choosing Courses

Students' decisions about academic programs are uniquely consequential, since enrollment and at least minimal success in courses are required for continued membership in the college community. Whatever else they may be doing, students must at least fairly often attend their classes, which therefore become the foundation stones of the daily and weekly schedule. Course selection fundamentally shapes how students will experience college, both in the enjoyment of the courses themselves and in the scheduling possibility for other activities. Courses also mandate a gathering of people, on a regular basis, with some definite sharing of attention. If those courses aren't good, they can reliably and routinely make a student miserable. When classes are poorly run, students feel it directly; classes are thus, in the eyes of the students, a key measure of the college's academic credibility. In all these ways, course selection shapes both a student's academic career and her nonacademic options.

Leaders who understand *how* students select courses can influence *what* courses students take—and thus, their entire college experience. So let's look at how students at the college go about choosing their courses. Two crucial facts emerge: (1) From a large number (roughly five hundred per semester) of initial courses, any particular student in fact actively chooses among perhaps a few dozen. Most courses are quickly eliminated early in the process. (2) Once those early parameters are set, students' decisions rapidly become quite local and contingent, made not on the basis of broad educational considerations but instead specific and sometimes minor factors: time of day when the class is offered, which section is open, or whether the classroom is close to the dining hall—in effect, factors of scheduling. What struck us was how frequently course decisions were made not from strategic considerations (major field, for instance), but simply from a desire to fill out a schedule ("find a fourth course") that would be minimally aggravating—a decent topic, not too much work, seats remaining in the class, etc.[1] Specific courses may in the end be chosen quite arbitrarily. This approach by students, we note, means that the arrangement of college course offerings and schedules can be surprisingly influential in what students are actually exposed to.

Before choosing courses, students *exclude* courses. Beginning from the entire course catalog (the online listing) a student makes a huge initial cut from 100 percent down to perhaps 10 percent of all courses. The vast majority are ruled out right at the beginning ("I'm not at all interested in that"). Some disciplines, for instance, are seen by many students as simply beyond their ability.[2] At the college, as is often true nationwide, many students avoid science and math courses when possible.[3] Their concern may actually bespeak not merely distaste or fear, but a belief in the fundamental incompatibility of their own personality with the subject matter. "I'm not a science person" is a common refrain.

> INTERVIEWER: Are there certain departments that you specifically have stayed away from?
> STUDENTS: Anything sciency. Yeah, I'm not very—I'm not really a science/math person, so I tend to take humanities. (Sarah, junior)
>
> I'm not much of a science person . . . as soon as they like start to involve lots of math, I just don't, I can't deal with it. (James, junior)
>
> I've never been much of a science person to be honest. (Hannah, junior)

In our research, at least, avoiding science is asymmetrical: no student ever told us, "I'm not a humanities person" or "I'm not a social science person." Students who pursue science, math, and foreign language courses report taking courses across all the disciplines, and their transcripts indicate that they do.[4]

Thus many students—wisely or not—have already ruled out entire swaths of the curriculum. Only then do they begin positively looking for courses they want to take, starting with their general interests. They then ask around about popular courses and professors, typically by talking with other students—roommates, friends, older students, whomever happens to live on their dorm hall, or next door—and sometimes (but less often) with professors or advisors. The range they explore may be wide or narrow—some students want to learn everything, some are clearly focused, and a few seem bored with life itself and have no visible interests.

Once a student has settled on her own area of preferences, she still faces a variety of structural barriers such as prerequisites. Since college curricula are generally organized hierarchically, many courses appearing in the catalog are in fact not open to all students, but are intermediate- or advanced-level offerings for upperclassmen. At the same time, juniors and seniors at the college are themselves sometimes denied admission to lower-level courses, usually on grounds that the class would be too easy or that they might compromise the classroom dynamics by intimidating the freshmen.

So what initially appears at a small college to be, say, five hundred available courses quickly becomes reduced to perhaps a dozen or so seriously considered by any particular student. From among these relative few a plausible coherent schedule is drawn up.

Only then does the student at the college—at this rather late stage of the game—meet with a faculty advisor, by which time, in truth, most of the major decisions have already been made. (Of course merely *having* a faculty advisor is a luxury unknown to vast numbers of American college students.) Some advisors have significant influence, when they actually exercise their power to deny a student registration, or when they meet with students early in the process, or when they have become trusted mentors. Some advisors can be a great help in solving minor problems, warning against planning errors, and finding that "fourth course." (Although a few students told us of "gaming" earnest advisors a bit by demonstrating great enthusiasm for what really was, in truth, just a fourth course.) Most of the time, though, the student's initial interests and fears rule out entire divisions of the curriculum, while professorial reputation, the fulfillment of necessary prerequisites, and the preferences and peculiarities of scheduling have already narrowed the choices severely before the student even talks with an advisor.

In the overall formation of a student's course selections, advisors (as distinct from true mentors—more on them later) are clearly minor players in the whole drama.

So preregistration meetings are frequently perfunctory. Anecdotally, some advisors seem to regard them as a mildly tedious formality.

Basically every [course] that I've done, I figured out on my own. I've been to [my advisor] three times: . . . preregistration the first semester, preregistration the second semester, preregistration the third semester—and it was just to have her sign [the registration form]. Basically every time I go there, she just says, "OK, looks good," and signs it, and I leave. (Dan, sophomore)

Actually I go to [my advisor] with all my classes picked out. (Liz, sophomore)

INTERVIEWER: Did your advisor try to push you any way or the other . . . ?
STUDENT: Not really. I've pretty much picked out all my classes for all my semesters, and my advisor has pretty much [said], "I will sign off on that." (Anne, junior)

Certainly some advisors take their role quite seriously. At some "open-curriculum" colleges (for instance, Hampshire College or New College of Florida) advisors and students really do sketch out multiyear educational plans, discuss specific steps to meet clear goals, and the like, a state of affairs reinforced by advisors' real power to say yes or no. When course offerings allow students to sign up for all of the courses they want and intend to take, this kind of advising can work. Whether such careful planning and execution are common, we don't know.

The final moment in the course-selection process is registration, which at most institutions nowadays occurs online. Here again, educational philosophies too easily fall victim to administrative and logistic necessities. (We will note here that judging from national surveys, seniors at the college are actually more satisfied with course availability than are students at some of its peer institutions.) Famously aggravating at many schools, registration is at best a kind of free-form dance in which students try to maneuver their way into courses they would plausibly like to take, given all their previous planning.

I ran out of options pretty fast actually. It became just a scramble really, just looking for any random course I could fit into based on the prerequisites and the schedule. (Mark, freshman)

Some students inevitably get to choose classes earlier than other students. At the college seniors register first, prioritized by an alphabetical rotation that changes each semester; within that sorting, early registrants pick first. Later registrants inevitably find that their already-limited options have suddenly become drastically narrowed, as they are "closed out" of favorite classes by enrollment limits.

The seniors take all the 400-level classes, and most of the 300-level classes, and, like, I could only take one class for econ even though I am a junior and I am an econ major. There was only one course that I could take. (Czengis, junior)

I think the worst thing is that . . . I've seen people who want to be government majors who get cut out of classes that are prerequisites to take other classes. And you can't really follow that course of study because obviously you're shut out of classes you need to take, to take other classes. (Jay, freshman)

Or juniors and seniors finding themselves unable to take up a new field.

I wanted to take an oral communications class, Intro, and I think it's too late [in my career] . . . I mean, I understand they're open for freshmen and sophomores, but I just, it's kind of rough when like if you, now you look back and you're like, "Oh, I wish I had taken this class." (James, junior)

Having worked through all the steps to finding classes they want and can take, students may still find themselves hunched over a computer terminal at 6:00 A.M. on registration day unable to enroll in that one class they *really* wanted. And at that very moment, online registration—so obviously advantageous, administratively speaking—simultaneously isolates students as they deal with this frustration and completely conceals their frustration from administrators, who aren't sitting alongside as the student struggles to find a course.

So then—on the spot, right then—our hapless student has to scrounge around, looking for another course that will fit. Whatever elaborate planning has taken place up until now, at this moment it's just "I need a course!" For students last in line, it's not pretty.

Well, the first time I was in first [registration] period, so I was OK there. But I was in the last [registration] group this time, and so now I'm [enrolled in] three classes that are at, like, 8:30 in the morning . . . courses that were my third selection on my list.
I got blocked out of my first, second, and third choice on one [slot] and my first and second choices on three others. [So] I got, like, my last three choices. (Jack, freshman)

Almost everywhere, we suspect, scheduling is peppered throughout with happenstance, frustrating errors, and sometimes serendipity. Only rarely can students put together an ideal "great college education" and then execute it without a hitch.

Much "advising," then, is done not by advisors but by the class schedule itself. More formally put, the course selection process, especially for third and fourth courses to "fill out the schedule," quickly becomes local and contingent. Course suggestions came from the kid next door, or a professor chatted with after class. Signing up depends on what other classes you're taking, whether a class meets right next to your dorm or a mile away, whether it meets first thing in the morning or right after lunch, and finally, whether you secured a good place in the registration line. Students set up a plausible schedule for themselves, and if they're lucky—given the obstacles of overenrolled classes, goofs in scheduling, and bad luck in registration—they get something they can, or must, live with. The students' willingness to take challenging, valuable courses matters—but so too does a college's administrative savvy in making those courses, and those teachers, readily available.

If the courses aren't there at the right moment, the students can't take them.

Finding the Right Professors

Courses are places to learn skills and information, but also—and more importantly—places to work with other people, especially teachers. In the lucky cases, classes are also where students find faculty mentors—as we've said, a luxury for students nationwide—who can profoundly impact a student's education and even life. Mentors influence not only what classes a student takes, and what other teachers they find, but more, what she learns in them, how exciting and engaging the courses are, and how she feels about the subject and about learning in general.

Many students in our research followed a standard pattern: they took classes, where they met teachers. Most then had a "professional" relationship with the teacher—perhaps attending office hours for extra help, or saying hello on campus, or being cordial before and after class. The professor (at this small college, but almost certainly not at many larger universities) knows the student's name, but little else; the relationship doesn't reach beyond academics.

Some of these relationships, though, eventually become wider ranging and more personal, and the teacher may even become a mentor. Mentors, we found, can have deep, lasting, positive results for students, and at the college, over half of the students develop such relationships with a faculty member. From our data and nationally, mentorship leads to better academic performance, certainly higher satisfaction with college, and even better success in finding jobs immediately after college.[5] Of course, it's hard to know whether the students who find mentors are simply those more likely to be successful anyway, but the correlation is still clear.

Classes, then, are not just a setting for learning skills and gaining knowledge. They offer a daily opportunity for intellectual relationships, a setting in which students and teachers meet each other regularly for a substantial amount of time over topics they presumably both enjoy. These relationships feed students' motivation, and motivation leads to learning—not only in the class at hand, but in other classes, and for years after college as well. In classes, students are exposed not just to ideas but to people; and while academic disciplines are important, they are as much a vehicle for meeting teachers as for ingesting important information. The transformative effects of relationships, that is, may matter more than even the cumulative effects of learning new material.

Teachers Matter

In describing to us the "good teachers" they enjoy taking classes with, students at the college mentioned four characteristics. None will surprise our readers, but the overall pattern is revealing. Students said their best teachers are: (1) exciting; (2) skilled and knowledgeable; (3) accessible—easy to find, available, and approachable; and finally (4) engaging. Notice, first, that only one of these characteristics—"skilled and knowledgeable"—describes professors' personal strengths aside from their relations with students. Certainly, a level of genuine knowledge and expertise is required. Perhaps at other institutions, professional competence is a problem. But at least for these students, at this college, professorial knowledge is not the critical factor. Rarely did we find students complaining about professors not "knowing their stuff," although obviously that shouldn't be taken for granted.

More importantly, three of the four characteristics are not really about the teachers *per se*, but about the students' *reactions to teachers*: good teachers are exciting *to students*, accessible *to students*, engaged *with students*. These qualities all describe a teacher who, however it happens, is regularly able to excite students about the subject; eager to talk with and listen to them; and generally able to connect with students, even starting from wherever the students are.

> He was really patient. Like, you could have asked him, "What's 2+2?" And he would have said—like, if 2+2 equals 5 on [my] paper—"Now you have to be careful there, you know, when you're doing arithmetic." "Careful," [he would say,] not "You're a stupid moron, get out of my class!" (Martin, freshman)

Then, good teachers begin to engage students with a kind of provisional equality.

> Professor Bates and Professor Cross place a heavy emphasis on, on like, student participation that's guided without being condescending . . . They're able to guide the conversation and make it interesting without making it drag, without making it feel like, you know, you're pulling teeth from half the class.
>
> It was really important for professors to recognize kind of what level, like, I'm ready to tackle. [They] treat their students—or at least, students that they really can see moving ahead in that field—as future colleagues, rather than someone who is just sitting in their class, you know, with their hand on their cheek falling asleep . . . It's the ability to recognize who wants to pursue something seriously, and then being able to feed that person material to help them pursue it. (Hannah, sophomore)

How do they do it?[6] In a series of comments, Murphy told us about half a dozen great teachers he had taken classes with; in every case, the teacher both stimulates and responds to students, in various ways compelling students' close attention to the topic.

> Professor Knox makes learning fun. For every fact he tells us, he tells us some funny story that makes us all like laugh and shocks us, but it really does teach us something . . . Professor Clark is tough as nails; like, everything you say has to be backed up, and she's driving you constantly for more information and more proof . . . She always has some counterargument . . . she'll ride you until the end and then she'll be like, "That was really good."
>
> Martin and Sarah are really good because they listen, and they're always quick with the jokes, and always thinking and relating things to real-world problems . . . When I disagree with something, they don't take offense.

Professor Nelson is always quick with a laugh and gives you quarters if you get really good ideas in his class. He's just honest about like, "If you're late, I'm going to pick on you today." And then Dwight, my ceramics professor, is . . . really great: he's just a ball of creativity, and always wants to talk about a new idea or a new thing you could do. He's always bringing in magazines and stuff with things about ceramics . . . (Murphy, sophomore)

As the institution's representatives, teachers are well resourced to pull students into being academically engaged. First, obviously, they decide on the students' grades, and indeed whether students pass the course at all. Second, students are, again, required to attend a certain number of class meetings in order simply to stay in school and eventually graduate. They have to show up. In the short run, for a substantial chunk of time—perhaps three hours a week—students are basically required to sit and listen to, and mostly watch, this one person whom the institution has selected. There are twelve, or forty, or (at larger schools) three hundred students in the room, but only one "professor." Third, this person (the professor) really is at the center of attention. She very typically is older, probably more formally dressed, standing while everyone else sits, and located at the physical focus of a room designed to make her the center of attention. That gives her a major advantage in dominating the room and coordinating what everyone else will do. Fourth, many college students will at least initially give the professor the benefit of the doubt; they'll see what she has to say. (At selective schools students have been admitted in part for their willingness to do this with good humor. They have a record of "doing well" in classes, of paying attention, of showing up reliably.)

Beyond these advantages, the professor is committed—and paid—to *profess*; she personally vouches for the subject. Being possibly smarter, probably more knowledgeable, and certainly more committed, the teacher has something to offer the students and a genuine incentive to try. She can be a true leader, going headfirst into the strange and deep thickets of Victorian literature, or music theory, or chemical physics, a person who takes the initiative, leads the way, and supports her followers. Crucially, the teacher guarantees that, in that thicket, anyone else who goes in will not be alone. Even if she's not the smartest person in the room, she is a reliable colearner: "If you want to talk about this subject," she promises, "I'm ready to talk with you." Having found such a person, some students gravitate to her.

Wielding such influence, professors matter in one surprising way: new students (almost by definition) know little about any particular field, especially outside of subjects heavily covered in high school (history, English, math). The first professor they meet in a discipline (geology, theatre, anthropology, engineering) effectively *is* that discipline to that student. When we asked about academic subjects, students overwhelmingly respond by talking not about the subject, but about their own teachers' habits, pedagogical styles, and personalities. Granted, at large research institutions with huge departments, students may realize that one professor (or T.A.) doesn't make a discipline. But students everywhere, required to choose classes, seem often to rely on seemingly idiosyncratic information—the teacher's reputation, personality, grading style—to form an impression of an entire academic field. Even in familiar fields, introductory courses seem to set a tone. That's reasonable; students have few other reliable sources of information. Students don't see disciplines in the way that faculty do, as elaborate divisions of expert intellectual labor. They see instead the specific living human being standing in front of them, and from that overwhelming face-to-face reality they extrapolate an entire discipline. Because of that impact, a good teacher can redirect a student's entire college career.

> I didn't want to take art history, but I had to because I had my writing-intensive requirements to fulfill. And I had one class with Professor Swanson, and I was hooked. From that second, I filled my schedule with art history classes, and decided to major in it. (Claire, alumna)

Not all teachers are good teachers, of course, and bad professors come in their own varieties. Some are simply dull, monotonous, or vapid; others demand too much busywork, or grade unfairly; others don't respect their students' abilities.

> The older I get, the more frustrating it is for me when professors . . . treat me like I don't know what I'm talking about, and like, I should just accept what they have to say because they're professors . . . Sometimes I felt underestimated by my professors. (Jane, senior)

Bad teachers are often described as arrogant, or maybe

> pissed off that they aren't teaching at Ivy League schools, and they just take it out on kids. Like, you know, "I'm socially inept; growing up I hated life, but I'm smarter than you." (Alfred, sophomore)

or

[they just] want to finish their little books, or whatever. (Marcy, sophomore)

or

[they] don't turn around [from the board] during class. Don't know any-body's name. Don't *need* to know anybody's name. (Mark, freshman)

Such professors can do serious damage in introductory classes, where as we've said they may be seen as a living embodiment of their disciplines. If the teacher seems intellectually lightweight, or tedious, or offensive, the discipline may itself appear that way. Introductory teachers thus, for good or ill, are gateways to their disciplines.

Initially when I came to [the college], I was really interested in [two disciplines] and those were my main passions. And I found [one] department very—not arrogant, but oh, I don't know, maybe "lofty"; maybe, you know, a little bit proud that they were publishing, and the students were second priority.

Whereas, I went to physics; they were very helpful, checked up on you. I thought my advisor was, you know, a physics professor and I formed a very close relationship with her. And the German Department, the two professors there are also very personable. And they still treat you, you know, more as a colleague.

So, I gravitated to those. (Jay, senior)

At the college, when a student reported to us a bad experience with a professor, she would typically state, unequivocally, that she would not take a course—any course—in that field again.

I had a teacher . . . She chose favorites and . . . her paper grading was en-tirely [arbitrary]. It kind of sucked . . . I definitely don't want to take another course [in that discipline] here ever. (Marie, sophomore)

Poor professors are "red flags" to students, signaling a kind of "danger zone ahead." In liberal arts disciplines, at least, students typically go no further. For students in our research, one off-putting professor can easily end a student's study of that professor's field.

She was, like, an extremely boring lecturer . . . We'd discuss [relevant current events] . . . They were cool things to talk about, and she made them boring somehow! Like, I don't think she would try hard enough to teach. She was teaching because she had to . . . That kind of made me not want to major in [her discipline]. (Kim, sophomore)

I just basically said, "I don't understand why [this paper] needs to be written this way." And he would say, "Because that's just the way I like it . . ." It was kind of ridiculous that the way I wrote initially was getting me, literally, Cs and low Bs on papers.

   And then I finally caved and said, "Fine, I'll write it the way you want me to." It was very simplistic, and it was very, I don't know, very middle school almost. And I got As. I, I was like, "Fine . . ." [But] I stopped taking classes in that department after his class. (Katie, senior)

There are important exceptions, to be sure. Premed students, if they continue making reasonable grades (not to be assumed), are often willing to put up with difficulties in pursuit of their career. So too are international students, who at the college are often more career focused than their peers, as well as some business-oriented students.

   At the college, most students have excellent teachers, whose courses they enjoy and with whom they typically develop a good "professional" relationship, focused on academics. The professor knows the student's name, may greet her by name when meeting, perhaps exchanges e-mails over a class topic, arranges to discuss a paper, and maybe extends a deadline. One step beyond simply an in-class connection, the "professional" relationship is close enough for a professor to write a reference letter, which for many students is the most they will ask, although the letter might not be very detailed. Such teachers can be excellent, valued instructors. These relationships are cordial but limited.

I remember Rosen would always talk to me after class if I had a question . . . he's a really good guy, and an interesting guy. So yeah, I really, really like him.

   But . . . you can't expect that a professor is going to, like, have friendships with all their students . . . it's only in certain cases where you can, you know, have a better relationship with them and talk with them about other things. (Sean, senior)

A fair number of students, including many men, as well as large proportions of international students and ethnic minorities, say they prefer that the faculty-student relationship be and remain at this strictly professional level. It's hard to know whether this is always a true preference; some international and minority students told us they were hesitant to attempt any contact with professors outside of class, whether or not they want it.

So the quality of the professors who teach introductory courses matters, both for engaging students and for legitimating disciplines. When students dislike a freshman-year course they frequently will never again take a course in that subject. Especially if the subject matter is new, an unpleasant first experience certainly may make students skeptical of the department, and fairly often diminishes their impression of the entire discipline. In a lab-science course, for instance, it could easily steer students away from the sciences altogether, unfairly or not. This dynamic is obviously critical when students exercise broad discretion in choosing courses.

Even at institutions where students arrive committed to a field, or are constrained by core distribution requirements, we would still suggest that introductory courses remain an important gateway mechanism. When they are staffed with weak teachers—untested visiting faculty, overworked adjuncts, underpaid graduate students, leftover "deadwood" professors working off some obligation, or even otherwise excellent professors who just aren't good with beginners—entire subject areas can be delegitimated. The academic enterprise starts looking, to new students, like perhaps a poor investment. Even when students remain in a major they don't like, or take courses they've heard are bad, the damage is done: physically students remain, but psychologically they have already left. They then fall into a "sophomore slump." Academic efforts sag, as students—some of whom showed initial enthusiasm for schoolwork—have been deflated by the realities of freshman-year courses; social life reigns supreme; and concerned faculty and administrators wonder what happened. It isn't big news to many professionals in student affairs offices, but it bears repeating: what happens in the first year is decisive.[7]

Meeting Mentors

The most valuable relationships students have with teachers are *mentorships*. These entail a significant personal and professional connection, lasting more than just one course or semester. They can't simply be assigned, but neither do they happen just by accident.

Nationwide, faculty-student mentorships vary dramatically by institution type, but according to Senior Surveys conducted during our research the college has a distinctly high number of them. The probabilities rise steadily during a student's career. Seniors looking back rated their relationships with "preconcentration [that is, freshman] advisors" as being "friendly and respectful (professional)" about 40 percent of the time, improving to "close and personal" about 15 percent of the time. Junior/senior advisor relationships scored better, with 40 percent judged as "professional" and a full 40 percent "close and personal." Finally, when the question was expanded to include *any* faculty member, not just official "advisors," nearly 80 percent of seniors said they currently had a "close and personal" relationship with some faculty member. That's not identical to mentorship, but it's still an impressive proxy result.

The defining characteristic of a mentor is a concern for the student beyond the immediacies of a course.

> We talk about everything. When it has to be academic . . . registration period . . . a deadline coming up; but other than that, it would just be, like, catching up! "So how have you been? How are things?" . . . "So what things are going on in your life?" So it's been really helpful. (Victoria, senior)

At the simplest level, a personal connection with a teacher seems to encourage students, even those just trying to get by, to work harder in classes.

> [Usually I take] a kind of capitalist approach: you do the minimal amount of work and get the highest, you know, outcome. Not so bad. But . . . this class I have right now with Professor Hinkes, I need to be prepared because I have this relationship with him, and I need to walk into class and know exactly what I'm talking about. (Herb, junior)

Some mentors draw students into close intellectual engagement.

> The first professor I ever met at [the college] was Professor Knox. My dad and I were up for an interview, and I sat down and had lunch with him and we chitchatted about history for a couple hours. It was a great time.
> I kept in touch when I was in Oxford because I was thinking of getting a doctorate in history. We e-mailed back and forth. I sent him some ideas. We were feeding off of each other's ideas, you know, we were trading books . . .

I'd hand in twenty to thirty pages [to him] here and there; and periodically, I'd give him like, you know, detailed outlines. Or we'd just sit down, and I would just talk. (Ruttiger, senior)

Two professors helped Hannah into courses and topics that challenged and expanded her intellectual range.

I kind of fell into the Philosophy Department, took a course with Professor Cross, and it was unbelievable. And my writing and my experience in the department was beyond that of my classmates, so he invited me in the spring to a senior ethics seminar. So I was a freshman, and I was a little intimidated . . . but it worked out, because it kind of clinched for me that I was going to pursue that as a major. And he also started to serve as sort of my surrogate advisor outside of the English Department.

He pointed me towards, you know, Professor Bates in the Anthropology Department who does a lot with linguistics . . . who let me into a course . . . It was Ethnography of Communication. I just really loved the material and wanted more of it. So I started reading, like, more than, than Julianna [Bates] was giving in class. And I started spending a lot of time in her office. And the more I read, the more I felt like, "Yeah, this is really what I want to study." I just felt really connected to what I was reading. (Hannah, junior)

Mentors can be supportive in various ways.

Professor Clark is really awesome. She's my advisor . . . She sort of turned me on to all this stuff, like, to my major . . . And she's been really, really supportive.

Our Chinese program for the summer got cancelled because of the SARS epidemic, so I sort of threw up my hands . . . She ended up calling me and saying, "Hey, I found these like three options that you can do . . ." She also taught one of my classes, but she's just been helpful like in and out of class all the time.

The really good ones, sometimes I feel like they're teaching me something just so that they can have a really cool discussion with me about [the subject] . . . (George, sophomore)

So how do mentorships happen?

In order to become a mentor, the teacher must first spend some time with the student. True mentors were almost always either course teachers or athletic coaches.

I talked to my math professor about it and he was the one—he gave better advice than my [official] advisor. I was just saying, "Why don't you become my advisor?" (John, freshman)

I'll keep in touch [after graduation] with my swim coaches for sure . . . They were the first people that would see me wake up, and the last people you see before you go to bed. It's just natural that you want to keep a relationship with them. Yeah, I'll keep in touch with them for sure. (Yi Jae, senior)

Again, this point may seem obvious, but it is sometimes ignored nonetheless: *when professors don't have students in their classes, mentorships can't develop.* When even an official faculty advisor doesn't have advisees in class, mentorship almost never develops. Frequent working interactions are a necessity for mentorship. The more contact, the better.

I drove from our camp in Nevada to Salt Lake City with Sarah, which was, like, a four hour drive alone in a car. And just hearing lots of stuff about her life, and about Martin's life, you know, and hearing about stuff from my other professors' lives has like really inspired me, and . . . given me guidance as to what kind of person I want to be and . . . what kind of values I want to hold. And so I don't really think of them as professors. I've housesat for Martin and Sarah for like weeks on end; I've, like, lived in their house . . . (Murphy, senior)

Because of the volume of contact time required, relatively few freshmen or rising sophomores at the college have mentors. With each subsequent year, they are more likely to find one: it takes time. By the junior year, many students have one, although again the fact of being one's official "advisor" seems not to matter at all.

Second, interest in mentorship must be mutual; both student and professor must want the relationship. We didn't study faculty, but students seem to feel that plenty of professors are willing. (A minority of professors, though, anecdotally at least, don't want to have any sort of personal relationship to their students. Some think it's inappropriate, others that it's a waste of time.) Among students, women as a group are far more likely to want a mentor, and may benefit more as well. Most women in our panel wanted and found one, even if too late to gain the full benefits, while no women expressed an active *lack* of interest in being mentored. A fair minority of men in our panel, on the other hand, didn't care about having a mentor—in fact, actively did *not* want one, and thought such relationships would be weird, awkward, or just not useful. These men were also the most "instrumentalist" about their education—they planned careers in business or law, expressed little interest in the liberal arts *per se*, and basically aspired to graduate with good grades and begin their careers. They were, again, only a modest portion of the men we talked with, but they had no female equivalents.

Third, mentorship and academic success clearly go together. But which comes first? In our data, students with lower grades—especially men—often have no mentor. But high-GPA students, both female and male, all have relationships with at least one professor, and often with two, three, or even four, that they describe as close. Maybe that's just because academic success attracts mentors, and that's probably true. In interviews, students themselves say that contact with a professor comes *first*, encouraging their work, making them pay attention, increasing their faith in the professor. Indeed, one of Dan Chambliss's senior thesis students, Kathryn Kroleski,[8] found in her research on mentoring that perhaps neither exclusively "comes first": a little success may prompt extra attention, which then leads to further success, and so on. Whenever it starts, mentoring helps.

Finally, activities that blur the distinction between professional and personal concerns open the door to mentoring. Such activities seem to have significant, sometimes even profound, impact. For instance, time and again, alumni both young and old told us of having been invited to a dinner at a professor's home, and how important the experience was for them. For many, it was a signal event in their college career. They seemed to feel that it symbolized the college's commitment to its students, or at least that professor's personal concern for students. It seemed almost magical to them, a kind of talisman.

But was the college's almost mythic "dinner at a professor's home" really so common? And did it really matter so much? For the answers, we turned to a more rigorous statistical analysis. Every spring, seniors at the college answer a comprehensive standardized questionnaire, produced by the Higher Education Data Sharing Consortium of colleges (HEDS), that covers a wide range of undergraduate experiences and attitudes. In 2006, our colleague Shauna Sweet, then engaged in graduate study in statistics and survey research, brought together seven years of these Senior Surveys into an integrated database of 2,018 respondents. In the course of her analyses, she looked at two questions in particular: (1) "Have you ever been a guest in a faculty member's home?" and (2) "Would you choose again to attend this college?" Sweet wanted to see whether, as alumni suggested, the two were correlated.

The overall number of home visits by itself was striking. On average, 85 percent of graduating students at the college had indeed been a guest in a faculty member's home at least once. Probably more impressive, a full 20 percent had been a guest "often" or "very often." By itself this seems remarkably high, certainly compared with the broad range of student experience nationwide.

But our question was different: does such personal contact *matter?* The initial finding, as a simple correlation, again seemed clear. Among women— generally more satisfied with the college—having *ever* been a guest raised their "choose again" response by 9 percent compared to students who had never been a guest. For men, the increase was a full 13 percent. These are large jumps in a sample of over two thousand, clearly significant both statistically and substantively. In other words, even a *single* visit to a faculty member's home during a student's four-year college career was associated with a substantial improvement in outlook on the entire college experience.

That still seems too easy a conclusion, possibly misleading. So both Ms. Sweet and, independently, Chris Takacs, performed more rigorous statistical analyses of the data. They measured both "choose again" and general "satisfaction" results, and they used both linear regression and ordinal logit statistical techniques. They controlled for all the major variables associated with student satisfaction, especially GPA, gender, and race, overall the most powerful factors. No matter what variables were introduced, no matter what analyses were used, no matter which researcher did the analysis, the results stood firm: a single visit by a student to a professor's home clearly correlated with the student's satisfaction and willingness to "choose again" to attend the college. In fact, visiting a professor's home had a greater statistical impact even than changing a student's GPA from a B- to an A-, a serious improvement in academic standing. Statistically speaking, this finding doesn't go away.

A critic might argue that professors invite their favorite—most eager, most already-engaged—students to their homes. In fact, the dinners aren't that exclusive; the vast majority of students attend as members of classes, not as individuals. There is little individual selection in reaching the "ever attend" group.

Our point isn't that all professors should be inviting students to their homes. It's that remarkably small actions can at least potentially produce huge results, noticeable even years later. Specifically: a one-time, perhaps three or four-hour effort by a professor (hosting a visit to her home) can potentially have a marked effect on dozens of students' feelings about their entire college career. Such actions—we will discuss others in subsequent chapters—seem typically to entail face-to-face personal contact of some sort. Small cost, big results.

Of course, this particular intervention may not work everywhere or for every professor and student. When we shared our findings with a colleague from a large Midwestern state university, she demurred. She had tried to invite her students for dinner and they were aghast; "It totally violated social distance norms." But for students who want such contact, even a very small action—a few hours out of four years—can have decisive impact, perhaps in opening the door to a mentorship.

One thing is certain: if a student never has contact, personal or at least professional, with a teacher capable of mentoring, the student has *no* chance of finding a faculty mentor. Only some professors are willing and able to be good mentors, and only some of them have contact with significant numbers of (willing) students. Both factors must be in place.

When they are, the results can be extraordinary. When we talked with alums five and ten years out about teachers who influenced them, we were surprised to discover that a relative handful of faculty accounted for a large percentage of mentors. Indeed, *a single professor*, recently retired from the college, accounted for a substantial—nearly 10 percent—of all positive comments we heard in our alumni sample. He was an exceptional mentor, no doubt, especially for a certain kind of student. He was also, crucially, in a department (Economics, as it happens) that saw lots of majors, and for a time he was the college's dean of students, where again his skills could be widely applied. The right person stood, in effect, in a rushing river of students, where he could positively affect hundreds, even thousands. And he did. Again, to find a mentor, a student must first *meet and spend time with* potential mentors.[9] And even the finest potential mentors can't help much if they don't meet a lot of early-career students.

Declaring a Major

One theme here has been how apparently small contingencies (a freshman dorm assignment, one's first teacher, the availability of a course, a visit to a home) can have lasting impacts on a student's career. This holds true for entire areas of study, where even the formally open, and important, choice of an academic major may be constrained by the vagaries of luck and smaller decisions already made along the way.[10]

At the college, students declare majors in the spring of sophomore year, and switching majors even after that is fairly common. Students believe that liberal arts education generally rests on the principle of delaying firm commitments to a field of study, valorizing the flexibility of thinking that presumably comes with studying a variety of fields and perspectives.

> I wanted to come to a liberal arts school because I really didn't know what I wanted to do, and I thought it would give me the opportunity to look and study in a lot of different courses and areas. (Mary, freshman)

> A liberal arts school is a school that provides many options for [you]. It provides . . . a way to try a lot of different things. [It's nice] to have that option . . . not being so, not being forced to make a decision right away. (Tom, freshman)

Waiting to declare a major certainly has its advantages. Many academic disciplines are not at all as entering students imagine them: undergraduate premed studies, for instance, are not really about medicine, but about chemistry and microbiology, and there's little or no contact with patients, diseases, hospitals, surgery, or medical practice. Psychology, which some students hope will help them negotiate difficult families or tricky relationship issues, often turns out to be a compendium of memory studies and neural transmitter articles. Economics, which one might think is about the stock market and making money, turns out to be a vastly theoretical elaboration of complicated graphs and esoteric equations. And because anthropology, linguistics, and political science aren't discussed at all in most high schools, they may be totally new areas of study.

Then, too, even many serious students in liberal arts programs may care less about their major than about their GPA and feeling successful; many don't seem concerned about their major's effect on job prospects.[11] Like other selective schools, the college admits students primarily for their high school records, grades especially, so it's no surprise that these students are good at massaging their academics to produce high GPAs. Rather than persist with subjects in which they aren't doing well, they will gravitate to subjects in which they're doing better—or at least getting better grades. Or they discover new disciplines they hadn't been exposed to, which they find more interesting. Or they follow—"major in," students say—a great teacher. In any case, they are often flexible about majors.

At the college, official declarations of a major often postdate the student's *de facto* commitment to a discipline. Declarations occur near the end of the sophomore year, allowing students time to explore a variety of subjects. Rather than commit to a major and then take the courses, many students take some courses, then declare a major. They take one course, then another, then another, often following a professor, sometimes a subject, that they enjoy. After three or four semesters, when it's time to declare a major, it is as if they look around and say, "Oh, I guess I'm an art history major," or, "I guess I'm a sociology major!"

> I kind of ended up with it because . . . sophomore year you declare your major. Well, I had my most classes in government; I might as well do that. (Anne, junior)

Declaring a particular major, that is, may actually *conclude* a sequence of events:[12] initial exposure to the discipline, probably in the first semester and certainly in the first year; no "red flags" or bad experiences in introductory courses; a positive experience with at least one professor; and decent information about the department and the subject matter. Once those conditions have been met, the student may be ready to officially commit to a major. Apparently small decisions, each made in the short term, lead to the serious commitment. Just as a wedding proposal nowadays typically concludes, instead of beginning, a courtship, so here the official declaration of a major simply ratifies what the little choices of daily life had already produced. One actually does "declare" a major, not "choose" one.

These patterns describe women better than men. Men at the college tended more often to commit to a specific career path (often business, banking, etc.) and then choose a major appropriate to it. Although family pressures and career concerns are an important factor for everyone, men in particular seemed likely to be pushed by their parents to find a career-relevant major. They would stick with a major almost regardless of their experience in it. The women seemed more influenced by the personal relationships they look for, and usually find, with specific faculty members.[13]

For Rick, one of our panelists, the process of choosing didn't work well; neither his own style nor the college's system seemed to help. He came to the college from a small, public school in rural New England, where he had developed an intellectual curiosity that valued, as he put it, "learning for the sake of learning." He wanted to explore a variety of fields and learn about numerous topics.

Initially, he was surprised at how much time he had to devote to academics.

> Pretty much the first month, I was just really, like, surprised by the amount of work. I was shocked, and at points I was, like, I wasn't sure if I could handle it. I felt sort of, like, sinking.

After a few months, he grew more accustomed to his academic requirements. At first, he considered majoring in government; the introductory class taken was interesting enough, but he wasn't ready to commit. He had a few good professors along the way, but none he really clicked with.

By late in his second year, Rick had realized that he had waited too long to find an academic home. His advisor, an English professor (one of Rick's many possible majors), was of little help, and only really offered him advice for English majors. Several possible majors were by this point out of reach, with unmeetable prerequisites. He also knew that in his last two years, it wouldn't be as easy for him to take courses in new areas.

> I was just kind of experimenting, and now when I look back on course offerings, I'm like, "Oh, I should have taken that course, and now I won't have time to . . ." Toward the end of the first year, I realized that I had taken courses that didn't, that didn't like pique my interest or anything. There weren't any courses that I thought I'd want to continue on with as a major after having taken them.

Rick repeatedly expressed his desire to continue exploring, not to settle on one field. He wanted to take more introductory courses (often closed to juniors and seniors), not because they were easy but because they could offer him new areas of knowledge. Small classes too, he felt, sometimes got in the way as students would be locked out of them. He found

> small classes a hindrance to students who want to learn: I'd say my main concern is that the size of classes kind of hinders students' abilities to take classes they're interested in . . . I just think they should allow more students [in].

In his junior year, Rick switched his major to mathematics.

I feel like I finally had direction while choosing classes this year. In the past, I was just sort of taking classes to sort of feel around . . .

However, he was still unhappy that he couldn't continue to explore other fields.

Realizing I would like to pursue, like, other areas, I feel like—I realized it too late, and a lot of, like, opportunities were kind of shut out to me because of, because of the system . . .

I just remember being like, say, the Physics Department. I just remember them, like, strongly recommending you have taken the two introductory courses—it's a year-long thing—by the end of your freshman year! And then I realized that, even if I wanted to take this route, it was almost kind of closed out to me.

Admitting that his major had changed "a million times," Rick explained that "my ideas for the future have changed and as a result, my intended major has changed."

By his senior year, Rick had changed his major one further time, back to government. Towards the end of his time in college he felt that it was more interesting than mathematics; but he wasn't really happy with government, either.

Rick entered and left college with an intellectual curiosity that many students lack. He talked about the content of his courses—the work, the ideas, their application, their meaning. But he was one of few students who, in our interviews, didn't talk about his professors, and he admitted not being close to any of them; he had good teachers, but no mentor. Unlike many of the students passionate about learning, Rick never found his niche. But with no mentor, no helpful advisor, no discipline that really attracted him, and blocked out by his junior year, Rick found no good choices remaining.

When we asked Rick what he disliked about the college, he would insist that it was great. Nothing needed to be changed. He was painfully hesitant to criticize. But when we asked him whether he would choose to attend the college again, his answer was clear: "no."

Making Decisions

After the overcontrolled boredom of many American high schools, freedom of choice is certainly one of the great attractions of undergraduate life. There are no assistant principals here, and the deans are often distant or unknown.

No one tells you to tuck in your shirt or lengthen your skirt; you don't need a "hall pass" to go to the bathroom, and you don't sit in class all day long. You can just hang out and nobody cares. You can choose from dozens, even scores, of programs. And at the end of the day, you go to bed when you want to (maybe even with another person!), and then sleep in the next day.

With all this freedom, college students appear to face a considerable number of decisions: What courses should I take? With what teachers? What friends would I like? Where will I live, and with whom? Should I join a frat? Do I try out for a sports team? There may even be too many choices, more than the student is prepared to make, with too many options to review and consider in an informed fashion.

But their choices are more limited than they seem. At the college, although hundreds of classes are listed in the catalog for each fall semester, an entering freshman, practically speaking, chooses from among a few dozen at most. The college itself helpfully provides a listing of classes "appropriate" for freshmen. From that list, realistically, weaker students aren't likely to sign up for (or make it through) introductory chemistry or physics. It's hard to be a music major if you're starting from scratch, or a biology major if you're coming from a poor high school. Similarly, only recruited athletes play on the basketball team; only strong singers, usually with some serious music training, can make the choir. There are structural limits as well to what students can do: prerequisites for all kinds of courses, enrollment limits for that program in Paris or Beijing, only so much time in one's schedule, and good or bad luck in the registration lottery.

Armed with limited information and working within a host of constraints, students who are picking classes quickly become opportunistic, looking for workable solutions to their current problems: What will be my major? What classes should I take? Which ones can I get into? Who's the professor? Is there room in this section? (it's at 2:30 on Friday!). Especially later in the registration process, they make decisions quickly and then find themselves carried along. They ask advice not from the wisest person, but from whomever is closest—a roommate, a friend sitting adjacent at dinner, or maybe a professor they chat with after class. This is one reason why daily friendships are so important: friends (and parents, often) are the people they first turn to for help and advice, and the wrong friends can systematically send them in the wrong direction.

They are "satisficing," as the economist Herbert Simon put it, trying to make a reasonable accommodation to the demands of the moment.[14] They are not looking for perfect answers, just for solutions that are good enough, or even just OK. Students have academic preferences, sometimes quite serious, but their preferences are neither fixed nor always decisive. Their choices often become local and contingent: based on immediate conditions, often idiosyncratic.

"Choosing" a Spanish major, for instance, might be only the final step in a long series of earlier choices. One Spanish class, which turns out to be fun, is taken with a brilliant young teacher in the department. Then another class, and another; soon the student realizes, "I'm a Spanish major!" Afterwards, the found commitment (to Spanish) propels a host of other decisions: taking a semester in Madrid, having Professor Lopez as an advisor, writing a thesis on Latin America. What initially appears a minor choice (to take this particular course, this particular teacher) in the fall of freshman year may in fact easily have a host of future consequences.

Casual choices create social commitments, unrecognized at the time, setting up a row of "side bets"[15] that lock a student into a path or pattern of behavior. Sports teams, we have seen, are a good place to find friends. But having joined, athletes don't want to disappoint their coaches by going abroad for junior year, thus hurting the team's chances of making it to the playoffs. And when all your friends are in the hockey or lacrosse fraternity, when you're the star player, you can almost never quit; everything depends on your participation. If your teammate friends are OK, they become your "crowd," and you quickly find yourself moving through college with them—in effect, stuck with them, since friendships with *these* people may rule out friendships with *those* people.

By the end of sophomore year, almost every student has faced and made a number of clear, official, institutionally recognized decisions: what courses to enroll in; what major to declare; what roommates to have, and where to live; whether to study abroad. Academic majors have been certified in writing and put on the official record. Fraternities and sororities have made bids and in turn received "pledges," a public declaration of intent to join. Even roommates, once assigned more or less randomly by the college, are now openly chosen; a student must come out and, in effect, declare, "I want to live with you." Even arrangements slipped into gradually or thoughtlessly soon become institutionalized.

Thus certain apparently small decisions that a student makes early on (guided by the easy availability of some options) can have a profound influence on the paths down which she will move from then on.

Early small steps matter, especially when they involve relationships, including those with professors. A dean we once talked with was skeptical of the importance we attribute to teaching, mentorship, and personal connections of faculty with students, especially those forged early in college. He had heard, he told us, *lots* of stories from graduate students in prestigious universities: on arriving in a PhD program, they were shocked to discover that their beloved undergraduate teacher was—well, twenty or thirty years behind the times in his discipline! The dean, seeing this as clear evidence of failure, proposed that his own institution, traditionally rather teaching focused, therefore needed to reemphasize professors' research currency.

But the dean, we think, missed the point of the stories. Look at what apparently happened with these students. They first studied with an undergraduate teacher who excited their interest. Then they took more courses, and came to love their teacher and their discipline; then they moved on to graduate school—at "prestigious universities," he said—where they continued to learn, and to correct their prior misperceptions. In the end they planned, in fact, to devote their entire lives to these fields of study. The dean, by his own report, had heard this story "lots" of times. That sounds to us like a story of remarkable success—not perfect, admittedly, but at least very good.

The students who didn't like their first teachers—however up-to-date those professors were as researchers—probably never even took a second course. So the dean never heard their stories.

4

The Arithmetic of Engagement

In a lot of the large classes that I take, there's just,
there's too much room for people to slack off. And, like,
you don't have to do the work. You don't have to stay
kept up on what's going on. So it's easy for people to
just become disengaged with the class.

(Harry, sophomore)

Let's stop for a moment at this halfway point in our narrative. Until now we've looked at students' experiences, and we've seen that apparently small factors or even chance can sometimes lead to very important outcomes; that apparently minor decisions can often have major results; and that teachers matter, not only by inspiring students but sometimes, unfortunately, by discouraging them as well. We've also seen that what students want is sometimes not what they actually need, even to satisfy their own immediate wishes: unattractive "high-contact" dorms can help to produce the friendships that students most require for success in college. Students themselves can understand such phenomena, if only in retrospect.

But for the next dozen or so pages, we hope to remind the reader that students learn within much wider organizational settings where one student's gain may be another student's loss. In this chapter, then, we pull back to the broader perspective of an administrator, and show how what seems to be obviously a good idea—from almost everyone's point of view—can in fact become quite counterproductive. Administrators' work can be organizationally risky, filled with unpredictable results and awkward trade-offs. We will try to show how this happens in one particularly vexing case. We will try to show what is wrong—even apart from financial considerations—with small classes.

When students choose courses, meet teachers, and select majors, they are sorting themselves among a limited number of educational opportunities. Not all students can capture all the good opportunities. Colleges offer students a limited number of good teachers (even allowing for different styles, etc.), convenient class times, appealing courses, and worthwhile majors. An entering student only gets one freshman dorm, four or five first-semester courses, a few extracurriculars, etc. Viewed from an administrator's perch, then, a student's choices are constrained by the probabilities of finding a good match. Sometimes the odds go up, sometimes they go down. Even when resources are lavish, as at the college, the odds remain finite. A conscientious administrator will work to make them go up, but there's no escaping the "musical chairs" logic of the situation. For any particular student to become engaged in college socially or academically, she needs to encounter the right people at the right time; but her chance of having those encounters is inevitably constrained, in part by what other students get.

We call this reality "the arithmetic of engagement": at any particular moment, there are a limited number of great opportunities for students to become engaged. Fortunately, however, even a small number of engaging people and events, properly located, can have a disproportionately positive impact on students' educational careers. Consider these findings from our research:

- While students may have a large circle of acquaintances, having just two or three good friends seems sufficient for most students to have an enjoyable college experience.
- Out of perhaps twenty-five teachers a student has during college, she needs only one or two "great" ones to feel that she has had an excellent academic experience.
- In a small college, a tiny number (say, five or ten) of excellent large courses can positively affect large numbers of students.
- Conversely, a single poor professor, teaching a large introductory course, can easily destroy scores of students' interest in a discipline.

These facts suggest that even with a limited number of available teachers, enrolled students, courses being offered, etc., a strategic use of such resources can lead to noticeably improved outcomes. An administrator who understands the arithmetic of engagement thus has some ability to escape the ruthless tradeoff between quantitative financial realities (which press for higher student-faculty ratios) and qualitative educational needs (which press for lower ratios).

In quantitative terms, the problem appears brutally simple. Since students create revenue, most institutions financially benefit from having a higher number of students per professor. So administrators monitor the enrollments of departments and courses, encouraging everyone to "carry their share" and handle large numbers of students, in order to pay the bills. Departments with low enrollments lose positions; departments with higher enrollments gain new positions, keep their roster of faculty, and maintain department budgets. "Enrollment management" nicely describes the administrative strategy involved: putting enough warm bodies in place to pay for the entire enterprise. In the worst cases, students are sorted into "empty seats" in available courses with little regard for their particular needs or interests, something like commodity corn being poured into hopper cars on a railroad siding, filling each to its grid-marked limit.

Qualitatively, of course, such massified education can quickly become so watered down as to be useless. In huge classes, students rarely speak up or ask questions, get little feedback from the professor, and often remain unknown. Grade inflation easily sets in as professors try to attract those warm (if sleepy) bodies, while entire departments acquire reputations for offering "gut" courses or a "joke" major.[1] In such cases, students in an oversized program, or with dull teachers, may actually be worse off than with no program at all—it may actually be *detrimental* to large numbers of students, by making them see the subject, or college, as a useless waste of time.

So it may seem that the answer is simply to offer a greater number of smaller classes (which, of course, cost more money). There's no doubt that small classes can be a valuable part of a college education. For the students in smaller classes, there are great benefits, hardly available in the huge lectures so characteristic of large universities. In small classes, students can speak up more, have their questions answered, and have their opinions valued.

I feel like in really small classes that we have, everyone's forced to be on top of the subject matter and it just helps in terms of, like, everyone participating and feeding off . . . what other people are saying, so that new ideas are being put into your head, not just what the teacher's saying. (Harry, sophomore)

Small group discussions can be tailored to the actual students in the room, with their own individual backgrounds and levels of preparation. Professor responses can take each comment seriously, pushing students to really pay attention and engage with each other.

> I took a class called Analytical Methods of Archeology, which was like a lab archeology class, and it was me and one other girl and two professors. And so, like, you can't get more interactive than that. There's four people in the room and two of them are the professors, you know. It was like a very interactive class, and it worked well for this topic because, you know, we're discussing, like, lab methods and the pros and cons of the different theories. (Murphy, junior)

At the college, students almost universally want more available small classes: the benefits are important, even irreplaceable, and small classes, they say, represent what's uniquely valuable in a small college.

A strategy of "more small classes" (perhaps freshman or sophomore seminars) thus might seem to be a reasonable approach to engaging students early in their college careers. But over several years of research and experimentation, we found—to our surprise, and in contrast to what the students themselves claim—that small classes are not a reliable solution to the problems of student engagement. Small classes or seminars can actually be counterproductive, by preventing students from encountering the professors and topics they need to become engaged early in their careers. Even wealthy institutions such as the college, with the best overall student-faculty ratios and an abundance of small classes, therefore can easily find themselves having misallocated their resources. In this instance, one may easily be misled by students who themselves don't fully appreciate or articulate exactly what they mean when they say that they "like small classes."

In 2001, as part of a new curriculum, the college began aggressively attempting to expand the number of smaller classes and seminars it offered. Student surveys and interviews, including preliminary work for our Mellon Assessment Project, had suggested that small classes were integral to education at the college and crucial in attracting prospective students. ("Small" and "large" are relative terms, of course. Many university students rarely if ever see classes with fewer than fifty students, or, as is often the case, fewer than several hundred. At the college, classes generally are far smaller, but our logic still applies to larger schools.) Some faculty and deans were concerned about a perceived "sophomore slump" in students' academic enthusiasm. The administration was also at least aware that the *U.S. News & World Report* rankings included a measure of "percentage of classes under 20 students." After much debate, the college launched a program of sophomore seminars, required for all students, as well as a range of "proseminars" (limited to sixteen students), to be widely available to freshmen and sophomores. The "soph sems" were to be the centerpiece. Each would be team-taught by at least two professors; topics would be interdisciplinary; and oral communication would be emphasized. The strict maximum of twelve students per professor was mandated to enable close student-faculty interaction. Dozens of these "soph sems" and proseminars were added to the curriculum, noticeably shifting faculty resources into those courses.

Two years into the programs, we asked students in our assessment interviews what they thought of all their small classes. To our amazement, many responded, "What small classes?" We were puzzled. Obviously the college offered the required sophomore seminar, plus scores of proseminars; these courses were filled with students. Our respondents, we surmised, must either be deceiving themselves, or perhaps were just complaining that they didn't have even more. We couldn't believe that their schedules weren't filled with the many small classes the college offered.

So we asked the college Registrar to print out complete transcripts for our panel students. We then sat at a table and began reading. It didn't take long. Simply flipping through this random sample of student records was immediately revealing. Most courses taken by most students were not, in fact, small seminars. Most students, it appeared, were concentrated in a handful of the largest majors, taking mostly midsized (twenty to forty–student) classes. Many had a moderate number of smaller classes or even seminars (with twelve students), but the "small classes" self-image of the college seemed a bit overstated.

To confirm this rough impression, our economist colleague Ann Owen undertook a more precise quantitative analysis of enrollment patterns. Using electronic records from the Registrar, she first looked at data on courses. She listed all courses taught at the college in the spring of 2005, the senior year for our panelists. She found that if these courses were arranged by enrollment from smallest to largest, the median class size—the one in the center of the distribution—was only thirteen students, an impressively small number. In fact, a whopping 74 percent of the college's courses fell under the "20 students" line that *USNWR* uses. The college had the same percentage of small courses as Swarthmore! At the same time, only 9 percent of courses enrolled more than thirty-five students—again, a tiny proportion compared to what happens in big universities. These numbers looked very good.

But then Owen looked at the experience of students—not *courses*, that is, but *students*. She collected electronic transcripts for the entire Class of 2005 (roughly 450 students), and for each student calculated the mean and median size of classes they actually took. The results were surprising, to say the least. Most of the time, a typical student was in a course with twenty to thirty students; the average course enrollment was 22.5 students. Most *students*, most of the time, were in classes with more than twenty students, despite the fact that 74 percent of the *courses* had fewer than twenty. And the "small class" opportunities were not distributed at all randomly; departments with few students per professor unsurprisingly yielded many more small classes.

What was happening? Why had such a huge initiative produced such disappointing results? Certainly the college offered lots of small courses, many of which quickly filled to their limits. But a basic, almost obvious—in hindsight—logical point had been missed: *by definition a small class is one that most students aren't in*; that's what makes it small! And classes whose enrollments are tightly capped are—again, by definition—those that, from another point of view, actively exclude the most students. If the total number of courses offered at a college remains the same, simply increasing the number (and proportion) of smaller courses only serves to exclude more students than ever before.

So why are the *U.S. News* numbers misleading? Because they ask colleges what percentage of all *classes* offered have fewer than twenty students, not how many *students* are in small classes. The college's *USNWR* numbers were quite high, around 73–74 percent—roughly comparable, as we said, to those at Swarthmore College, a perennial "#1" contender in the "National Liberal Arts" rankings. *USNWR* asks colleges for "the percentage of classes with fewer than twenty students"—the number of small classes, divided by the total number of classes, and multiplied by one hundred.

USNWR treats classes—not students—as what social scientists call the "unit of analysis"—the thing being counted up, the thing you want to know about. But a moment's reflection will show why classes aren't the right unit of analysis. Classes are not the point of college. They are a tool, a useful means to the end of educating students. It's perfectly possible to have a huge number of small classes—or for that matter, excellent classes—without producing much good education for students. Classes and students really are different things, different kinds of things, and what's good for one may not be what's good for the other.

Imagine you're the dean of faculty at a ten thousand–student university, and you want to inflate the university's *USNWR* "small classes" score. The best strategy would be to establish ninety-nine tiny courses—tutorials, with one student assigned to each. Then you assign the other 9,901 students to a single immense lecture course, held in the football stadium. Maybe you could show some movies. The college could then report to *U.S. News*—with absolute veracity—that 99 percent of its classes were small (very small!) while only 1 percent of classes (the stadium lecture) had more than forty students (to be exact, 9,901). So while 99 percent of *courses* would have small enrollments, just over 99 percent of *students* would be in the single huge class. Classes and students are completely different units of analysis. When Professor Owen looked at student transcripts, she saw results by student, not by class, and thus explained the discrepancy.

The flagship "sophomore seminars" launched at the college in 2001 crashed on the rocks of elementary arithmetic. With a limit of twelve students per professor, they aimed at being small. But when they were also "team taught" with two professors in the room, any actual student was in a "seminar" with as many as twenty-six people—hardly a setting for active speaking engagement. Because they were "interdisciplinary," few of them fulfilled departmental major requirements, so professors had to choose between the program and their own departmental needs. Finally, the most popular courses filled quickly, leaving many disgruntled students studying topics they didn't care for, with professors they hadn't preferred—and excluding huge numbers of students from engaging with the most appealing courses and teachers.

So the presence of a large proportion of small classes can actually make most students worse off, although neither students, nor professors, nor department chairs are normally in a good position to see this problem. When *students* are asked their opinion of small classes, they think—reasonably enough—of small classes they've actually taken. But of course those were classes (1) that to some extent they chose, and (2) in which they successfully enrolled. Ironically, through the arithmetic of engagement, the more small classes a college offers, the lower the real chances for any specific student of (1) getting the great teacher or subject they chose, and (2) actually enrolling.

Professors think small classes are better because, like other people, they know what they see; and what they see are the students *in their classes* who indeed may be well served. These, of course, are the students who got in; those turned away at registration are elsewhere. Professor A's small class has produced Professor B's larger class, and Professor B may not even know why his own courses are so large. (Some professors will say, perhaps correctly, that "my pedagogy requires smaller classes," but they're arguing in a circle: having committed to a small-class pedagogy, they then claim they "must" have small classes.) For any individual professor, as for any one enrolled student, small classes certainly look like a better arrangement—but partly because they don't see the students who aren't there. And for the students who aren't there, the college is, at least to some extent, a worse place in terms of learning.

Academic departments can also benefit by selectively reducing the size of their classes, so long as they don't lose faculty positions in the process. With tighter enrollment limits or tougher grading in introductory classes, a department can effectively off-load students to other departments or selectively admit better students. Attracting fewer, but better, students makes teaching more enjoyable and can certainly raise a department's prestige. In one case we know of, a department collectively decided to "raise our standards" and become more rigorous—a praiseworthy goal. They tightened their grading, increased student workloads, and reduced class sizes. When department enrollments fell (of course!) they were aware of it, but cited the "increased rigor" as an improvement worth the cost in numbers. Perhaps. But the "rigor" they added was only applied (of course!) to the students who remained; it couldn't be applied to those no longer in the classroom. The newfound rigor couldn't be applied to students who now never encountered that field of study at all. The total number of students getting rigorous training thus may actually have gone *down*—but the department faculty never saw that result, since those students were no longer in their classes.

Administrators overseeing multiple departments are better positioned than anyone else to understand that the quality of a course only has impact if there's a quantity of students in the room. Enrollments matter, and not just financially; the term "enrollments," after all, is just administrative jargon for "actual students in courses," that is, people at least potentially learning something. But some of the usual measures of academic quality can easily mislead even savvy administrators. Student evaluations of professors, for instance, even if perfectly fair and objective, are only completed by students who took the professor's class. They aren't filled out by students who deliberately avoided a professor known for, say, a bias against women or contempt for weaker students. They also aren't completed by students who couldn't get into a class, so their dismay goes unnoticed. So almost paradoxically, the most quality-sensitive leaders may come to believe that smaller is educationally better, not simply more selective.

And of course, even educational *researchers* find small classes to be better. Careful, scientifically controlled studies show that *ceteris paribus*—other things being equal—small classes are probably better than large classes, because of the engagement benefits, increased feedback, and chances for active participation.[2] We don't doubt this finding at all, as a scientific result.

But here, alas, social science trips on its own shoelaces. In the real world, *ceteris* aren't *paribus*; other things aren't equal. Small classes necessarily—by the sheer fact of being small—limit student access to teachers, topics, and experiences. A class doesn't exist independently of a teacher—a particular teacher, who may be wonderful or deadly. Then too, classes don't exist apart from a specific content or topic (chemistry, art history, Japanese language) that engages some students but not others. Education scholars sometimes promote some pedagogical method or "best practice," citing quite good research that shows "it" works better. But there is no "it," standing alone; other things are never equal. No method—active learning, small classes, whatever—is actually practiced independently of the teacher using it, the topic, the time of day, and so on.

This inescapable interlocking of factors—teacher, topic, method—also helps to explain the frequently disappointing results of freshman seminar programs, a perennial favorite of reform-minded deans. Freshman seminars ought to work. They promise intensive engagement, close student-faculty relationships in the first year, a building of strong foundation skills, all advertised with snappy new "interdisciplinary" course titles. But in college after college, after years of debate, faculty legislation, votes, preparatory workshops, and significant reorganization (all urged along by stipends, course reductions, and rousing press releases), freshman programs too often stall, bogged down in the realities of departmental priorities, a shortage of truly good seminar teachers, and—given the necessary exclusivity of any small class—lots of freshman finding themselves in their third, fourth, or fifth choice of a course. Sometimes, of course, the seminars do work—if the best of the faculty are truly and deeply committed. Often, though, freshman seminars are just another "neat idea" that continues to disappoint expectations.

Ultimately, large classes really do have their own educational value. Financially, of course, they provide at least the theoretical possibility of an inexpensive way for lots of students to learn, to be engaged, to have access to quality education.[3] Critics say lectures do not exemplify "active learning," but whether they do or don't is an empirical question; some certainly do. Physics students in Richard Feynman's legendary introductory physics course at Cal Tech in the 1960s certainly didn't feel unengaged. Some classes are large—huge, even—because they're so *good*; everyone wants to take them. Large classes can expand students' exposure to the few great "performer" teachers, and can create common experiences that form the basis of intellectual communities, with books that everyone seems to have read and be talking about. By contrast, students who do not share at least some part of their curriculum with their peers will struggle to find common ground around which to create intellectual discussion.[4] Consider why adult reading groups work: because everyone has read the same book, and everyone is prepared to dive right into discussion and debate. At the college, one large course we heard about served this "common ground" purpose by single-handedly providing a shared base of knowledge—a shared reading list and lectures—to almost a quarter of the student body at any given time. Students talked about the course and its readings often. Everyone had something to say about it, because so many had taken it.[5]

Large classes put more students in a single place and thus create more opportunities for interaction between the students themselves.[6] It may be easier in a small seminar to create an emotional synchronization among participants, since there are fewer people to appeal to and a better chance to accurately tap the feelings of each. But there remain some professors who can mesmerize a large auditorium, engaging dozens in discussion—and when they do, more people benefit. Many colleges have their versions of courses in art history (Yale, Williams) or psychology (Cornell) or ethics (Michael Sandel's at Harvard) that are huge, enjoyable, and intellectually rigorous. If your college has professors who can give great lectures, why not take advantage of them?

That's a brief introduction to the "arithmetic of engagement." Given a few basic numbers—the student-faculty ratio, an average number of classes taught per professor, and an average number of courses students take per term—there exist only a finite arrangement of bodies (students and teachers) in space and time. Whenever a class in one room is smaller, a class in some other room must inevitably be larger. And realistically, there are a limited number of truly engaging professors, although fortunately different professors appeal to different students. For academic leaders, then, the challenge is to arrange classes, professors, and students so as to maximize educational engagement and success. Even money invested in low student-faculty ratios won't solve the problem, although it certainly does create more favorable odds; and certainly, the more great teachers of any sort on the faculty, the better chance a student has of studying with one. But low student-faculty ratios reduce access to the institution itself, by raising tuition. The most reliable educational tool isn't really small classes; it's *good* classes—interesting, motivating, rigorous—that lots of students are actually enrolled in. "Quality" courses without good enrollments are wasted—teaching into thin air. A "good department" without many students isn't really doing much good, sad to say.

The best protection against misallocation of resources is to measure the quality of outcomes for *students*, not for classes, professors, or departments. As we've seen, a college can have lots of good, and small, classes without necessarily helping many students. Similarly, an academic department can, if taken by itself, be evaluated as excellent while perhaps not really contributing much to students. And if professors are rated solely by the "quality of their teaching," apart from how many students they teach, then their quality won't help many students. Careerist faculty could just cherry-pick a few star students, keep their evaluations high, and concentrate on doing research. In such a system, one can be known as a "good teacher" while not actually doing much teaching. The best solution to such problems is to measure student results, not faculty "skill." The unit of analysis must be the individual student.

College works by selecting certain people, putting them in one place for a few years, and giving them a regular framework for routine meetings, formal and informal, centered on academic topics. The arithmetic of engagement is about placing people to maximize the odds that any given student will meet friends and encounter good teachers, with all the benefits that can result.

5

Belonging

I'm kind of shy . . . But I'm in rugby, and that's good for
meeting people. And let's see, what else? I'm in jazz and
that's good . . . And then there's sailing, but we're not very
active so it's hard to meet people. I'm a member of the
College Democrats, and I meet people through that. I go
to [gospel singing events] and I meet people that way. And
I'm in the Philosophy Club, I'm the treasurer of that . . .

(Joe, sophomore)

By the middle of sophomore year, almost all students at the college *belong*.
They have publicly committed themselves by declaring a major, by choosing
or refusing roommates, by selecting a faculty advisor, by sticking with or quit-
ting a sports team, and by joining, leading, or leaving a number of extracurricular activities. Some students are members of the campus "alternative" crowd:
living in a co-op dorm, eating on the vegetarian meal plan, maybe studying
photography or art.[1] Others are sorority officers, maybe planning to study
abroad in Italy while majoring in art history. Some like Joe, quoted above, are
deeply immersed in extracurriculars. Some spend six hours a day in the gym,
while others are engrossed in experiments in a chemistry or neuropsychology
lab. Almost everyone identifiably belongs to particular informal and formal
groups on campus—a gang of friends, a yearbook staff, an intramural softball
team, a fraternity. They have made their choices and found their places in
a manageable combination of academic study, extracurricular activities, and
hanging out with friends.

Students' strenuous efforts to "fit in" and find a place are well spent. Over
and over, researchers have found that integration is crucial to students' remaining in college,[2] and most students' main concern at college is to find a

and universities; it also promotes solidarity within the membership of those institutions.

Putting these four factors together, Collins argues that when a group of people physically gather, with a shared focus of attention, common activities, and a degree of exclusiveness, something happens roughly akin to reaching "critical mass" in a nuclear reaction: excitement grows, and begins to feed on itself, in a self-reinforcing rush of emotional energy.

> I really enjoy being surrounded by so many people similar to me in so many different ways . . . I like having so many people the same age group as me, the same interests as me, the same kind of academic intensity . . . they're open enough about themselves and about other people to keep themselves open to new things. And I like . . . that I can meet a lot of different kinds of people, and get to know more people than I would in another kind of environment.
>
> If everybody was all the same, it would be very boring. And if nobody had anything in common, it wouldn't be as much fun either. (Mark, freshman)

People start bouncing ideas around, talking back and forth, mimicking each other's gestures and emotions; they all laugh together, making the laughter that much more boisterous; or they begin to cry together, as at funerals, each mourner's grief feeding the grief of others. They see that the others are feeling as they do, down to the level of the fraction-of-a-second coordination in the back and forth of call-and-response, of "being in synch," of being on the same wavelength. They move together, physically and emotionally. When lofty words are spoken, everyone feels lifted; when sorrow is expressed, all are sad together.

But if this emotional coherence is predictable, its direction may not be. The presence of a dominant figure—a teacher, or a class clown, for instance—can move the group off in some new direction, presenting a point of view (an angry one, for instance) or a topic (the stupidity of academics) that may readily itself become a shared topic, a rallying point around which the group creates its moments of excitement. Such a person can "set a tone" for the group, which others join for the emotional pleasure of being in synch with those around them. Regardless of the particular direction taken, the sheer feeling of being with others seems, at some fundamental and even biological level, deeply satisfying to human beings. We like it. We want that connection.

An increase in the four factors, Collins says, predictably leads to increased emotional energy, the development of moral enthusiasm, and sometimes increased hostility to those who challenge the group's core values. (Conversely, as copresence, shared activity, shared focus, and exclusivity go down, the result is less emotional energy and group solidarity.) "This is right; we are right," they come to believe. As they feel more connection to each other, they also feel stronger bonds to the values that define the group itself. A successful sports team values athletic life; other groups, if they work well in harmonizing people, come to value the things that command their attention—a religious doctrine, certain ideas, a cult of a leader, a music group or style, or (for instance) intellectual pursuits.

For academic leaders, Collins's theory provides two crucial insights. First, it highlights the fact that motivation—enthusiasm, energy for doing work, attachment to institutional activities—is highly variable. It goes up and it goes down. The NECASL studies show that engagement in academic work rises and falls for individual students, from one course to another, and even day by day within different courses. (Professors in particular affect this engagement.[9]) Second, Collins's theory details how such motivation depends on definable, concrete conditions: physical copresence, a shared focus of attention, ritualized common activities, and exclusivity, implying that leaders can, if they wish, deliberately shape students' motivation in various directions.

Football, Dormitories

Colleges produce such solidarity all the time, both deliberately as a matter of policy and serendipitously as a matter of chance.

Consider football. A critical concentration of individuals is assembled to start practices in late summer—a recruited cohort of players. They all enjoy football; they begin to meet regularly, in close physical contact, to play football and practice the techniques of the game. Their university has deliberately brought them together, perhaps even paying (through scholarships) for some of them to be there. The college provides coaches, facilities, and equipment. The players focus on football and on their coaches, talk among themselves about football games, sharing their excitement when the team does well and their disappointment when it fails. Even a poorly performing team can create strong bonds, as the members share—and know they share—the strong emotions that go with an athletic season.

> It was just complete utter anguish, losing as many games as we did. That's no secret. We [only] had two years in the 1980s, and a couple of years in the 1940s and '50s where we had a winning program. But I would still say it was a really worthwhile experience. There are some of the people that I'm still friends with. And as gut-wrenching as some of the losses we had . . . my college experience wouldn't have been the same without it. (Luke, alumnus)

By being together, they affirm the value of football; their very presence says that this is not silly or a waste of time; it matters. The players come to love football, not just as an abstract collection of rules, statistics, techniques, and plays, but as an entire stage of life they share with these particular other people, to whom they now feel close.

From inside, this kind of microcommunity feels like a great group of friends, or a "really tight team"; members feel welcome and are eager to participate, and *esprit de corps* runs high. Its rituals, from the team meetings and practices to the very public ceremonies of Saturday afternoon games, all the way down to the casual greetings, standard jokes, and shared repartee, pull them together. Members know these rituals and enjoy them, finding them fun and energizing.

On campus, team members and outsiders alike recognize the team's distinctive style and bearing. The players appear confident, successful in some sense, and relatively assertive: "sure of themselves" is probably the best description, precisely capturing that they know who they are (members of the football team) and feel good about it. They appear as a clique, an exclusive group that others may envy, admire, or even be afraid of. Even if one doesn't want to be in the group, there's something appealing about it, and that something is the carriage of its members, who enjoy a level of confidence and strength that others lack. They seem to know where they're going, whom they're with, and what they're doing; they seem to be "at home."

That confidence then creates a chain reaction of energy, activity, and organizing. The football team feeds new pledges into a couple of fraternities; players take courses with a few favorite professors; they live in and shape the culture of certain dorms. Through concerted efforts, they can come to dominate student government. Having gained real resources, they then attract further supporters—team boosters, affiliate sororities, fans, faculty advisors. In their Greek-letter societies, they may form a linked network of societies ("the Pan-Hellenic Council"), absorbing large numbers of members, in turn defining appropriate college behavior in all sorts of ways. When players become alums, they will follow the team's season, maybe give some money, and defend the program when it's attacked. And in years to come, ex-players' love of football binds them to the game and its performance, to current players and coaches, and to the institutions that make it all possible.

Tight-knit football teams are deliberately produced, even if some of their by-products are unintended. But solidarity can emerge even where it's not deliberately produced, and even a very small college includes a host of informal "primary groups" whose members know each other by first name: "crews" of friends who sit around talking, eat meals together, and share a dormitory suite; or a laboratory group in the sciences who have pizza every Thursday night; or sorority sisters going to France together for study abroad. Actors in a theatrical production can become such a microcommunity; so can the "regulars" at a campus coffee shop. Through its own choices and resources, the institution certainly fosters these groups even if it doesn't officially charter them.

Consider, again, dormitories at the college. Dormitories provide especially fertile ground for meeting peers and making friends and connecting with broader networks of peers. But why? To begin, the college brings together a highly selected group of people. Certain kinds of students are admitted, sometimes into particular dorms (theme housing, freshman dorms, etc.). Residents have thus already been screened for academic ability, for some level of ambition, in some respects by social class and ability to pay, by gender (keeping a rough balance is important), and always by whatever attracted them to the institution—the appeal of an aesthetically attractive campus, or perhaps by a liberal arts education.

> A lot of people are happy to be here, and feel good about being here. And I think as a result, you mostly get people who are, you know, excited . . . My high school had 2,800; but of those 2,800, you know, maybe six or seven hundred actually took things seriously, you know what I mean? Whereas . . . everybody [here] wants to kind of advance . . . they're at least somewhat intellectually curious and, you know, they want to do better in life. (Russell, junior)

The college puts this selected body of students together; residentiality reinforces the connections already prepared by their commonalities. Students are already on the same wavelength, but the dormitories put them in closer contact so that the waves, so to speak, overlap with each other and sometimes even harmonize.

> The best thing is the fact that you can go through many aspects of your life with the same types of people . . . [who] play the same sports and take the same classes as you, and are interested in the same things . . . To meet people on different levels . . . that makes you grow more. (Jay, freshman)

Second, in dormitories students must spend time closely together with other students. Even the shyest residents see the same people day in, day out, while those who are outgoing quickly learn the names and faces of scores of their peers.

> There are always people walking around the halls. Like, if we don't have our door closed and locked, then there are always just people coming in and out of the room. And Vanderbilt [dorm] is also fairly central, so when people from Vernon [dorm] come up the hill and they have an hour to kill, they end up hanging out in our room . . . (Dan, sophomore)

As Theodore Newcomb recognized half a century ago, "one cannot very well develop peer group relations with persons whom one has never met."[10] The conditions under which people meet each other are central to the development of social ties. But Newcomb also recognized that chance meetings alone are not enough to foster lasting communities and relations. These also require particular institutional arrangements that increase "the frequency of *persisting* peer group relationships that originated in chance encounters facilitated by propinquity, as in dormitory residence or classroom attendance."[11] The constant presence of other people produces repeated, unavoidable encounters between students, whether friend, stranger, or enemy, accelerating the process of meeting people, forming groups, and reinforcing existing ties.[12]

Third, on a residential campus, with students present around the clock, both time and space are used flexibly, in multiple ways. There's little of the strict separation of function so characteristic of our modern, production-driven economy.

Someone I know described college as a full-time job with really weird hours
. . . fellow students are more like coworkers, kind of . . . (Martin, freshman)

At any particular time, some students will be sleeping, others studying, others eating, and still others just hanging out, playing video games, talking, or
looking out the window. Traditional "dinner time" may still be honored, but
so is the 2:00 A.M. "breakfast" break. The quad at midnight becomes a convenient place to "hook up"; the old boarded-up fraternity house becomes an ideal
place to smoke a joint; the library morphs into a social center, the fitness center into a pickup spot. Any specific locale gets used in multiple ways, exem-
plified in the all-purpose dorm room: a scene for partying, sleeping, lounging,
e-mailing, and studying. Thus dorm residents see each other in a wide variety
of situations and roles: as dormmates, newspaper editors, athletes, students (in
very different subjects), lovers, partygoers, slobs, druggies, or friends. There is
little room for "role segregation," where one appears in a single guise, keeping
observers ignorant of all the rest. Such a mixing of work and play contributes
to making the college a classic *Gemeinschaft*—a community.

As part of this "community" experience, roommates must endure an almost complete lack of privacy, an intimacy previously shared only with family members. The disadvantages are obvious. Freshmen especially, with little
choice of roommates and new to independent living, often suffer the most.
Problems—messiness, loud noise, unpleasant music, uninvited intrusion by
girl- or boyfriends, dirty laundry and food spilled or stolen—all become
not the quirks of a weird neighbor but problems occurring literally in one's
own room.

I came in one time to my room and on my desk is a pair of dirty socks . . .
just on my desk, on my papers! (Jim, freshman)

I had one really great roommate and then two really bad roommates . . .
One of them definitely had a urinary problem because he'd get really drunk
and pee on everything. (Murphy, sophomore)

I woke up this one weekend, and there's blood all over my room . . . I walked
in the bathroom, and there's just blood in the sink. One of my roommates,
like, cut his hand because he punched a window, and was bleeding all over
the place . . . He was pretty drunk at the time, and he had stolen like a case
of beer, and bottles of orange juice, this water, and a keg cap, and I don't
know. Supposedly it was pretty funny though, because he was running

around without a shirt on [in midwinter], and there were like five Campus Safety guys running after him trying to get him. (Alfred, freshman)

On the other hand, students consistently told us that living close to others, even when unpleasant, positively affected both how they act and how they think. Loners for instance can be pulled out of their shells.

I was kind of a hermit in high school . . . I saw college as being a way to get away from that.

The three of us [roommates] not fighting, we called ourselves "Switzerland," because everybody else would come in and talk about their roommates and how much they were annoying them . . . We were also at the top of the stairs, and so everyone would walk past our room and be like, "Hey, are you home?" you know, stop in for five minutes. That helped me come out as well. (Jade, junior)

This can certainly affect how openly students talk about, say, politics—as is well described in Binder and Wood's book, *Becoming Right*.[13] They found that the style of students' political expression varies based on their college experiences, on their social and cultural lives, and on the organization of the campus. On our small, close-knit campus, fear of stating one's views openly is probably widespread, but Russell saw it more positively.

You sleep in the bed you make, you know what I mean? . . . If you're living in New York City, you could flip somebody off and not really hear about it . . . But here, you do something, you know, to piss somebody off and, you know . . . it really does get around . . . I really do feel like we're in a community . . . In order for the community to work, people have to respect one another. (Russell, junior)

Some students describe, too, an increase in their psychological awareness or sophistication, especially in an appreciation of the less public, less noble elements of human behavior. Perhaps more than anywhere but in the military or their own families, young people in residential colleges can get to know other people well enough to understand even their subtler motives. It's one of the great benefits of communal living. Before college, as Dex told us, "you only know the way your parents do things, and the way, you know, things are run in your house. And you come to college, and you're put in a room with a bunch of other guys from all different places, and you end up seeing—well, maybe the way he cleans and organizes the room is a better method . . ." (Dex, sophomore). Jared felt "more able to discern superficial relationships from meaningful relationships." For Jenn, living with three roommates "helped me realize that my first impression of people maybe wasn't the right impression."

> I have become a lot more cynical . . . When I came here, I used to trust people a lot. Like, I've been hurt by so many people, that now I have a lot fewer friends . . . I'm a lot more suspicious of people. (Jenn, senior)

And Alexandra has

> become more wary of a lot of people, you know. A lot more wary . . . More aware of, of people's reasons; people tell you something that they think you would like to hear. I'm more worried about actual interpersonal relationships . . . I've been—not deceived, not lied to, but "misled" on a couple of instances about friendships.
>   I feel like I can read people better, a lot better. Like, I can tell more when somebody is hiding something . . . I think I've become more aware of how to, like, understand people and their motives. (Alexandra, senior)

One final factor may heighten the influence of dorm living: isolation from the rest of the world. Many universities and colleges are physically set off from their neighborhoods not only by the walls of buildings but also by iron fences, dramatic gates, or imposing stone archways; some are set in a parklike greensward even when in cities, sometimes with virtually their own towns (Ann Arbor, MI; Princeton, NJ; College Station, PA). The college itself is rural, surrounded and set off by spacious woods and rolling corn fields. This isolation means that academic life can exist in a bubble, or – to shift metaphors – in the "ivory tower" so consistently criticized by outsiders. "The bubble," a term used by students at the college, describes a self-contained culture geographically and epistemologically cut off from the rest of the world.[14]

> This is the first time, I think, in my entire life I've not known everything that's going on in the world around me. That was something I wasn't expecting in college, actually. I honestly have no idea about this [Afghanistan] war we're in . . .
>   And that was something that definitely shocked me. I'm sure that's probably true at all colleges, but it's . . . just like a bubble. (Liz, freshman)

For some students the bubble is an attraction—they can focus on their work and social lives without the distractions of "the real world." In such a setting, they feel protected, in some cases almost completely secure.

> I can leave my books out, my CD player, out in the common room, in the lounge, and I can leave the dorm for an hour or so. I'll come back and find my stuff still there. I can leave my door open. I don't even lock my door at nighttime. I just close it, but I mean it's just, I can go take a shower, and leave my door wide open with my stereo playing . . . A lot of people respect the dorm. (John, freshman)

> The best thing about [the college] is, I guess, that feeling you get on campus where you do feel at home . . . (Patrick, freshman)

This combination of factors—a selected group of residents, close living around the clock, meeting and interacting with others in a variety of roles, multiple uses of time and space, separation from the rest of the world—produces the lifestyle integration that makes the residential college experience so intense and memorable. At too many institutions, of course, dormitories may not be physically safe environments,[15] and wandering freely down the hallways can actually be dangerous. But when dorms are safe, a student who belongs to this community can make connections that are multidimensional, intense, and almost unique in one's life experience. For many, it becomes a home.[16]

Networks

An inner circle of at least one or two friends is necessary for psychic survival at college; finding those friends was the subject of Chapter 2. But a broader network of acquaintances strengthens a student's feeling of being "at home," as if this is "my campus." Even a prospective student visiting for a weekend can sense this atmosphere at the college.

> The one thing that I noticed right off the bat was the tight-knit community of the [college] campus. There are only 1,700 kids here, so everyone knew everyone . . . We'd just be walking around, like, through the campus, and [my host] would say hi to just about everyone that we passed, just because everyone knew everyone . . . I thought that was really nice. (Frank, freshman)

Such a filigree of acquaintanceship happens when the initial friendship group opens outwards, connecting friends of friends, joining contacts through contacts already made.

> I met some people during the orientation groups. I met some people during the first night, and a lot of that just kind of branched out from there. You know, you meet a couple people, you go to their room to hang out, you're meeting their roommates, you know. [Then] their roommates have people come over. (Dex, sophomore)

> The majority [of friends] I met because we lived together. It was me and my two roommates, and the quad of girls from across the hall. Outside of that, it was people I met on Outdoor Adventure. And then from there, it kind of branched out to other roommates and other acquaintances and other friends. My group of friends is really big. (Ashley, freshman)

> I met a lot of people through the football team. I also met a lot of team-mates' friends, like my teammates and their friends that are not on the football team. (John, freshman)

Students who initially make friends then quickly tap into broader networks, which expand geometrically out into the college at large.[17] Just as students who excel in freshman academic courses receive new opportunities as research assistants or for field trips or advanced classes, success in early social networking leads to still more networking.

> We have sort of a group of friends, we're all connected in some way . . . we all know each other from different people that we have friends in common from high school . . . [And also I met] two [friends]on the soccer team that I made in the beginning of the year, and now I have five friends on the soccer team because we just met through people. (Sarah, freshman)

Such "weak ties" with the friends of friends are an excellent source—the best source, really—of jobs and information, as sociologists have known ever since Mark Granovetter framed the concept in the 1970s.[18] But they are also an excellent source of interpersonal contact and general social support in daily life. Acquaintances say hello in passing, give a nod of recognition and a greeting, the face brightens a bit when they look up and see you: "How's it going?" Those greetings matter, making the recipient feel like "I am somebody."

Without them, one becomes entirely dependent on close relations and less at home in this broader world. When weak ties are common, even ubiquitous, they reinforce the feeling that "this is my home."

Of course, students expand their networks not just through meeting individuals, but also through joining organizations.

For John, a football player,

> I think choir and the singing have . . . really broken me out of my shell. People look at me as a stereotypical football player, and they're like, "You play, you're a football player, and you can sing and you dance?" And, like, people who never have ever said a word to me . . . they'll see me and they have no fear of coming up to me and are like, "Oh, I saw you perform the other day. You did very well." It's just allowed me to reach different groups of people. (John, junior)

In other words, some campus organizations—choir, in John's case—act as network "brokers," connecting individuals by linking different kinds of organizations and individuals.[19]

Any one student may thus be a singer in the college choir, a neuroscience research assistant, one of the "cool crowd" in Watkins dormitory, a devoted intramural softball player in the springtime, and a tutor in the college's Writing Center. One panelist took out a sheet of paper and drew for us.

> If this is a Venn diagram, I'm in the middle: [there's a] big blob of, like, very musical people with like a little, some people that I know from like [a student theatre group], and a few random people that I know from my major, and classes; and then, like, the friends of my friends . . . (Jane, junior)

Each of those "blobs" gives Jane support and motivates her to keep engaging in those activities, seeing those other people, and moving through college with a strong sense of purpose and validation.

Students without those connections feel the lack.

> I wish I'd gotten involved in more things, because I think that's really what made me feel more at home at [the college]—like getting involved in activities and getting out and meeting people . . . The community really doesn't exist unless you go out and, like, become a part of it. (Anne, senior)

By taking part in socially "central" activities, some students are better placed to find new friends and become more broadly linked with the college community at large.

Figure 5.1 shows in visual form how certain activities, by sharing students, link those students to new friends.[20] In that sense, it shows the core and the periphery of student activities (including academic majors) at the college. This chart can help us understand how students integrate into the college.

In the center is a dense mass of linked activities, including majors such as government, anthropology, and English, as well as all sorts of music activities: the music major itself, *a capella* groups, the indie music group, and participants in the annual musical, while choir in particular holds an obviously central position.

Student tutors at the Writing Center are also here; they meet lots of students from all over the campus and are thus socially well integrated, structurally reinforcing the cultural prominence of writing at the college. This may pay off in learning, as we'll see in Chapter 6.

Off to the far-right ("east") side of the diagram is a cluster of "multicultural" organizations (POSSE, Rainbow Alliance, Brothers, and others), which are clearly interconnected. Football, a high-enrollment activity in the central cluster, anchors an important link to minority-student men also in the Brothers group and thus to a variety of other campus activities.

Except for Sorority 5 and Fraternity 3 (center core, south), fraternities and sororities are *not* centrally located. Indeed, they are typically off in one of the peripheral clusters. At this college, such comparatively ingrown organizations can actually limit a student's connections with the broader institution, as we will see later in this chapter.

Interestingly, around the perimeter (especially southwest) are a sizable number of sports teams (softball, cross-country, swimming, baseball, hockey, tennis, soccer, golf), suggesting that these teams may also be relatively self-sufficient social groups that are to some extent isolated from the core. This is likely because the time demands on student athletes are so great that they cannot participate in other activities. Major exceptions are football, rugby, and lacrosse (in the core). Rugby is a club, not varsity, sport demanding far less time. Lacrosse's centrality is, for us, a mystery, although women's lacrosse may benefit from being one of the most successful teams at the college, having recently won a national championship.

Figure 5.1
Campus activities:
core and periphery.

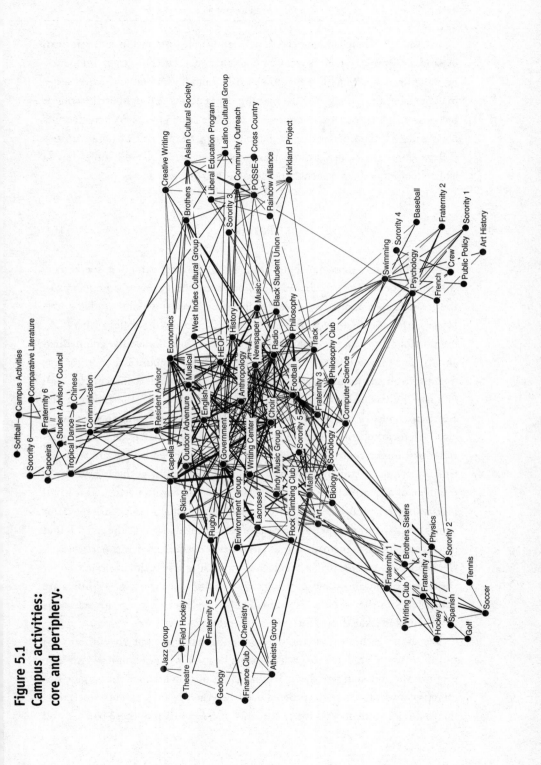

In sum, the diagram suggests how membership in certain activities can expand or limit student networks. Students in relatively large, frequently meeting groups (music, large majors)—call them "high-contact" activities—may have better opportunity for making connections throughout the college by connecting, through acquaintances, to other large groups. When students have widely linked networks, it opens to them the wealth of opportunities college offers. In comparison, certain varsity sports may tend somewhat to isolate team members, probably because of the time demands.

Parties

The fundamental importance to students of having extended social networks—of belonging to a broader campus community—might help explain the irrepressible popularity of large drinking parties at undergraduate colleges. Although most students we interviewed credited the college with making possible "the best friendships of my life," they simultaneously complained about what they called the "boring social life" on campus. This finding was quantitatively striking in survey results: respondents rated the college high on fostering friendships, but low on providing "social life." The apparent discrepancy vanishes when one recognizes the qualitative difference between close friendships (and the ubiquitous "hanging out" that makes them possible) and looser acquaintanceship opportunities. "Friendships" are with intimates, while in student parlance "social life" refers to gatherings of large numbers of acquaintances and strangers—in particular, to parties. This small Northeastern liberal arts college lacks the revelry of major university spectator sports events, and the mellow relaxation of sunshiny days on the quad found in warmer locales. Instead, a few large drinking-and-dancing parties each weekend become the prime venue for expanding and enjoying one's larger circle of acquaintances and meeting new people. Once those possibilities are exhausted—as they soon are at a small college—"social life" in this sense becomes limited indeed. But for a time, it works.

We didn't gather systematic data on student parties, but given their centrality to many students' experience of college and to "belonging," we here propose the following analysis. It's based on our own experiences, plus numerous conversations with students over the years. Many students—certainly international students and many students of color—dislike these parties, and

researchers have described how drinking parties are often somewhat dangerous scenes of excessive drinking and drug use as well as sexual harassment and
assault.[21] But why do they remain so appealing?

Here's how we think it works, at least at the college. Even when students
head out to big parties, close friends remain key allies. Friends—"teammates"[22]—are one's home base, a place from which to start. Early on a weekend
evening, a group of friends will gather in someone's dorm room, to "pregame,"
in the metaphor taken from sporting events: dress up, drink a while, and talk
themselves into going out on one of the odysseys[23] that characterize the party
scene.[24] They psych up, they talk about what they plan to do; they try on this
dress, or that shirt and pants, testing them out on friends before later trying
them out on strangers. And odysseys they are—the group moves from place
to place, one party to the next, to a game, then to a party or two, then to the
late-night diner, then back to a dorm room, in search of the adventures that
lend the weekend its special appeal.

The challenge of the night is to impress not only friends but also other people, less well known. The point of partygoing is to enjoy the larger community
of acquaintances—or at the very least, to see and be seen by lots of other people. While intimacy may be a result of the evening ("hookups" being a goal
for many and certainly a topic of speculation and gossip for all[25]), something
considerably less demanding is routinely expected and enjoyed: just being
with lots of people, interacting at a deliberately superficial level—but no less
important for that superficiality.

A few standard features of college parties foster the kind of unserious
conviviality that allows for satisfying exchanges between relative strangers.
Nighttime scheduling helps to convey a sense that "this is not work," that
normal daytime rules don't apply; the darkness of nighttime (and of the party
room itself) tends to anonymize the revelers, soften one's less attractive physical features, and allow bumblers a quick escape from social failure. After a few
drinks, even shy people become more gregarious, ready to talk with strangers and acquaintances. For many students, drinking *per se* is not the point
of parties—after all, one can drink alone, or with small groups of friends,
and it's probably easier to get drunk with one's own hard liquor than while
standing in long lines to get a foam-filled cup of cheap beer. Yes, holding a
drink—imbibing some—is a necessary part of "joining in." But alcohol is a
facilitator of interacting, and not an end in itself for most students.[26] Loud
music is crucial: conversations can't be serious or deep when it's hard simply

to be heard, so conversations are reduced to a bare minimum of greeting and simpler gestures—"Hey! Great to see you!" "Wanna dance?" And dancing—physical communication in its simplest form, moving in time with the obvious rhythms of "dance music"—gets everyone in the room immediately on the same "wavelength" (literally, in the sonic sense). With the music playing, entire groups coalesce, facing inward to their circles, holding beer cups, swaying or twisting in time. Sometimes, for a popular song, the entire room will sing along; often couples will break off and head to the center of the floor to dance with each other, enjoying the elemental eroticism of the most basic sort of physical coordination of two bodies, devoid of—even denied the possibility of—any more nuanced verbal exchange.[27]

Parties are built around elements (night, drinks, loud music) that foster an anonymous intimacy among acquaintances, and even among strangers. After all, for partygoers the fun isn't just in being with friends, although they are a necessary base of support. Parties are about seeing and connecting with occasional contacts—broadening the circle, as it were. On a single evening's journey, one student may see and greet dozens, even scores, of other people. Most encounters are quick—"Hey, how're ya doin?" followed by a friendly, even exuberant reply. Nothing much is demanded of the other person, so giving and getting attention is, mostly, cheap. The goal seems to be simple affirmation, repeated time after time, over and over, that "I Belong Here"; "These Are My People"; "I'm an OK Person." (Worth noting again: many students in fact don't like the party scene at all, and find it alienating.) One's social acceptability and interactional competence in the community is being affirmed—certainly, with some high peaks of excitement or attraction thrown in. The superficiality of these interactions shouldn't hide the fundamental importance of what they communicate. After all, many students are afraid to go to parties, or don't like the scene, and some who initially do go and try find they can't really pull it off. It does in fact require a degree of skill.

Some party stars, experts at what Georg Simmel a century ago called "pure sociability,"[28] shine in this setting. They know everyone, say hi to everyone, are greeted enthusiastically as they move from one cluster to the next, almost magnetically picking up enthusiasm, confidence, energy. But even lesser lights can enjoy a feeling of acceptance and belonging. The weekend odyssey is a journey filled with the excitement of new rewards, and some risk (although one can always leave), but it's an amazingly immediate (if not always accurate) way to check one's status and competence: Am I cool? Attractive? Do I have friends? A few or a lot? And although there is certainly competition, the results are not so unambiguously hierarchical as the Dean's List, or a fraternity bid, or being preferred as a potential roommate. It's about status, but it's a pretty widely available status.

Partying is thus really about testing who I am as a member of this community. It's about belonging—again, a major challenge for most undergraduates. At smaller institutions like the college, the scene fairly quickly wears thin, as the available pool of strangers is exhausted. Within a couple of years, everyone knows who you are. But at large universities as well as small colleges, when partying works for the participants, the students can return to their daytime lives with a bit more confidence, with the assuredness that once everyone's hair is let down, I can move pretty well with the best of them, that I fit in here, that it's my world.

Insular Groups

For some students, though, it isn't "my world." Some close-knit groups or even lone individuals become detached from the rest of the community, even entering a downward spiral of alienation from the rest of the college.

This "failure to belong" to the larger community seems to have several possible sources. Occasionally small cadres of international students or students of color would coalesce quickly and then, feeling alienated from the general campus, withdraw into their own groups. On a larger scale, one or two of the major fraternities at the college drew members mainly from two or three varsity sports teams; "blocked" their members into a couple of dormitories (there are no fraternity houses); and then socialized almost exclusively with each other and with one or two sororities. Their solidarity was fortified by a culture of (nominally illegal) drinking parties and the more general student resistance to the alcohol policies of "the administration." In these fraternities, even brothers with lots of friends were in fact both socially and even physically somewhat separated from the larger communities. Herb, a member of one such fraternity, realized that

> my social network is getting to be somewhat limited. I'm in a fraternity . . .
> I live with these guys, so I hang out mostly with them . . .

I'm a pretty lazy person, and so I got the opportunity to meet other people who are pretty lazy . . . You know, the guys in the fraternity are going
to look for guys who are like them. And so presumably if I got, if I entered
this fraternity and the guys who were in before that, would be lazy also . . .
So, like, I live with an entire [dormitory] suite of people right now who are
all "Type B, we don't do anything" people. And I have to wonder if I would
have met them [without the frat]. Probably we all would have just sat on our
couches and not even met each other.

But I mean it also is limiting to a certain extent. (Herb, junior)

Our surveys showed that fraternity members were, in broad averages, more
likely to be dissatisfied with the college than non-Greek males.

Sorority women, far more likely to actively participate in other extracurriculars, did not exhibit such dissatisfaction. Many of the sororities actually
required membership in other extracurriculars, while most fraternities did not.
In addition, for many women a sorority was a transient affiliation, a convenient
way to meet other women. They made good friends, but kept other options
open. For men, though, a fraternity membership itself was often a major goal
and an achievement in itself, sometimes seen as an avenue to career success.
Many fraternity members participated only in two activities: their fraternity,
and its associated athletic team. This pattern is suggested in our network diagram of campus organization participation.[29] Fraternity men were more likely
than any women, affiliated or not, to be somewhat isolated socially.

Too exclusive a focus on one activity—often a sport—can likewise limit
a student's network. Katie almost fell into such a pattern "because of swimming—it kept me away from people outside the sport . . . And since it started
so early, you know it starts in October . . . but that's when you're supposed
to hang out with your roommates." Later she deliberately worked to make
friends in classes. Romantic relationships, despite their obvious appeal, can
also sometimes have negative consequences, for female students in particular,[30] as couples may ignore broader friendship networks in favor of this one
relationship.

If my boyfriend lived on campus, you know, he would be around all the
time . . . But instead, I feel obligated to spend like half an hour, or an
hour, on the phone with my boyfriend every night, which is a bunch. And
then—he's six hours away! So if one of us goes to the other, that's twelve
hours of my weekend that is committed to driving—twelve hours that I

really needed to spend studying. So, like, it is a drain on my time. (Cynthia, junior)

It certainly takes up a lot of time, which is also part of why I didn't do that much with extracurricular activities or things like that . . . We lived, like, right next door to each other in Vernon [dorm]. I don't know if that was such a good idea. (Sean, junior)

Romantic relationships consume time and energy that could otherwise be spent with friends, on school work, or in other activities. Further, social life at the college is not organized around long-term romantic relationships, but instead, typically around diffuse friendship groups. Partners in romantic relationships often struggle to "fit" their relationship into their friend group, and vice versa.

So campus life here isn't like it is at many large public universities, where Greek-letter organizations and spectator-sports events have historically been the social foci.[31] At the college a different form of social organization has emerged, characterized by core groups of friends that expand outward to larger networks of "weak ties" generated from dorm contacts, teammates, and the extracurricular activities in which a student participates. Students who live in "high-contact" dorms and participate in dispersed activities will routinely meet and befriend a wide range of people. Students spending time in more isolated settings (apartments, small but demanding teams, ingrown organizations), will not have that opportunity, and their acquaintance networks will suffer accordingly.

Finally, a few individuals we saw, maybe from the mismatch of their own personalities and the available opportunities, never really connected socially or academically. Frank was recruited into the college to play a varsity sport. To protect his privacy, we'll omit some details, but his story represents what can go wrong. He had attended a small, private prep school and wanted to go to a college where he could play the sport he loved, get a good education, and enjoy a good social life—a real college experience, as he suggested. He admitted to not being the best student academically, but he knew how to avoid really bad grades.

When we first interviewed Frank, he had just a few weeks earlier learned that he would not be invited to join the team's regular fraternity. Being rejected soured Frank on the fraternity system; it was clear that he had expected a bid, and was disappointed not to have received one. Despite this, he continued to play his sport. Frank admitted later that he didn't really have many friends from the team, rare for athletes in our sample. He felt socially rejected from the team. Such friends as he made were from his freshman dorm.

Meanwhile, he was drifting academically. He had a C+ average (not good) during his first year, with no idea of what to major in. He did find a couple of professors he liked, and asked one of them, an English professor, to be his advisor. He "knew what . . . was going through my head, and knew what was probably the right thing for me to do . . . His advice was helpful." But the relationship was not inspiring to him—it was helpful practically, but not intellectually stimulating.

During Frank's second year, he "hit a wall" in English, taking a class with his advisor that involved far too much reading for him. He dropped the class, but took a studio art class which he enjoyed. He decided to major in studio art—the work was fun, the faculty was nice.

During his junior year, Frank overslept on the day he was supposed to register for classes, and was effectively forced to take four classes he had no interest in, and then simply "hated." One was taught by a professor who was "a jerk"—he "took tenure for granted and didn't care about his students . . . He was just mean . . . Every day was awful. I mean, somebody would try to answer a question, and if it was wrong, he would just be incredibly mean about it. It was ridiculous." Frank mentioned this professor in each of his subsequent interviews. On the other hand,

> I've been having a lot more fun this year, because freshman and sophomore years are all about wanting to be in a fraternity. So not being in one, I think this year it's like . . . I don't worry about [not getting in one] . . . I just got over it, basically.

Frank also began to feel more comfortable with his major and the associated faculty in the Art Department. Despite finally feeling better about his place in college, both academically and socially, when we asked Frank whether he would have chosen to attend the college again, he responded, "God no, I'd probably go south; the weather at the college is terrible." Frank still spoke poorly of the college's social life.

We talked with Frank after he graduated, and he vividly remembered some of the things he struggled with—his rejection from a fraternity, his awful experience with a terrible teacher, the lack of social life, the cold weather.

With some distance from his experiences, he recognized something that had become clear to us during his first few interviews.

> I wish there had been a little more guidance as far as figuring out what I wanted to actually do with my life, when I was there . . . I took too long to figure out that [business was] what I wanted to do. Had I had more guidance, and someone to bounce ideas off of on a more regular basis, that would have probably been very helpful.

Membership

The social world of college spreads out from a small circle of two or three close friends, to a wider group of routine acquaintances in the dorm or sorority or classes, to a much wider, looser network of familiar faces and recognized groups. Emotional links to the various people may be almost nonexistent or only passing, or quite strong. When all of these networks, different for different students, begin to move in roughly the same direction, we might say that the college constitutes a community.

Colleges and universities aspire to be *membership* institutions, not simply vendors of a commodity service. They would like, first, not to accept every student who can pay the fees; prestige—selectivity—is measured mainly by how many willing customers a college actually turns away. Then too, what a college sells (beyond the diploma) is typically very loosely defined, certainly not promised with the kinds of long, legalistic contracts that characterize, say, buying a house or a car. Students want to be a member, not a customer. "Be a Longhorn," says the University of Texas's website. "Wildcats: start your engines," says the University of Arizona on their admission page, to students who want to enroll. "Welcome, new Ducks"—the University of Oregon. Or even at the University of Phoenix: "Become a Phoenix." They also sell tradition, even when (at some) it's a tradition of rebelliousness, or innovation, or the "fighting Titans," or of being the right place for up-and-comers, or of being the home of future great scientists or leaders of tomorrow. Once enrolled, a student has access to a wide and often loosely defined range of services and opportunities: classes, clubs, entertainment, housing, and dining options, use of the gymnasium and fitness center, even that sunbathing space on the quad when the weather is nice—in sum, a whole range of "rights and privileges thereof," as the diploma typically says that its graduates are "admitted to." The comprehensive fees often are quite high, but once they're paid, the identification of a person with an institution is fixed; after graduation, the identification can be virtually permanent.

Fellow alums know this. Encountering each other for the first time in New Zealand or Brazil they may embrace, share jovial greetings, even have dinner together. When a new graduate goes looking for jobs, alumni networks might help her out. Associations of former students of a college or university often are mutual-aid societies—although why alumni want to help their fellows is rather mysterious, beyond wanting to maintain this community itself. An "extended family" probably overstates the principle, but often not by much.

These "imagined communities"[32] also spread back and forwards in time as well. Very old colleges are proud of their age and celebrate their major anniversaries and centennials—although again, it's often not clear what they really have in common with the institution of, say, two hundred years earlier. A physical location is often important as well—Yale in New Haven, for instance—while old buildings and nostalgically beloved settings make colleges locationally conservative in a way that very few businesses are anymore. Colleges and universities need to preserve their local communities, and college buildings *look* like college buildings, which in turn students and alums feel sentimental about, as alums remember favored places of their youth. Colleges, of course, sell this nostalgia, to the youngest prospective applicants as well as to the oldest living alumni. The tradition is a lasting institutional commitment that incoming students can count on, and will carry for the rest of their lives. Colleges project themselves into the future as well—as students need them to. That mutual aid only works if older alums believe they share something with current students.

Belonging, we have tried to suggest here, doesn't just happen by accident. The institution shapes the available pathways into membership's inner rooms, making it easy (or not) for different students to fully join. Elizabeth Armstrong and Laura Hamilton precisely describe this dynamic in their book *Paying for the Party*, showing for instance how a confluence of favorable locations on campus, easy majors, and access to university policy-making support a Greek-driven "party pathway" for well-off students at a large Midwestern university.[33] The college, in contrast, closed down its fraternity houses in 1995, breaking up the easy pathway to Greek life, and possibly leading to the kind of "noncentral" location of some frats we saw in Figure 5.1. Fraternities that had been at the pinnacle of a well-defined campus hierarchy became one admittedly important group among others—the vibrant group of choral singers, a collection of tutors from the Writing Center, an "alternative" crowd living in the vegetarian co-op, or a tight-knit band of chemistry majors.

Students like Frank who never really belong are left floundering. But those who are able to meet with peers regularly, share significant activities, and find a wider network at the college gain (as Collins suggested in his theory) in their motivation to be there at all. That motivation, in turn, is critical to learning.

6

Learning

I have to do my school work, I have to go to class—
teachers care about what's going on. There's an emphasis
on the process of learning. You get an assignment, you
meet with the teacher, you work on the paper, you discuss
it, you rewrite it . . . They actually care about what you're
learning. And, you know, I feel like they want to be
engaged with you in class, you know. They want you to
participate, they want you to talk, they want you to listen.

(A.J., senior)

By their junior year, most students at the college are at the top of their game.
They have met and passed the challenges to enter college, choose a direction,
connect with teachers, and belong to various groups. They have friends and
participate in activities. Many are leaders of some sort: soloists in musical
ensembles, stars in college theatre, the social chairs of sororities, editors of
student publications, initiators of class discussions. Though not officially captains of their sports teams (those are seniors), juniors are frequently the *de facto*
leaders of squads.

They are more confident, too. As freshmen, they were hesitant in our interviews, asking for clarification, and tentative in responding; now they launch
at length into their opinions and histories. Transcripts physically show their
self-assurance: their answers are now longer, more detailed, clearly more articulate. They are noticeably more voluble, expounding on what they're doing
and what it means. Yes, some of this is "maturation," but maturity might be
just a word for describing that one has a clearly established sense of who one
is. Having mastered the more personal tasks of leaving the home, finding
friends, learning the bureaucracy, picking roommates, and choosing courses

and majors, they are now immersed in the official task of students at the college: academic learning.

In our interviews, they report doing lots of academic work. In a sense, juniors are consolidating their collegiate education, seriously improving and refining the skills that define a college-educated person. Academically they are focusing on specific skills, knowledge, and methods. Their classes typically have prerequisites and are more advanced. In their majors, they are taking research methods courses, conducting apprenticeship research, and writing longer term papers; public speaking becomes more frequently required, as they have the background to really know enough to present a topic to others. Speaking before a group becomes, if not totally a pleasure, at least not so terrifying. Writing has become far easier to do at a higher level. Reading difficult material and making sense of it, picking out the arguments, has become simply what one does each week for classes.

However, even in this chapter, which focuses on academic work, students' concern for personal and social connections will be evident. Friendships comprise possibly the most frequently cited gain by students at the college, along with the confidence born of facing and completing challenging tasks.[1] Individual students themselves typically have multiple goals and can enjoy various positive outcomes which need not be mutually exclusive.[2] Put differently: students can both gain friends and be good students at the same time. We have proposed that for learning to take place some relationships are virtually necessary, first to simply survive daily life, but then to motivate learning. Scholars such as Alexander Astin and Vincent Tinto have exhaustively demonstrated the importance of integration to keeping students in college—an obvious prerequisite to their learning anything while there. Students need to "get into" college emotionally.[3] We've added that they need to "get in" logistically as well: for students to learn course material, they must first be in that course—an important if obvious point, sometimes neglected when colleges schedule classes and assign teachers. Pathways to learning have to be available to those who want them: seniors who want to take a new subject should be able to find open courses, for instance.

Once they're in courses, they need to do the work. There's a rich recent literature on student learning and its proximate causes, demonstrating the importance of hours spent studying ("time on task"), the use of proper study techniques, the volume of pages written, and working to meet challenging standards. These tasks must be faced by each individual, and students studying alone seem to perform better than those working in groups, according to recent studies.[4] The correlations of these activities with learning are well established. They are true, they work, and we don't dispute them. "Time on task" and "deliberate practice"[5] really do matter, as Dan Chambliss has argued elsewhere.[6] If you work more, you'll learn more—certainly.

But why would anyone—let alone, say, a nineteen-year-old away from home for the first time—want to do more school work? *Motivation* is crucial for getting all that work to actually happen, and emotional connections to others and to a community provide the strongest motivation. While students arrive at the college highly motivated, that motivation is not fixed and can't be taken for granted. Even these excellent students find that their enthusiasm for learning goes up and down,[7] depending in part on their relationships to others—teachers, peers, audiences. And in those relationships, surprisingly simple things can dramatically improve that motivation: a single meeting with a teacher, a single required class presentation, a single intense conversation with a dormmate.

Writing

In many undergraduate colleges writing is a fundamental skill, taught as part of the general education program and often embedded in core requirements. Central to the operation of all modern organizations, clear writing is helpful for middle-management employees and crucial for professionals. For undergraduate students, the discipline of writing also helps them to formulate their thoughts and to present their ideas clearly to others. In that sense writing is a social as well as intellectual activity, requiring that one has at least a modicum of empathy with one's readers.

Do undergraduates actually improve their writing skills in college? And if so, how does that happen? To learn the answers, we conducted a five-year blind-evaluation study of student writing at the college. All of this work—a huge, expensive, half-decade project in itself—was supervised by Sharon Williams, director of the Hamilton College Nesbitt-Johnson Writing Center, who was indefatigable in her efforts. Ms. Williams and our research team first assembled an archive of student papers from panelists as well as other students. The archive comprised the following documents: (1) From each of the panel members, we requested one paper written in each academic year, of their own choosing, from their last year in high school (a graded class paper, submitted with their college application) all the way through their senior year of college: a total of five papers, over five years, for each student. These papers were usually collected at the time of the student's annual interview with our project team. Assuming that students pick their very best high school essay to submit with a college application, and given that many of the freshman essays in particular were prepared for writing-intensive classes, the early papers especially should represent their best work. This selection method, we hoped, would make improvement more difficult to prove by raising the baseline—a "conservative" sampling method. (2) Over the same period, we gathered hundreds of other student essays, written for a variety of classes at all college levels. As with the panel papers, we oversampled writing classes for freshman and sophomore essays, while upper-year papers were gathered more by sheer availability. Again, this procedure arguably makes it more difficult to show improvement, by raising the floor—the early years—as high as possible.

Thus at the end of four years, we had an archive of 1,068 usable student essays; hundreds of others didn't fit our sampling, length, or content criteria. This archive allowed longitudinal tracking of individual students as well as contemporaneous cross-sectional analyses of performance by grade level (freshman, sophomore, etc.). We could also, to some extent, make comparisons between graduating years, since every year we collected some senior papers. All identifying information (names, course titles, etc.) was removed from the papers and a code number was assigned to each.

Ms. Williams and her team next recruited outside readers (mostly directors of writing centers at peer institutions) and trained them in an eight-item evaluation rubric (designed by Williams and Professor Ted Eismeier), using a seven-point scale to rate papers on each of the eight items (for example, grammar and usage, coherent paragraphs, etc.). Since readers would not know the assignment or the course for which papers were written, the evaluations would be essentially technical, based on the quality of writing isolated from its course purpose. The readers were given training and test runs to ensure the reliability of their ratings, although due to cost we could only have one reader per paper. The readers then read and evaluated—blindly, knowing neither the author nor the course for which a paper was written—all 1,068 papers, all mixed together. Over the four-year collection period, they contemporaneously evaluated several hundred papers each year. The scores for every paper, on every item, were then entered into a computer database. We could then see, objectively, whether students' skills improved.

Over the same years that the papers were being collected, we continued our interviews with our student panel, asking them among other things about their writing and the writing instruction they received. We also compiled, from our annual Senior Survey, the answers that students gave to questions about writing. Thus when the Writing Study results came in, we were able to integrate objective evaluations of students' writing, their own subjective assessment of improvement, and what they believed affected such improvement—all in one study. The college faculty, when presented with the design, were admittedly a bit nervous: this was a blind, objective evaluation of whether students actually improved over their years at the college. There could be no pretending.

When the reader evaluations of the papers—on eight criteria per paper—were completed, all the data went into a computer database. Then Professor Jennifer Borton, an experimental psychologist who teaches statistics, ran three different kinds of analyses: (1) longitudinal comparisons for panelists who submitted papers for all five years (including high school). Unfortunately, there were only eighteen such students (collection of panel papers proved very difficult, for instance, when students studied abroad); (2) longitudinal pairwise comparisons for any individual for whom we had papers from any two different years. These comparisons were enabled by our collection of large groups of papers from certain courses and professors, so *any* student whose work appeared in two different years could be evaluated; and (3) cross-sectional analyses of different class years (for instance, sophomores and seniors).

The findings were clear. First, to the immense relief of the college's faculty, students really did improve. Hypothetically, imagine that a "blind" reader was handed a randomly ordered, five-year set of papers written by one student. According to our analysis, that reader could, on average, accurately sequence those papers from high school up to the junior year of college by their improving quality: 1,2,3,4. Junior and senior papers were indistinguishable. The improvement over the first four years was usually statistically significant; even when it wasn't, results always fell in the upward direction. Objectively, students really did improve their writing.

Second, we found what we call the "college effect": the biggest gains occurred not just early in college, in the freshman and sophomore years; some occurred *very* early, in the first weeks of college. Several students themselves mentioned in their interviews that this happened. It may result from the extra work students put in, higher levels of expectation, or a desire to please a new set of teachers.

> Professor Stinson is a hard professor, but I thought he was very fair and good . . . I was shocked that I needed improvement . . . In the beginning . . . there were hundreds and hundreds of criticisms. I'm shocked at his response to my papers, and other professors' response to my papers, [but] rather than just getting the way that I was expressing my point, they were actually interested in what I had to say. (James, alumnus)

The college effect may come from students' sense that more is expected, and so more is delivered. A shift to "what college teachers want" seems to be involved—a shift in audience, or to a sharper awareness that one *has* a real audience. Apart from any technical information or instruction being passed on, going to college itself seemed to improve students' work.

Third, the weakest freshman writers scored the biggest gains on the numerical measures. Some number of initially low performers were international students, very high achievers in most respects but still just beginning in English. Their language skills improved rapidly and their writing showed it. In a sense it wasn't writing improvement *per se*. And, in fairness, it is possible that improvement by the weakest writers may just be what statisticians call "regression to the mean": cases at the extremes of a normal distribution (the weakest writers, for instance) are likely to move towards the average, simply because they can't go any further to the extreme. In a sense, maybe the weakest writers improved because they couldn't get any worse. Whatever it was, they still improved.

Interestingly, the top-performing writers out of high school showed the least improvement on our objective measures, suggesting that perhaps the college's program does better helping the weak rather than the strong—"raising the floor," we might say. That's plausible although several facts weigh against such an interpretation. For one thing, it would contradict much of the extant literature on college performance, which clearly supports instead a "Matthew effect"[8] in which the better-prepared students also gain more from college. Second, statistically it becomes more difficult to move up on a seven-point scale if one begins near the top. Third, on the HEDS Senior Survey, the (objectively) best freshman writers were twice as likely to say that the college had "greatly improved" their writing. Finally, among our panelists some of the best writers said they improved tremendously, especially in their abilities to self-diagnose writing issues and to communicate with different audiences. All of these points suggest that the top initial writers did in fact improve.

Regardless of the details, here is a program that clearly works, an institutional effort that really pays off. The college requires writing across the curriculum, enforcing "time on task" and rewriting. Students must take at least three "writing-intensive" (WI) courses to graduate; in practice many students take six, seven, or more. The WI program reflects a long-standing institutional commitment to making sure that students are proficient in writing before they graduate. All departments, not just English or literature departments, offer WI courses, and students themselves report that many courses not officially designated as "WI" should be, since writing is emphasized there as well. Since the WI courses automatically have an enrollment limit of twenty, faculty have an immediate incentive to offer them. Overall, so many writing courses are offered, and are so widely dispersed, that *the courses can't be avoided.* The college houses a first-rate Writing Center, with a large team of well-trained (and rigorously chosen) student tutors, an excellent director, and a guiding committee of dedicated senior faculty. Basic messages are repeated, time and again: have a thesis; use topic sentences; keep paragraphs coherent; cut the excess. Time on task really does work. By the time students graduate, even the weakest among them generally write fairly well—nationally speaking, very well indeed.

The writing program was not simply added on to an existing curriculum. Writing as an emphasized skill is deeply embedded in the college's history, self-image, and culture, a fact the college website announces on its front-page banner. Prospective students want that emphasis, are attracted by it, and in some measure are selected for their relative expertise in it—a graded high school paper, along with a personal essay, being required on the application. Entire departments—English, History, and Philosophy among them, all with large enrollments—have made all of their 100-level courses writing-intensive, and self-consciously emphasize their attention to writing. Graduates brag about the program and their own writing skills. In a sense, this isn't a program so much as a core value of the college.

In learning to write well, students say, the most important step for them is professorial feedback, both written and spoken.

> We got our first paper back today . . . She's read each paper six to eight times . . . These were long papers, and she typed up, like, a response, [what

she] felt about your paper, and it's a four paragraph response. She gave us a rough grade, and then she went on to say if you'd like to revise, you should do this. "You have exactly eleven sentences that are not grammatically correct." Yeah, it was insane. I was like, "That's dedication!" . . . I just want to revise it because I feel like she's put all this effort into [it] . . . (Susie, freshman)

We hand in a paper, and then when [the professor] hands them back he has, like, a full typed page of his thoughts . . . He writes on the paper as well, like all the, you know, grammatical stuff, but then . . . for each person, he types out his own page of suggestions on the subject matter and stuff . . . It was really helpful. (Jenny, freshman)

[We get] *extensive* comments . . . At first, you know, naturally you're offended because, you know, "I worked really hard on this! I poured my heart out to you, and personally, I think it's goddamned perfect just the way it is!" But then, you kind of sit there and you realize . . . when I took her advice, it made a really big difference. (Sasha, sophomore)

Even more than written feedback, though, students told us that conversations—one on one, private, face to face—about their written work made the biggest single impact on their writing. They especially talked about the times—even a single time seemed to work—when a professor sat down with them, in an office, and talked about their writing.

He always encouraged us to come and talk to him in person about our papers, and I think that helped me the most, more than just the comments that he wrote on paper . . . Something about the act of conversing about a topic just helped me. (Frank, freshman)

It's phenomenal because you sit down with the teacher, and go over your paper before you turn it in, which I think is really good. I would say that the only thing that could make it better is maybe . . . if every teacher sat down with each student after they turned in a paper, and went over the paper with them, and really took apart what went wrong or what was right with it, I think that would just do the student wonders. (Jay, freshman)

Interestingly, students' comments were almost never about classroom instruction. And while many appreciated the support and instructions of peer tutors, even that was not the driving force for improvement. Nor were they most impressed with the professor's technical knowledge—after all, most professors have little specific expertise in composition or rhetoric.

What mattered from professors was the sheer fact of their paying attention: she took the time; he helped me. Attention says to the student, "Writing matters"; but more, it says, "*Your* writing matters."

Students learn from this attention paid by an important person. They learn that with careful work, their writing can improve; that writing is a craft; that what they say counts. By taking easily defined steps, one can make a paper noticeably better. Technically it's not so difficult; the information needed is readily available in books, handouts from classes, peer tutors, professors. It need not be mysterious. The real issue, then, is motivation, which is heightened by knowing that an audience—really, a person—cares.

Speaking

Speaking is another core liberal arts skill, though less widely emphasized in most colleges than is writing. It takes a variety of forms: speaking in classes, participation in seminars, collaborative conversations in labs or on field trips, delivery of a report in class, presentation of a senior thesis, or sitting for an oral examination. All of these activities are resource intensive, requiring a low student-faculty ratio, but the skills can be very useful in later life, and the practice itself has some interesting side benefits.

Students at the college are regularly required to speak in classes—called on to answer questions, to take a position, to agree with or refute an argument, and to speak up even when they're shy or nervous. They are exposed to embarrassment; in seminars they are virtually forced to cope with and at least minimally overcome this fear. Sometimes they must debate a superior—the teacher—in ways that were probably discouraged in high school, and sometimes they simply have to convey their ideas under tight constraints.

> What's helped [my speaking] the most is probably working at the Writing Center [as a tutor] and just talking to people, you know, in all of our appointments; and really having to learn to explain yourself clearly and concisely, with not a lot of time . . . trying to express what you're trying to say as quickly as possible without sounding, you know, rushed or confused. (Jane, senior)

Students say that sheer experience improves their ability and confidence in speaking.

It seems like every class I've taken, we had to do some group project we had to present to the class, which helped me get over nerves . . . Every class emphasizes participation in class, as well as my [extracurricular] organization, you know, it's just given me an opportunity to talk to large groups of people and present my ideas. So I've definitely become more confident in speaking. (Jack, senior)

Probably through a lot of my classes being really small and being largely discussion-based I've become more comfortable, you know, speaking to other people or in front of other people . . . It's just something that comes with practice. (Jenny, senior)

You definitely have a chance to improve upon your communication skills just through . . . speaking in class and, like, making comments, and asking questions. And just to be in an environment in which you're constantly hearing people make arguments, and present ideas, and communicate effectively. (Sean, junior)

To learn how students improve their more formal public speaking skills, we compiled the results of four studies: (1) Our colleague Dr. Jim Helmer assembled and evaluated an archive of 288 videotapes of student talks given in students' sophomore and senior years. Given the lack of a public speaking requirement at the college, only some students gave such talks or were available for taping, and we often couldn't obtain tapes of specific students giving talks in both years (sophomore and senior). Within those limits, though, Dr. Helmer prepared a written report comparing sophomores to seniors. (2) In our panel interviews, we regularly asked students about their oral communication skills, both in public speaking as well as in class participation. (3) The annual HEDS Senior Surveys included questions on oral communication. (4) Finally, our alumni interviews included questions about oral communication skills. We evaluated the results from all of these, looking for consistent findings.

Several conclusions emerged. First, despite the fact that the college no longer has a systematic program to improve public speaking (for many years, ending in the 1980s, it did), improvements seem clear. On the videotapes, seniors obviously speak better than sophomores. This finding, tentative because of our sampling problems, is bolstered by the self-reports on both Senior Surveys and in the panel interviews: many students certainly believe they have improved. Some of this they ascribe to maturation, but many "mature" adults are terrified of speaking in public. After several years at the college, these students are not.

Being an RA helped public speaking . . . [In RA training] they teach how to command an audience, and how to get their respect very quickly. You don't talk down to them; . . . it's just a matter of comfort level talking in front of all these people. And, you know, by junior year, when one of my idiot advisees, who almost got suspended, asked in the middle of the first meeting, "So when can we buy a keg and bring it into the dorm?" I was able to laugh it off . . . But as a . . . sophomore, I probably would have peed my pants. (Jonathan, alumnus)

Second, small efforts seem to produce significant results. A student need not give a twenty-minute presentation to gain these speaking skills; a very short talk—two or three minutes—seems to work. This isn't rocket science.

In the fraternity, you know, we had weekly meetings, and just speaking in front of forty people every week gets you comfortable in that sort of situation. (Jack, alumnus)

There is a true art to rhetoric at higher levels, of course, but that's not what we're talking about. The sheer act of talking to a reasonably sympathetic audience, perhaps with a modicum of feedback (for instance, using video recording, even one time), produces improvements, with relatively little investment of either class time or faculty expertise.

Third, there's a mildly surprising side benefit: the emotional intensity of public speaking brings with it a variety of other academic and personal gains. When they talk, formally or not, in front of a group, students have no choice but to be engaged, especially if they "belong" to the community and care what their fellow students think about them.

We had thesis meetings, me and my advisor, and then there'd be five or six other [students]. And just . . . trying to ask questions about others' theses is indescribable . . . [You are] just trying to . . . fully comprehend and speak intellectually a lot of the time, you know, and not sound like an idiot. (Jack, alumnus)

Embarrassment is an immediate incentive, so the student speaker does more work, learns the material better, and is far more emotionally engaged than with almost any written work. They then learn the irreplaceable value of preparation: "I really *knew* what I was talking about," they told us.

year to the end of their sophomore year. This would translate into a 43 percentile gain, indicating that if these freshmen entered higher education at the 50th percentile they would reach a level equivalent to the 93rd percentile of an incoming freshman class by the end of their sophomore year. Crucially, this category of high performers includes students from all family backgrounds and racial/ethnic groups, as well as students with different levels of academic preparation.[11]

This suggests that hardworking students of all backgrounds at good colleges (such as the one we studied) are likely to improve their critical thinking quite a bit, rather quickly.

Arum and Roksa's book also shows in detail how a major factor of student progress is basically "time on task"—that is, time spent reading, writing, and doing classwork. We did not use the CLA at the college, but we did ask our panelists whether they believed that their critical, analytic, or thinking abilities improved. When interviewed during college, most responded with a carefully modest "yes," saying that perhaps they had simply matured. But when asked the same question four years after graduation the hesitations vanished; a significant number believed that their "critical thinking" abilities had indeed improved.

Students credited two kinds of experience with enhancing their critical thinking abilities. First, sheer exposure to a diverse set of roommates and friends forced many students to reexamine their own views on issues.

> I come from a really small town in Massachusetts . . . I really haven't been outside of the U.S., plus everyone in my town was, you know, white middle class . . . Freshman year my roommates were from Uruguay and Korea . . . and one of the kids [who] became one of my best friends was from England. And then another [had] taken time off before college and done a lot of traveling in Europe, and lived in Greece . . . [these friends] are much more critical of religion and God—they're atheists! And it was definitely an interesting experience, which was difficult for a while . . .
>
> But then over time everything changed, you know, I changed, like, the way in which I saw things. (Sean, alumnus)

In these cases as in others, it was the emotional engagement of face-to-face relationships that often prompted students to think "critically" about moral as well as intellectual questions.

Nationwide research supports the same conclusion. In July 2007, Dan Chambliss reviewed findings from interviews conducted, as part of the

Wabash National Study of Liberal Education, with freshman students at a sample of colleges and universities across the United States. When asked to describe major developmental experiences from their freshman year, students almost always mentioned a difficult or challenging personal situation, often requiring ethical decisions, with individuals personally known to them. These situations frequently involved competing loyalties—between groups of friends, say, or between friends and parents. The moral dilemmas presented were stark. They were not abstract or hypothetical cases, as they might be in an ethics class. They involved real people. On such occasions, according to the Wabash interviews, students often sought out a trusted adult mentor, and sometimes then recalled and saw the personal relevance of classroom discussions. Critical thinking and moral reasoning was no longer a game.[12]

Critical thinking—at least, the intellectual side of it—is also directly promoted by professors' actions in their courses.

> Professor Rosen would say something, and he'd say, "What do you think of that?" And a student would respond; and then Rosen would argue a *completely different side of the issue.* [Eventually] you'd get about eighteen different points of view, and you would feel like you were never, ever right. (Anne, alumna)

Or:

> I did this whole lecture with Professor Nelson in Intro to Anthropology, and . . . at the end of the class he said, "I made this all up!" In looking back, you were kind of, "Yeah, none of this made any sense to me . . ." And he was like, "Well, all of you wrote it down, because I was your professor" . . . No one had the guts to raise their hand and say, "I don't think so," and he was just like, "You have to question me, even if I'm your professor!" (Murphy, alumnus)

Some professors seemed routinely to challenge their students' views on a wide variety of issues, instilling in them the habit of skepticism.

> I take a lot of religion classes, and I take a lot of biology classes, and they kind of look at the same thing from very different perspectives. They're both looking at, you know, How do you define the world? What does everything mean, basically?

When you look at it scientifically, you have to go through this whole scientific method where you formalize the hypothesis, and then you make observations, you analyze your observations, and then you form your conclusions . . . From the religious aspect, it can be . . . more subjective where, like, your personal emotions and spiritual beliefs are [required]. So we have these . . . different ways of approaching observations . . . (Harry, senior)

Just as the students are taught in their writing classes to take a position ("state your thesis"), in many other courses they are pushed to criticize, or at least question, the authors whom they read and the professors they study with; they may even sometimes (as Nietzsche urged) develop the courage to challenge their own beliefs. Critical thinking then becomes more than just an academic skill, or a technique employed to solve particular problems; it becomes a habit, or even a personality trait.

I will hear something on the news . . . and not automatically assume it's fact. I'm going to think, "Why are they doing this? What's their motivation behind it? Who's the decision maker behind this? What's their motive to follow through with this action?" (Jonathan, senior)

And this is, again, not simply an isolated skill.

It's more of a lifestyle . . . No matter what I look at or what I read, I kind of see more of the inside of it, what's deeper . . . My whole [comparative literature] major, that's basically all we did . . . After reading so many books and writing so many papers, and just looking at things more critically, it's just become more like habit. (Victoria, alumna)

Science

Two other relatively "exclusive" academic programs benefit large numbers of students at the college: extensive work in the natural sciences, and study abroad. In each case—although for very different reasons—benefits can obviously be substantial, but gaining access to the programs is also difficult.

In the natural sciences, these difficulties themselves probably produce one of the major benefits—prestige. By "sciences" here we mean the laboratory or field-based study of the natural world, including at least physics, biology,

chemistry, geology, and neuroscience.[13] Serious work in these fields often requires both expensive equipment (costly for the institution or the foundations,
firms, and donors who underwrite it), and a strong high school education
(calculus, good work habits of the students). Within academia, the "hard"
sciences represent something like a prestigious and well-funded elite sector.
"STEM"—sciences, technology, engineering, and math—education in general has received a lot of attention in national discussions, since it's seen as
crucial to the nation's economic productivity and competitiveness.

For many years, the college required all students as part of their general
education to take at least some science courses. Students frequently met that
requirement, as they do everywhere, by enrolling in what they thought might
be the easiest courses—some local variant of "Rocks for Jocks" or "Physics for
Poets." But in 2001, the college dropped its distribution requirements altogether. There followed a modest, but not huge, drop in the numbers of students
who took lab sciences. Many students had, in effect, already been avoiding the
tougher ones. If they wished, they could now avoid the sciences altogether.

There's more at play here, though, than simple preference or lack of interest.
A sizable number of students in our panel expressed a deeper resistance to the
whole realm of mathematical or scientific work. Faculty advisors frequently
hear the phrases "I'm not a science person" or "I can't do math," as students
describe a lack of inborn talent for scientific study. They see themselves as perhaps incapable of doing the work, and regard this as a kind of personality trait.

> Yeah. I'm not very, I'm not really a science/math person, so I tend to take
> humanities. (Sarah, junior)

> I've never been much of a science person, to be honest. (Hannah, junior)

This sentiment comes out even when, grudgingly, they take a "nonmajor" science course.

> [I'm taking] Scientist's View of Nature with this professor. I like the course.
> I'm not a science person, but my advisor suggested I take science because
> he's really anal about that. So I decided to take that course because it's not,
> like, major science. (Katy, freshman)

We have no way of knowing, based on our data, whether this occurs nationwide, although research has strongly suggested it has. Study in the natural

sciences has somehow come to be seen as implicating one's identity.[14] (Perhaps the closest analogy would be arts performers—"I'm a photographer" or "I'm a dancer.") These students have successfully entered the world of college, as we said in Chapter 2, but they regard entering the sciences as beyond their innate abilities.

Even if they wanted to enter there, some structural barriers hinder them. As science educators have long known, the pipeline for science students is continually narrowing, with curricula that are clearly sequential and hierarchal. Because a student must pass earlier levels to go on to later ones, students are continually "ratcheting out"; with each passing year, fewer students remain in any one discipline. At the same time, almost no one enters these tracks later on, since to begin at the beginning would entail a significant additional expense of both time and sometimes money. When—as at the college—distribution requirements don't exist, many students don't take any science in their first year; if departments don't offer nonmajor courses then or later, those students are effectively separated from entire branches of human knowledge. Finally, when students expect to receive dramatically lower grades in science courses, a sizable number won't take those courses, fearing their GPAs may be lowered. Under such conditions, science departments have in a sense created their own admission standards.

But if students outside the sciences are alienated from those fields, how do insiders feel? To explore the issue in a little more detail, we assembled a small group of science majors. When we asked about their studies, they quickly asserted that science students really are both different and—they hesitated to say it directly—a bit superior to nonscience students.

INTERVIEWER: How are science students different?
STUDENT NO. 1: I should be nice.
STUDENT NO. 2: I guess in terms of skills, science majors definitely focus more on the quantitative data analysis . . . Yeah, I don't want to be mean.
INTERVIEWER: How are science majors different?
STUDENT NO. 1: Well, for starters, I have eleven more hours of class time a week than a humanities major.
STUDENT NO. 3: Yeah, it's really like taking an extra class with each lab.
STUDENT NO. 2: It's kind of like two or three extra classes.

The students all agreed: science majors put in more time and work.

Second, they regarded scientific thinking as more rigorous, more rule bound, demanding definite right and wrong answers: "In the sciences, you can be right about something, or wrong about something." "Opinions don't matter as much in science. [Even] when I have political discussions, I back up my data with a lot of statistical research to figure out why I believe in something like this." "There are rules," compared with other fields: "It would bother me to talk about things day in and day out that don't have a definite answer." These students value the empiricist rigor and evidentiary thinking that the sciences require.

There's clearly a moral judgment in their attitude. One student in our group explained.

> Some people—I'm going to stereotype now—will say, "I'm a creative writing major. I don't know what I want to do yet—maybe move to Europe for a few years, maybe try and go into journalism or something."
>
> I'm so horrified [by this attitude]! I try not to bad-mouth them, and make them feel like crap, which I do sometimes. Some days [these non-science students] get really angry at me, and honestly I don't care—I have another four hour lab I gotta go to . . . I'm learning skills I'm going to have the rest of my life, and you're talking about creative writing!
>
> . . . In science, you're either going to do research; you're going to stay in academia; you're going to a private company and do research for them; or you're going into medicine, that's pretty much it. You know that you will always have a job . . .

Even within the "Temple of Science" itself, as some refer to the lavish new building, students perceive a status hierarchy among the disciplines.[15] Such distinctions are more joking than invidious, but they are distinctions nonetheless, reflected in the occasional intimation that "certain departments don't deserve to be in the Science Center." "Deserve" here implies a level of accomplishment or legitimacy as yet unachieved. Even among the clearly "legitimate disciplines," competition continues: a biology major, for instance, spent a summer working in a chemistry lab.

> STUDENT: I always got a feel . . . that chem people feel themselves superior over bio, for sure. We would always be, like, in the lunch room during research breaks. We'd be sitting there and one of the bio majors would walk by wearing shorts; and everyone in the Chem Department was like, "Oh, bio, that's just weak, wearing shorts" and whatever,

because you can't wear shorts in the [chemistry] lab. That was the biggest deal of the day! They were mocking bio for the rest of the week because one of the researchers was wearing shorts . . .

INTERVIEWER: They don't have to worry about wearing long pants because they're not working with those chemicals?

STUDENT: Right . . . If you're in the lab, using chemicals, you have to wear long pants . . . You have to wear safety glasses and stuff. A lot of the safety stuff is more relaxed in bio. And I feel the chemistry kids, they're like . . .

ANOTHER STUDENT: Hard core!

STUDENT: We're intense because we have to wear all this safety protection all the time.

A biology student argued back.

I wish they would come up [to the bio labs] and deal with keeping workplaces sterile. That's one of the biggest issues we have with microbiology, and doing it every day—keeping things sterile, keeping things, you know, uncontaminated—it's a pain.

That summer we spent most of our time talking about other departments and [whether] we were cooler, which was uncomfortable for me because I was a biology major working in chemistry—still am.

At this point a psychology major jumped in: "Because I am a psych major, I feel like we get crapped on." (Another: "Yep.")

I think a lot of chemistry, biology, physics, neuroscience people especially, they just crap on us and say we don't deserve to be in the Science Center . . .

[Psychology is] a lot more people-based, I guess kind of . . . [But] there's definitely still that quantitative aspect as well as research reports, research and lab reports . . . There's definitely still a lot of hypothesis testing. It is still a science, although people do call it more of a social science. I get a lot of crap for that.

She went on to note that "psych majors are, I guess, less intense and kind of more relaxed." (Another student: "Chem majors are crazy.")

Prestige in science, as here described, is clearly connected to being "hard core" in terms of intellectual rigor, seriousness of purpose, and danger of lab work. "The intense science majors, like chemistry, are really superintense beasts. They're like, 'This is what you've got to do!' and a lot of them are premed so that adds another layer . . . The premeds are very cutthroat . . . whereas psychology is a lot more, like, it's nice and fun and laid back."

The huge expense of science research and equipment also enhances prestige: a professor in one of the lower status departments ". . . is going to be bringing in million-dollar machinery in the next few years or something like that, so he's legit." As a student noted "You also get to play with really, really expensive toys . . . Within your first year of doing chemistry, you're working on a multimillion-dollar instrument every week."

But overall, the students based their respect for chemistry on its difficulty.

STUDENT NO. 2: In terms of the number of difficult classes you have to take, chemistry is possibly the hardest.

STUDENT NO. 1: You have to take Orgo I; you have to take Orgo II; you have to take P-chem; you have to take either Advanced Organic or Advanced P-chem.

STUDENT NO. 2: And Super Lab! . . . Super Lab is a really intense lab techniques course, and it's a lot of time, and it's super hard.

STUDENT NO. 1: I think if you could make a list of the top five most feared classes on campus—one of them would be Psych Stats, P-chem, Super Orgo, Super Lab, and the other Orgo. That's how many chemistry majors have to take, but nonscience majors have more electives, hence easier classes.

"The most feared courses." Prestige here reflects danger, of hard work, of "brutal" standards, of being "hard core"—a kind of academic machismo, stereotypically masculine. So where do women fit into this world? In the Science Center itself, one student noticed, the physical location of departments from the basement up to the third floor actually seems arranged by gender of students: "As you go up, the ratio of guys to girls flips . . . I know one, there's one or two female physics majors [in the basement labs]; . . . it's virtually all guys. [On the first floor] chemistry has a few girls, but it's still mostly guys. And bio [on the second floor] is fairly even, and psych [on the third floor] is mostly girls . . ." Location in a building is probably fortuitous, but it's no accident that the proportion of women in different fields varies in relation to the centrality of human beings as the subject of study: very heavy in psychology, medium in biology, and almost nil, for instance, in physics.

Women also seem more concerned than men with the quality of teachers in their courses, more influenced by the grades they received, and less committed to any particular major or even career track. Three examples from our panelists illustrate the point. Sheena initially planned to major in psychology, but she took the introductory course and "realized I could not do that for the rest of my life." Another discipline's introductory course she found to be "not necessarily bad, it's just taught terribly and doesn't give you any motivation to learn anything. The professor on the first day was like, 'I don't like teaching . . . I'd rather be doing research.'" In still another science the professor was "horrible, horrible . . . he can't teach." Eventually she found Professor Grand. "He was just a brilliant man, and when I declared my major he was chair of the department . . . He was just a great inspiration." Her teacher and then mentor was crucial in her selection of fields.

Men, on the other hand, seemed more committed to disciplines than to teachers. Joe started on a premed track. After receiving a C- in Organic Chemistry, he realized that medical school would not be an option. But he didn't change his major. He liked science, no longer worried about his GPA, and eventually graduated with a science major and went to law school. Similarly, from the beginning Jay was committed to studying physics. Initially there were big lectures, but he didn't mind. He appreciated good teachers and advisors along the way but they didn't affect his choice of courses or major; in that sense, he didn't really care whether they were good. With decent grades throughout, he completed college and entered a career in which his intellectual strengths were rare and highly valued.[16] The gender difference might suggest that anyone interested in attracting more women to science should consider the role of teacher quality, especially in introductory courses.[17] Once missed, that chance won't come again.

The challenge of attracting students to science has not been lost on policy makers and concerned faculty. Since the late 1980s, a "research-based" model of undergraduate science education, encouraged by the National Science Foundation as well as by private foundations, and enthusiastically embraced by many science faculties, has enjoyed prestige as the preferred pedagogical method. *Science* magazine itself, the Journal of the American Association for the Advancement of Science, regularly promotes what it calls a "hands-on" model of "doing real research," in which students are taught to "think like a scientist" and are introduced, via "investigatory labs," to the "excitement of research." Such language consistently dominates conversations about the natural sciences in liberal arts institutions such as the college. Promising to reverse widely perceived declines in scientific knowledge and interest among students, research-based education borrows from the prestige of "being a published scholar" to entice students into the lab. More broadly, the model has been expanded by some colleges to include senior projects, independent studies, and sometimes summer internships or research apprenticeships; it has expanded into the social sciences and, a bit haltingly, into the humanities. Studies published in *Science* and elsewhere suggest that the educational benefits to students who actually participate are substantial.

Participation, however, can't be taken for granted; the problem is that most students don't participate in the first place. For average college students, we suspect that research-based teaching won't work. It takes as its implied task the preprofessional training of scientists rather than general dissemination of knowledge about the natural world. Students are treated as if they are headed for careers as research scientists, an assumption that for the vast majority of American undergraduates is obviously incorrect. It can easily reinforce the notion that science is only for future scientists. If departments pour all of their energy into research-based training, they may unwittingly be abandoning the vast range of undergraduates, some of whom might potentially become interested in science, and all of whom need some basic scientific education. It would leave most college graduates woefully ignorant of the biology of reproduction; the evidence for global climate change; the basics of health, nutrition, and human physiology; fundamental knowledge of what genetics, and evolution, and stem cells are—the list goes on. In effect, research-based pedagogy could confirm the isolation of the natural sciences from most American undergraduates. It may be—although this is itself debatable—the correct approach for attracting and developing research scientists. When adopted by masterful undergraduate teachers, as it has been in many places, the model works quite well. But we suspect it does little to solve the broader problem of inadequate science education for the great majority of college students.

In facing a serious college science curriculum, the average graduate of the average high school encounters a daunting array of intellectual and motivational challenges: the inescapable need for precision; an emphasis on memorization of a large number of facts; the nonhuman scale of scientific topics (from the submicroscopic to the literally astronomical); the heavy emphasis on methods and techniques over perhaps more intrinsically interesting content; and the simultaneous manipulation of multiple abstract concepts. Successful science majors know they are different: "I feel like I go to the Science Center University," said one. The imposing building, its departments, and its students almost comprise a college within the college, with its own higher standards, more demanding workloads, and—certainly from science students' point of view—a deservedly higher place on the academic prestige ladder. For everyone else, across the nation, poor high school preparation, curricular structures that preclude late entry, and a culture (reinforced by tremendous pressure on faculty) in which research holds such great importance may conspire to leave too many students out. They then graduate with a substantive ignorance of the natural sciences, a sense of personal inadequacy to the task, and a lingering and probably lifelong feeling of bafflement in the face of numbers, data, or any information about how nature works. The problem here is not with the elite standards of science programs. It's that too few students actually encounter and then meet those standards.

Study Abroad

In our panel, virtually every student who studied abroad praised the experience; many, in fact, cited it as their single most valuable educational activity in college. Like majoring in the natural sciences, study abroad is an "elite" or special experience reserved for a minority of college students, although here the selection criteria are less academic than financial. Students at wealthier colleges—and this group overlaps with the most selective—are far more likely to study abroad. In 2009, only about 15 percent of American college students studied abroad during their college careers, but at wealthier schools such as the college that number is approaching 45–50 percent or even higher. While most students nationally will certainly never be able to afford the yearlong experiences of many students at the college, understanding the benefits of study abroad might help us find ways, at a smaller scale, to replicate the experience more cheaply.[18]

Study abroad exemplifies, in a different context, the fundamental principle of our book: college works best by bringing students together with the right people at the right time. Residential college juniors have already lived away from home for several years, formed new friendships and found teachers in a new and somewhat unstructured situation. Many have studied a foreign language and can thus solve at least basic living problems in another country. The college helps them select a country (Czech Republic, Costa Rica, Thailand, etc.) and find a well-run program. The language departments in particular offer a clear pathway, providing structure and support, and making logistics easy. (The college's own programs in France, Spain, and China, for instance, are quite organized and academically rigorous.)

Friends and prior commitments to programs are also important in the decision to go abroad. For some students, yes, the choice reflects an educational goal of broadening one's view, expanding horizons. But the specifics—where to go, when, for how long—are shaped by language programs, and by one's friends. Students with double majors, locked into a sizable number of required courses, can't afford the time away. Athletes heavily committed to their teams—or whose coaches, needing their talent, pressure them to stay—often decide not to go, almost always to their eventual regret. Occasionally students with romantic involvements stay on campus as well. "I was dating someone who went to a different school than me, but had come to the region to be close to me . . . And I felt some sort of responsibility . . . to show the same kind of commitment . . ." (Alan, junior). Relationships already formed (academic, athletic, romantic) increase or hinder the chances of taking this one major opportunity, which students will most likely never have again in their lives.

Going abroad is a bit like starting college again—a major life change, requiring significant adaptation to a completely new environment. It requires self-reliance in overcoming fears of social rejection, looking foolish, being alone—all the fears once overcome in the freshman year—and beyond that, fears of being lost, getting sick, or even being kidnapped. It demands new skills: workable mastery of a foreign language (although the most popular destinations are in fact English-speaking countries, where that's not the problem), settling into an apartment without the immediate assistance of parents or college staff, getting one's own food, learning to travel in a different society—and just adaptation to local customs and conditions.

> While I was in [Vietnam], it was very hard. I didn't speak the language . . . there were all these bugs, the food was disgusting to me . . . and it was hot. (Cynthia, junior)

It is a new world to some extent—a dramatic, maybe scary, and memorable reconfiguring of everyday life.[19]

> I just couldn't believe seeing a group of fifth graders standing outside at noon with their lunch smoking cigarettes. And it's very, very fashionable

. . . the typical French stereotype. With my friends on the subway, if we were speaking in English, we were so much louder than any French group—and the image of Americans is very noisy, loud, disruptive. In a French café, everybody can be having a conversation, but you can't hear a word. And if an American walks in, everybody in the café can hear what they're having to say . . . (Jen, senior)

Entering a new culture entails not just a few isolated tasks set against a backdrop of fixed, known routines, as they were back in college ("Now I'll take calculus; it's next in the sequence and it's required for physics"). It's an entire package of dramatically new experiences and challenges, coming all at once. When the transition works—and relatively few students give up entirely and go home—students feel a tremendous gain in self-confidence. "I go to a big city today in the United States and I feel like it is a piece of cake" (Downey report). To simply survive, one has to expand perspectives and mature: "I grew six years in six months."

I was forced to be independent in a place I wasn't familiar with. I had to find my own place to live, had to find out where to get my food, and I had to figure out how I would make the 40-minute walk from my housing to the university. It changed how confident I am in being able to do things that I am not familiar with and knowing that I can do those things. (A male student who spent a semester in South Africa on an SIT program. Downey report)

I didn't come home for an entire year. My parents visited me once or twice; but aside from that, I was on my own for a year in a foreign country, you know, 3,500 miles from home . . .

I had already had the academic discipline, that wasn't really—that wasn't a problem. I needed a social discipline to be able to take care of myself, you know. Like, I had—essentially, like an apartment; so I had to like take care of bills, and all that. I kind of had to grow up a little bit. (Ruttiger, senior)

Study abroad is, in some ways, a foreshadowing of life after college, life on one's own. For many students, it will be their only major college activity lived with (initially) no friends or acquaintances. It requires meeting new people, rapidly learning things about one's new surroundings, and reorganizing one's daily life.

Almost all who go abroad find returning to college a difficult challenge, a kind of reverse culture shock. Returnees feel "too mature for this," recoil at the silliness in undergraduate life, frequently say to themselves, "Why am I here?"[20] Their friendships are not the same; often their social circles have moved on, and many returnees never again feel fully integrated into the college. It's probably part of an unavoidable growing away from the provincialities of the college, and of the country, too.

> It was hard coming back to the States, period. It was, I—there was more culture shock on the way back than going there. Because going [to China], I was prepared for it to be somewhat totally different. Like all those things that we don't like to talk about—being American, eating too much beef, the servings that we eat. It's mostly food for me, I got nauseous; I came back and saw hamburgers, and it made me nauseous because [food is] so much healthier there. (George, junior)

But all say, nonetheless, that the experience was crucial and valuable.

Even though study abroad for a year is prohibitively expensive for most college students, some of the benefits—the exposure to other cultures, the "real-world" connections with academic work, even the "on-your-own" challenge—might be replicable, at a smaller scale, in field trips to "real-world" sites, service-learning projects, or internships. We know professors at modestly funded colleges who organize trips abroad—one or two weeks—that, with good planning, can be managed even on tight budgets, with tremendous benefits to the students. Even with exposure to a foreign culture, the difference between "never" and "ever" is huge—a single, relatively brief trip can be not only enlightening but a great motivator for further exploration as well.

Why Do Students Learn?

From these various examples—writing, speaking, critical thinking, science, study abroad—what might we conclude about learning in college? First, it seems that many "college" skills (writing, speaking, organizing, time management) are not really esoteric. Teachers of both writing and speaking don't need much special expertise to instruct students; the goal is solid basic craftsmanship, not artistic fluency. Most teachers at the college, from what students told us, don't fuss over the technical language of English syntax, nor do most students learn public speaking through the formal study of rhetoric. It's not that detailed technique doesn't matter, but rather that such technique is easily available—in books, from teachers, on the Web, or by simply imitating work already done. For speaking especially, students need to be comfortable, organized, and clear; this alone puts them well ahead of their peers in the general population. In the case of critical thinking, while different disciplines certainly teach elaborate analytic skills, the valuable lessons taken from them seem more generalized than professional: learning how to establish causal relations, how to evaluate evidence, and how to draw conclusions from a variety of data. In the fine arts and natural sciences, techniques certainly receive greater emphasis, but for most students, the arcana of a specific field are less important than the general lessons learned from mastering them. Students benefit most from teachers who are professionally competent, but more importantly who simply pay attention, try to improve students' work, and take the time to talk with them—in a word, teachers who *care* about the subject and the students.

Second, students come to understand that methods of writing, speaking, and even thinking can, in fact, be learned. College students find that there are clear steps one can take to produce better papers; that writing is always done for a particular audience; and that while it may take a good deal of effort, there's no magic to constructing a solid, clear, understandable written argument. Similarly, in public speaking many realize that with a bit of practice and a few basic techniques ("make eye contact," "don't read your talk," "don't juggle multiple topics") they can actually improve rather quickly.

Third, students don't think all skills are equally learnable. Statistical analyses of thousands of seniors' responses to survey questions, and findings from our interviews, showed this quite clearly. For instance, as we've said, students think that writing is very learnable—it's a craft, and with some basic techniques and hard work, almost anyone can do it reasonably well. Public speaking is learnable too, but some people have more natural ease or talent with it. Finally, quantitative skills (as well as scientific savvy) are, in the eyes of students at the college, essentially a gift—you either have them or you don't. Remarkably, even math majors believe this—although this may only hold in America, where "math phobia" is widespread. This threefold pattern precisely matches the college's varying emphases: work on writing is absolutely unavoidable; public speaking is readily available although rarely required; quantitative work can mostly be avoided.

Finally, notice how in every case, *connecting with, or relating to, a fairly specific audience is central*; and the *most motivating audience seems to be a face-to-face audience.* Scholars of teaching have long known that the more rapid the feed-back, the better; and there's nothing more immediate than feedback from a live audience. This is because interactions—the more immediate the better—engage people emotionally, and motivate them to act and to change. Oral examinations, public talks, theatre or dance performances, and singing all entail an immediate exposure to an audience's response, so they are power-fully motivating.

College works when it provides a thick environment of constant feedback, driven by the establishment and maintenance of social relationships. Do I fit in with my peers? Will the English teacher, or other students, think I'm stupid? Am I up to the science standards? Am I valued and respected? In almost every case we've found, the strongest motivation to work on basic skills comes from an emotionally based face-to-face relationship with specific other people—for instance, the one-on-one writing tutorial with a respected professor who cares about *this* student's work. Speaking improves under the immediate social fear of embarrassment—either of talking in front of a class, or of performing in an oral exam, or of talking in front of one's peers in a seminar. Serious, engaged consideration of ethical issues arises when students have personal conflicts with peers. Such fundamental motivators work in education as they do any-where else, and the college that wants to educate its students will tap and use them. The "college effect" we found in student writing—that is, writing improved quickly in the first year, even without technical instruction—results from students' freshman-year effort simply to fit in, to "make the grade." They haven't necessarily learned more; they're just trying harder, and trying works. It's a concerted effort to "join the group" in the face of overwhelming, con-stant feedback from other people.

The concept of "skills," then, artificially isolates one element of a much larger organization of living activities. Learning fundamental skills is not simply about picking up little boxes of techniques and rules ("keep paragraphs to one topic; use parallel sentences for parallel ideas"). It's about relating, and *want-ing* to relate, to this teacher, these peers, this college, or, for students studying abroad, to the natives of this (very different) country. Writing is really about clarifying one's ideas for others, asserting one's conclusion, and respecting one's audience. Public speaking calls for a deep, comfortable knowledge of the subject and some ease with standing up in front of a group. Critical thinking is less about the details of data analysis and more about the willingness—even courage—to challenge others' arguments. And just as clearly, when students don't care about relating to others in these ways, learning stops.

Students best learn skills in a supportive community, with relationships that value and encourage those students and those skills. *The real people involved*—not the abstract "programs"—are crucial.

7

Finishing

The best part of it is not from classes. It's coming from
just a whole college experience: learning to live on your
own, learning to take care of yourself, learning to live on
your own schedule, and learning to budget your time,
and learning to meet new people and deal with your
relationships and new issues. Because at college, you learn
something new the first day you walk on the campus.
(Keith, junior)

For students at the college, senior year is a time of pride and fear—pride at having surmounted the challenges and learned so much; fear at the approaching end of this phase of one's life, and of being forced (unless graduate school intervenes) to finally face the "real world" with its shocking shortage of safety nets. It's a time of transition, a bit like when they first came to college, of leaving one world and entering another. It's also a time for summing up, for realizing what one has gained.

Their immediate challenge is to remain fully engaged in the present. Most seniors have outgrown the college social scene; they have mastered the techniques of college work and college play; those who went abroad almost certainly feel a bit too old. It seems to them juvenile to gossip about dorm life, to troll the parties looking for hookups or even for the light thrills of drunken flirtation, or to win points by impressing freshmen. As incoming students, they were eager to learn the tricks—where do you get alcohol if you are under twenty-one? Which parties are the best (and worst)? Who teaches the easy courses? But for seniors, these tricks have lost their magic.

You get to a certain point, the social sort of options are limited . . . You know, you're going to the same bars and the parties . . . not that you feel above it, but you're looking at new people at these parties and—they're only freshmen! You're kind of thinking, "Wow, this has sort of been going on for the last three years." Maybe you're ready for something different, maybe a little bit more sophisticated. (Jay, alumnus)

Seniors told us that college social life itself has become "dull" or "boring," but, of course, it is they who have changed.

I've done everything here, you know. I've hung out a lot. I've—I've played all the games, you know: I've played the drinking game, and I've played the sports game, I've played the student game . . . I've played the being lazy game, and I've played the being a hard worker game. And [now] . . . I'm ready to set the world on fire. (Alexandra, senior)

Trying to stay engaged, some seniors reach out to explore new areas they've never studied before—take a first course in philosophy or dance, maybe, or try that geology professor everyone says is so great. More reliably, senior research projects and theses build on students' academic interests and allow them to "show what I can do," often on a project of their own choosing. Theses can require students to undertake a major synthesis of skills to meet a range of challenges over the course of a term or an entire year.

I did a thesis in physics, and it was really a project that was sort of beyond me . . . It took a lot of . . . confidence to work through the various problems that they threw at me . . . It allowed me to realize that, you know, the subject matter and the difficulty of it really don't matter when you're trying to put together a project or accomplish a goal. (Jay, alumnus)

Our panelists enjoyed pulling together all of their skills in an "authentic" project that mirrored to some extent what they imagine "real-world" work to be like—managing their own time, working together with other professionals, and producing and presenting their results at the end.

Looking back, I'd say that [the most important activity in college was] the relationships I formed with professors and doing a thesis at the end, the small group work, and completing the thesis . . . Wrapping up four years of studying and learning, that was probably the best experience. (Sarah, alumna)

The thesis project seems to illuminate the relevance of the major and what's been learned from it. More than that, a successful thesis can synthesize all of the gains a student has made while at the college.

Contemporary critics of higher education tend to talk as if skills, especially those readily measurable around the time of graduation, are the primary benefit of a college education. But that's a very limited view. In fact, different colleges produce a host of different positive results: technical skills, historical knowledge, personal and organizational connections, deeper religious faith, military training, intellectual awakening, cultural awareness, and others. (We're looking here only at primary outcomes—gains that are carried intrinsically by the graduates, not those accrued secondarily such as jobs, income, families, etc.) The college is a particular institution with its own specific mix of results. As they graduate and leave the college, students talk about at least three different kinds of positive results: skills, confidence, and relationships.

Skills

To the general public today, the purpose of college is to impart skills that will enable students to become productive members of society, skills that point to an imagined future in some kind of job. Explicitly or not, selective liberal arts institutions such as the college train students in the skills of the upper middle or professional class: these include analyzing data, compiling and making sense of different kinds of information, and finding general patterns amidst multiple situations; communicating with different groups of people via writing and speaking, in both standard and specialized English; and working effectively with others while organizing tasks and managing one's own work, sometimes over long periods of time with little oversight. These practices are built into the weekly or semester-long routines of students at the college. In specific ways, the Big Three academic skills—writing, speaking, and critical thinking—in fact habituate students to the management and leadership of others. For instance:

Writing.   Writing requires a willingness to present one's views and knowledge to an audience. At the college, students are routinely required to "make an argument," using declarative topic sentences and assembling arguments and evidence for their positions. Through the college's writing-intensive program, students become accustomed to expressing themselves in a clear, organized fashion—appropriate for persuading others, giving directions, and managing large group activities.

> Well, I know how to write a paper, which I did not know when I came here.
> And I feel like that's a symbol of something bigger, as far as being able to think about things in a very organized way—like being able to sort your thoughts, and put them into categories, and make them neat so you can show them to somebody else, and be like, "Well, this is what I think." (Madeline, senior)

Two years after graduating, Cynthia expressed the same point well.

> Writing [helped my thinking], you know—the central idea, your supporting ideas, where the supporting ideas come from, and how to move between them and particularly when we came to the conclusion . . . That kind of thinking was not a thing that I learned in high school; it was a thing I learned in college . . . (Cynthia, alumna)

Alums find that writing well really is a rare skill in the outside world.

> I am shocked at the number of people I come across in my area of work that can't write . . . What seems very basic and elementary to me, they can't do . . . Like—write a memo and have it make sense; having it be organized, and make a very strong argument in, like, a one-page memo. They can't do it. Just overall structure and grammar! People aren't very good writers. (Kathleen, alumna)

Although students learn to write for different audiences, the styles they learn are not informal or offbeat, aimed at fitting into local groups or idiosyncratic subcultures. College writing emphasizes standard English, widely used around the world, employing shared idioms and syntax, so that anyone who knows English—anyone in the world—can understand the message. It's about giving information and instructions to many people of varying backgrounds. These are not the skills of low-level service workers, whose words are scripted out on computer screens or in training manuals, whose actions are monitored by closed-circuit cameras and tracked by computer-keystroke monitoring. And the requirement, so common in freshman writing classes at the college, to "state a thesis"—to make a judgment—by its very nature forces students to stake out, for the moment, a leadership position.

Public Speaking.   Speaking in public, both in the give-and-take of seminars and in more public talks, similarly requires a willingness to unambiguously claim a leadership position—a situation in which rejection can be instantaneous.

> The presentation requirement [in a seminar] . . . was tough, but you learn a lot about your weaknesses, and you learn a lot about your strengths . . .
>
> Feeling comfortable in a big group of people is really important because if you can do that, you can really do anything . . . If you understand the material, you can, you can talk about it with large groups of people . . . That confidence is invaluable. (Tom, senior)

When students practice speaking, alumni tell us, they gain both skills and confidence that are invaluable in their working careers. A person who is willing and able to speak up clearly and persuasively rapidly rises to the top of many groups.

Critical Thinking.   Critical thinking, too, prepares one for leadership, for making informed decisions. Consider what concretely happens in the classrooms of schools like the college. Students routinely examine difficult texts, making sense of them, scrutinizing and evaluating the arguments put forth by some of the most intelligent people who have ever lived, and their successors in the disciplines: Plato, Dostoevsky, Adam Smith, Rene Descartes, Charles Darwin, Karl Marx, Albert Einstein, Sigmund Freud . . . Over and over, liberal arts students must engage with the ideas of committed, highly skilled writers and thinkers, artists and scientists. They become habituated to thinking about very big issues, and to debating those issues with informed opponents, both those physically present and those "virtually" there on the printed page. Furthermore, many discussions in liberal arts classes (literature, philosophy, history) are in essence about ethics—about what *should* be done, and about the inevitable tradeoffs involved—the kind of discussions leaders routinely engage in.

Such critical thinking, as we've suggested, is more than a skill; it can become a lifetime practice, and even a commitment to identifying as a certain kind of person.

Some people are willing to be a functionary and just do things the way that they've already established . . . Other people are confident enough in their ability to analyze the problems with a different set of standard operating procedures, or whatever it is, that they can figure out and improve it.

[For me,] the persuasive aspect may have come from the creative writing [classes]; the confidence and analytical skills probably came from the philosophy classes . . . the ability to analyze different conceptualizations of the same thing. (James, alumnus)

Finally, students learn the conventions of fair debate and discussion that allow one to win a debate while preserving the underlying relationship.

You get into friendly debates with people that are always going to challenge your beliefs and your values. I don't think you can value your beliefs [at the college] without being able to have some way to back those up, because someone will come along and probably will challenge you . . . I just remember something I said because [my friend] went off for, like, three hours on every single topic. And we both argued until we were blue in the face . . . (Anne, senior)

Though few students will learn these things formally, the numerous opportunities they have to speak and debate, to participate in class discussion, and to see other students debate (expertly or poorly—both can be instructive) will feed into their latent understanding of how to navigate contentious and critical meetings.

Seen up close, there's nothing mystical about how college skills become ingrained. Their practice is routine, daily, built in as part of the schedule. Writing, for instance, is structurally and culturally central to the college's program. Admission literature emphasizes it; students choose to apply and attend in part because of that emphasis; many faculty enjoy teaching writing-intensive courses; the entire program is supported by both students and the faculty. As part of the inescapable academic component of attending the college, students must write a lot and become reasonably proficient at it.

In the series of challenges that is college, students keep learning new things, overcoming hurdles, one after another. Advanced courses are designed to be more difficult than introductory courses. The sequentiality of majors is consciously intended to strengthen students' abilities year by year. Even when programs aren't linearly sequential, good advising and course selection can help to insure that students each year do things they couldn't do the year before.

This accumulating skill development in college seems to operate at most institutions. In their nationwide study of college outcomes, Pascarella and Terenzini find "evidence to suggest that the undergraduate experience provides cognitive skills that increase one's capacity for lifelong learning and continuing intellectual development. Overall, the trends in intellectual growth shaped by the undergraduate experience continue on the same trajectory after college," though such trajectories "depend to a substantial extent on the degree of intellectual stimulation and challenge in the post-college lives of alumni."[1]

Ideally, skills become self-reinforcing, improving over time. Reading, for instance, can become enjoyable in itself. When students are assigned interesting books and articles, then they become more likely to read for the rest of their lives. The greater potential benefits of college may lie not just in learning discrete skills, but in acquiring the habits and attitudes that support learning and make it intrinsically enjoyable. This is one reason why measuring student achievement at the end of a course, or even at the end of college, doesn't really work: it leaves out the far more important long-term results. A narrow focus on the short term can lower student motivation—love of learning—which really matters more in the long run. If a college does its work well, its best results won't be evident for years.

Confidence

As students improve their skills and master the series of challenges named in our chapter titles, they gain confidence. Our alumni panelists almost unanimously felt that they acquired a noticeably increased feeling of what psychologists call efficacy—a belief that their own actions work, particularly (but not only) in the specific skills they mastered.

> I've just become a stronger person. I know what my interests are; I know my personality; I know myself a lot better. I think I'm stronger . . . knowing that I can go abroad to Paris not speaking perfect French, and sit in a classroom full of French students . . .
>
> [I learned] how to prioritize and juggle so many different things: every day [in my job] I'm going to work, I'm juggling a ton of priorities, I'm on the phone with customers right then and there, helping out my staff, planning long-term strategy. Your brain is in a million different places, and you have to learn how to prioritize and juggle. [The college] teaches that extremely well. I had an internship; I was a lifeguard on the swim team; and with all

my classes, it was a lot to juggle. You really, really learn how to prioritize. (Claire, alumna)

[College faculty] kind of push you to do interesting things. For example, getting a grant . . . I never really thought about it until my professor was like, "Why don't you go for a grant, and do research this summer?" "Oh, OK." Just stuff like that . . . like taking Chinese! Like, I never really thought I would be able to do Chinese and study abroad. (Maudie, alumna)

My [football] coach said, "John, we need you to be more vocal." That was very hard for me, to break out of that shell and help my younger teammates . . . I was definitely forced to kind of reach out and introduce myself to people . . . And that transferred over into the workforce where, you know, I see people I'm not necessarily working with—I'll go out of my way and say, "Hello, my name is John, and you know, I'm working next to you . . ." (John, alumnus)

I've learned, if you can stay calm and go through something in your head before you act it out, you're way ahead of anybody who just gets frantic and panics, and tries to do too many things at once . . . You have twenty things of homework to do. If you can just sit down and do it, one by one, instead of just start pulling your hair out, it goes a lot easier . . . If you're driving your car and you get lost, instead of just making crazy turns, you know, pull over and ask directions! (Jim, junior)

The confidence comes from trying and learning new things in a relatively low-risk setting. Just as pilots learn to fly in simulators that let them pretend to deal with emergencies without catastrophic results if they fail, students practice living away from home, with no parents or close friends nearby; running a club or editing a newspaper; joining an intramural team; giving a talk, starting a relationship, maybe living abroad. College is a place almost designed for such efforts, in which failure has relatively little cost; not much long-term damage is done. Internships or service-learning opportunities provide something similar. People who don't attend college face new challenges too, and bigger ones. But they may have too much "skin in the game," working in settings (a job, for instance) where failure imposes real cost, with lasting damage. Such conditions don't encourage experimentation or risk taking. College, though, lampooned as a "bubble," or as "not the real world," is *supposed* to be a bubble—a protected environment in which to try things out. It's almost a program to enhance self-esteem: progressively more difficult challenges, with clear feedback but little real downside risk.

I don't think I'm the bravest person . . . I needed atmospheres which are open and supportive, and the kind where if you fail, you fail; and then you try something new . . . to be able to sort of get my foothold . . . I was much more timid about trusting people, about new situations, about taking risks all over, not just academically.

But [by] joining new things, and volunteering for things . . . I'm [now] much bolder in the things I'm willing to try; I'm much more articulate in the things I believe; and I'm much more trusting and adaptable in my friendships with people because I have a better—I have a better hold on *me*. (Judy, junior)

Amy directly attributed her intellectual confidence to how she was treated—lifted up, really—by her professors.

There's a certain poise, a sense of self that I developed while I was there . . . [It comes from] being treated like—sort of like an equal in a way, more like a colleague than being condescended to by professors. I think that's really important; being viewed as a fellow intellectual, if you will. And carrying that into the real world, I think that you can continue to believe that everyone will perceive you that way. And when you *believe* that people will perceive you that way, they do. (Amy, alumna)

Confidence—justified or not—is a valuable job and life skill that can measurably improve one's mental and even physical health.[2]

[The college] prepared you to interact with the rest of the world and be a strong advocate for yourself and your views. I see people, all the time, where they'll just roll over because somebody smarter than them, higher up than them, says, "This is what's going to be." Where I feel [the college] helped enable a rebellious streak . . . and to have that opinion come across intelligently . . . (Brandon, alumnus)

Social confidence tends to increase among college students nationwide, as Pascarella and Terenzini conclude: "Solid evidence indicates that students make statistically significant freshman- to senior-year gains in leadership abilities, popularity, and social self-confidence. These gains are apparent in longitudinal studies of large, nationally representative samples, even when controls are in place for students' precollege characteristics."[3]

Even if the confidence is misplaced, it can have positive effects.

The kind of people that I associated with gave me more confidence, which is kind of double edged . . . You're under this notion that you're something special, and you really aren't . . . that was the bad part. The good part is that . . . you're among people who are striving to be leaders and success stories . . . All my professors pushed me to do my best work. And that's really a mindset that they ingrain in you . . . [But] you get out in the real world, and realize . . . not everyone has that certain ingrained mindset. (Jay, alumnus)

Relationships

"Friendships" may well be the most frequently mentioned positive result of attending the college, with "relationships with professors" and improved writing not far behind. Throughout this book we've emphasized the central importance of these face-to-face relationships in the undergraduate experience. Finding friends is a prerequisite to a student remaining in school; responding to professors' personalities is important in choosing courses and majors; belonging or not to friendship groups shapes choices to go abroad, remain on teams, engage in extracurriculars, and so on.

Relationships affect students intellectually as well as socially. Many students told us, in detail, how close living with other college students effectively forced them to consider other points of view and to clearly express their own, even on the most important or personal beliefs.

I've never had a single [room] . . . I lived in a quad, and then a double, and then a double, and then I'm in a quad now. I think just by living with people around, always around you, you're constantly being challenged because, you know, you can't just say something ignorant or stupid and get away with it when there's other people there listening . . . You become more open-minded and more, you know, careful and, you know, less ignorant of others, how other people behave and interact. In classes, I think some of the statements I would have made in a class as a freshman, I would never, I would never say now . . . (Kim, senior)

Well, my roommate—who's been my roommate for four years—is a Republican, so that's been very interesting, because I'm very much a Democrat . . . She's my best, closest friend here. But we very much differ on things like abortion and gay marriage, and stuff like that. So it's sort of been interesting to communicate and talk to someone who I definitely care about, but at the same time, like, "How can you think that?" (Laura, senior)

I've hung out and just gotten into interesting discussions about, you know, the nature of God, and the nature of human nature, and political things, and how that all sort of ties together . . . It's from those discussions, in particular with people who are very, very different from me, that I've sort of been forced to find words to articulate beliefs that are so private . . . but never was actually able to explain to anybody else. (Judy, junior)

More diffusely, friends shaped the experience by encouraging or discouraging a whole range of activities, for good or bad.

I definitely did what my friends were interested in . . . It was nice to have friends that were also econ majors; that helped in some of the classes I took. I took [economics classes] because . . . [friends] could help me with issues . . . I also wrote for [the student newspaper] . . . because my roommate freshman year had written for his high school newspaper and wanted to get involved.

I didn't go abroad because none of my friends went abroad . . . My friends . . . shaped the decisions I made . . . (Keith, senior)

Sean, known among some professors as smart but not hardworking, revealingly told us that "none of my friends really spend a lot of time on academics or, like, studying, and I think that's, that's, like, fairly common throughout, you know, throughout the school. I think a lot of people can get away with not doing a lot of work" (Sean, junior). Such peer influence can, of course, be quite detrimental.[4] Even so, our interviewees routinely praised the friendships they made and have maintained, often for years after college.

Close relationships aren't the only human connection students want. As our discussion in Chapter 5 of extracurriculars, networks, and parties suggests, they regularly look for ways to find acquaintances and thus join the larger community of the college. They are looking for, and often find, *membership*, a membership closely shaped by this particular institution.

The meaning of membership of course depends on the character of the particular institution one is joining. The college certainly has its own character, which first attracts and then shapes its students.[5] Its size and location are crucial—a small, beautiful campus in the Northeast; the long, very cold winters with the forced intimacy of long dark winter nights in a dorm; the rural seclusion of the campus, simultaneously derided and cherished. The students are of traditional age and are predominantly middle and upper middle class. In an act of mutual selection, the college attracts (and picks) students who like and care about the campus aesthetics, the astonishing physical beauty. There's a "homey" feel to many dorms. Sociability, too, is highly prized in the much-vaunted "friendliness" of the campus—although it would be going too far to say that everyone is friends with everyone, the campus environment is clearly an amiable one. Conviviality is rehearsed weekly at big parties. And intellectual life here is valued, if not always the only priority—it's a mark of status and capability that "I can do the work," even if not always spending much time on it. Academics are taken quite seriously, but often as a job to be done well, not for a career in the academy or for the sheer joy of thinking and debating. Publicly recognized achievement is clearly valued in admission standards, in the huge array of prizes and awards given, and in the alumni magazine. Financial pressures, while very real for some students, are at least not a daily or weekly problem; generous financial aid packages allow a longer-term perspective, freeing up time for concentrating on academics and socializing.

Graduates then find that they share attitudes about work and achievement; they share, too, the history of a lived-in commitment to certain ways of doing, thinking, playing, socializing, and working.

> For instance, [the college] has very high educational standards . . . You can't just walk into a class and get an A. You really have to work to get a decent grade. And not just work really hard, but really differentiate yourself from the other students in the class to get an A, or a top-level grade . . . When you're in those classes, you know that those around you are probably on a similar level . . . You know that there's going to be people challenging you there, intellectually. (Keith, alumnus)

Membership in this community confirms that the graduate is not only the possessor of certain skills, but even a certain kind of person.

> You don't really recognize the influence or the significance of [the college] until you've actually graduated. For instance, when I say, "Yeah, I went to [this] college," you're kind of thrown into this immediate group of "Well, he's smart enough." They don't second-guess your ability. (John, alumnus)

Institutions clearly differ in what they practice and revere. At some, knowledge is seen as a means to an end—curing sick people, making money, enhancing one's prestige—while at others it has value "in itself." In some colleges, students routinely cheat; in others they don't; and across different colleges, what counts as cheating varies quite widely, at least in the students' minds.[6] In some they work hard and enjoy it; in others they work hard and hate it; and in many they don't work hard at all. At some colleges daily prayer is required; at others, marching in drill formations is. All of these college communities provide students, more or less, with a base of support: a viscerally known place and institution showing that serious, good people act "this way," whatever way that is, reminding students that they are not alone in believing one should do these things, and act this way. Employers, for their part, are exquisitely aware that different colleges, in whatever fashion, turn out very different kinds of graduates, so they favor graduates of the colleges whose style they like. West Point graduates have an advantage in the Army, in part because of the strong West Point network, but also in part because West Point graduates can be safely assumed to offer certain attitudes and habits that the Army wants to promote.

Colleges provide community support for different values or even identities, and when an alma mater and its graduates stay connected (West Point and career Army officers; Notre Dame and fans of the Fighting Irish) the graduates will continue to rehearse those attitudes and values. A look through an alumni magazine might suggest what a college values, at least among its alumni: Does it glorify quirky, offbeat types? Captains of industry? Solid members of the local community? Are the "class notes" in such a magazine a listing of achievements, prizes, and honors, or do they feature family events, or musings on personal developments? Are the lead articles about faculty research, or about the new buildings, or about controversies on campus? For many years there really was such a thing as a Yale Man; when alums tried to be a Yale (or Dartmouth) Man, they knew what it meant, and they tried to live that style. Many students entering college seek such an identity by virtue of their college choice, and some will find it. We aren't romanticizing this notion of "membership," or saying that it always happens. But it's certainly true, and sometimes implied by alums, that one's attitudes can be reinforced by having belonged, and still belonging to, the *community of values* represented by their college.

At the college, the connection for alumni is virtually permanent. Graduates can't be fired or expelled. In a sense, they can't drop out even if they want to; that line on the resume can't be erased, and will always matter. In this sense, alumni never leave. Many never lose their networks of friends from college. Many marry fellow alumni—there's a permanent community for you, right under one roof.[7] They keep getting the literature and the fund-raising phone calls, and to varying degrees even strangers still identify them with their college. Their job-hunting networks still work, even if they didn't like the place. Those connections last for a lifetime, not just a few years. In America today, it really is an astonishing act of continuity, a remarkable perseverance of tradition in a rapidly changing world. They return for reunions, time and again, often bringing their children and sometimes their grandchildren. And fifty years from now, graduates of the college will return to the campus for June reunions, see some of the same old places, and meet some of their old friends and perhaps even one or two hearty old professors, back for the event. They will talk of what they did then and have done since, a community of good and bad experiences shared from a formative period of life.

Even as a financial strategy, such community building seems to work, at least in the long run. The college attracts a large number of applications, far more than it can accept. Having been accepted, students are typically excited to be going. They arrive; they spend four years mostly happy to be there. They pay huge amounts of money to attend, sometimes borrowing over $100,000 to pay the required tuition and fees. They graduate very satisfied with the experience; then they begin—in any one year, over half of them—to give money to the college, even though their alumni donations produce for most of them no tangible benefits at all. Many continue to give for their entire lives, and when they die, some leave small fortunes to the college. Sometimes we hear that institutions of higher education should be run "more like a business." But how many businesses, fifty years after the sale, still have former customers annually sending them substantial cash gifts, just for the pleasure of helping out?

It doesn't work for everyone, of course: for Julia, tied to her hometown friends and her newly divorced parents, who never fit in and soon left; for Kristy, overwhelmed by academic challenges, who also left; for Frank, who floundered for years, never really connecting, but stayed anyway—and regretted it afterwards. On the other hand, students who successfully found this community had only a few small regrets, most commonly, not having taken advantage of the educational opportunities. John, whose football coach urged him to "be more vocal," and who reached way out to win a part in a musical, still felt he hadn't done enough.

To this day I punch myself, or kick myself, every day for not doing Spanish
. . . I remember meeting one student that came to [the college] not knowing
a lick of Spanish, came out speaking fluent Spanish after four years.

Seeing other people pick it up and, you know, going abroad and learning it, like, really, really fast just made me kind of jealous, envious. (John,
alumnus)

As early as senior year some realize that they should have reached beyond
their initial interests and friends. Maudie, who met the Chinese professor
who changed her life, said,

I feel like I probably wasn't as involved as I should have been, previous to
this year . . .

Freshman year, I think I was just trying to get settled, and didn't even
acknowledge that I was not doing much. And then sophomore year—I have
no idea what I was doing sophomore year . . . And then junior year, I was
abroad [in Beijing]. And then junior year coming back the second semester,
I was still trying to, like, get used to being in America . . . And . . . I started
doing the dance thing. So that was kind of getting involved, and it was very
good. And then this year, I was just like, "All right, let's go to it!" . . . I wish
I had done other stuff, because you meet other people . . . It's my own fault
. . . (Maudie, senior)

Even a good starting spot could become limiting, as Judy the choir enthusiast
found.

I found my niche really quickly, and I just sort of stayed there because I
loved it and it worked really well for me. And it provided me with such a
great support system, and fun, and things to learn. But I never . . . I didn't
try enough things . . . I wish I'd done more things that are outside my normal sphere of "white suburban Judy who sings in the choir." (Judy, senior)

Others were held back a bit by their social group. Herb, "lazy" by his own
account, felt stuck in his fraternity, and Stephen too realized the effect the
wrong group of friends might have.

Most of my closer friends did not get involved . . . We sort of influenced
each other, in that we did maybe more of our own thing, versus really getting involved with the school and the openness of professors.

I was taking classes I probably shouldn't have been taking; I didn't know what else to do . . . I wish I'd gone abroad . . . I also wish I had taken advantage more of my professors—this sounds bad—of their availability and meeting with them more. [If I could do it again] I would go to the Writing Center, taking advantage of various offerings the school had, and getting involved a little bit more academically. I look back on it and see all those missed opportunities . . . (Stephen, senior)

Even with those regrets, though, a large majority of our panelists felt—both as seniors and several years later, looking back—that their time in college was valuable. More than 84 percent of the college's seniors say that if they were back in high school, again considering where to enroll, they would at least "probably" attend this college. For women especially—more willing to drop an unsatisfying major, more likely to follow a great teacher, more willing perhaps to leave altogether if things didn't work out, more deliberately guided by relationships—the experience seemed better. And *none* of our panelists, even those who were dismayed about the very high cost, ever expressed to us doubts about higher education itself. For most of them, the pieces—entering, choosing, belonging, learning—came together well, and college worked.

For Russell, everything worked; all of the challenges were met, the breaks all fell his way. He came from a huge public high school, enticed in part by a generous merit scholarship. He *entered*—let's italicize the key moments here—this comparatively small new community smoothly, living with three roommates in a dorm where *it was easy to meet other people.* He joined the choir ("like a 'B' fraternity," he thought) and then auditioned for and was admitted to one of the student-run singing groups. With a strong freshman academic record (he made the Dean's List), he considered transferring out to be with his high school girlfriend, but the friends he made in his first year held him at the college. Initially interested in music and creative writing, Russell *had a good teacher* in his fall-semester economics course whom he followed the next semester, leading him eventually to become an economics major with a music minor. "Basically, [the fields were] as different as you can get . . . so the people . . . are very different people." Working in disparate fields "kind of force[d] me, by having to write in a lot of different areas . . . to actually say what I mean . . ." He found most students at the college to be both intellectually strong and socially personable, which contrasted with his high school, where maybe 25 percent of the students were academically engaged. He *found several other good teachers*: a religion professor whose "personality carries over into what he's teaching, so it becomes very interesting—even if what he's saying is kind of dry"; and an economics professor who likewise "makes something that could be obscure and kind of hard to grasp, very logical . . ." And "she doesn't judge students . . . if they come up to her with a stupid question. You know, she's very helpful no matter what." He studied with a series of good music teachers, one after another.

Because *he cared what those teachers thought of him*, Russell worked hard to think, write, and speak better. In an interview one Tuesday, he told our researcher that the previous Friday he had prepared thoroughly before going to ask a professor a question about an upcoming paper. "I don't want to seem like an idiot in front of a professor . . . You know, they are really smart people, and I don't want to seem like some jerk that just came into their office with nothing to say . . . So, a lot of times, I'll make sure I have at least a rough idea . . . Strangely enough, I think that has been at least some sort of incentive for me to improve [my] thinking . . . [I'm] trying to seem, at least, confident in front of people you know are smart . . . The main thing is just to really think through what you're going to say." His writing improved when teachers— some with memorable "pet peeves"—pushed him; one recommended him for a Writing Center tutor position, which boosted his confidence, and in which he came to realize that no amount of editing can save an incoherent idea. At the same time, *close living with smart dormmates* led to the classic "philosophical discussions": "Some girl was freaking out about nobody liking her [and so despairing of getting married]. It led to this really interesting, like, theatrical discussion about "Did humans make up marriage or was marriage a 'real' thing? . . . Do we create these things or . . . were they natural first?"

When Russell *went to London* for a semester, "what had been an intellectual exercise of seeing various perspectives became quite real. I went in knowing that people over there spoke with a British accent, right? So, you know, I was expecting that . . . Sure enough, I got there, and they do speak with a British accent! But what's funny is, I [had] never thought of myself having an American accent. I just thought I had 'the' accent, you know what I mean? And I think most people actually think that way; they don't think of themselves as having an American accent . . . That represents me realizing now that, you know, I'm just part of a larger whole as opposed to something more in the center . . . It's hard to break out of that—you know, you're the center of everything 'mentally.'"

As much as he loved music, Russell knew that careers in music are hard to pursue. After graduation, living in New York City *with several other alumni of the college*—they helped ease the transition—he fell, almost by chance, into advertising. The ad business required "a lot of thinking about problems in sort of a subtle and complex way; if you can articulate that, you're pretty much going to get noticed. Probably the one thing . . . that has distinguished me from other people at my age or experience level [has been] my ability to *clearly articulate thoughts in speaking and writing.* Writing and speaking—if you can't do that, you're cut off . . . I was ready to have a conversation with more senior people. I felt I was ready to write e-mails to more senior people."

Within four years of graduating from the college, Russell was vice president of a small advertising agency in Manhattan. By 2012—seven years after college—he was in a senior executive position with an international marketing and advertising firm.

One potential outcome of college, rarely mentioned in national debates, in fact embraces and transcends all the others. "Alumni satisfaction" probably describes what we have in mind. That sounds easy to measure, and satisfaction is indeed frequently evaluated through student and alumni surveys. But the limited "satisfaction" one gains from a consumer product isn't quite what we have in mind here. Something more pervasive is involved, something like "fulfillment," or even "happiness."

For most Americans, attending college is expensive in terms of both time and money. College isn't a discrete product like an automobile, or even a house. Four, five, or six years of one's life is a huge investment and personal commitment. And every year it seems that college costs more, even dramatically more. And yet, every year more people enroll and more people want to enroll. Perhaps at this writing America is experiencing an educational financial "bubble," destined to burst in a shower of collapsing college tuitions—but at this writing, there's no sign of that happening. Wisely or not, students and their parents are willing to take on enormous debts to finance a college education, even as state governments continue to reduce or severely limit their own expenditures on higher education.

Students (and parents) make the financial and personal sacrifice because they believe that college will make their lives better. Primarily, of course, they believe that something about college—the skills, the degree, the connections, the prestige—will almost certainly improve their economic well-being. Many students learn definite occupational skills—nursing, teaching, administration, engineering. Some students learn how to write, and then become advertising copywriters. Some find a wealthy mate. Some have fraternity brothers who start running businesses, and they go to work there. All of them believe that something about college will secure them a job, or a series of jobs, a liveli-hood, even a career or profession. They are largely correct, too; the research is unambiguous.[8] Along the way, some also escape from an unhappy home life, some find joy in learning, and many seem to have fun.

"Choir Judy" has been quoted frequently in these pages, not for any un-usual success or failure, but because she really has thought about what college meant to her. She and her parents, blessedly free of anxiety about her eco-nomic future, were looking to those broader results.

> Just coming away with the memories that I have, and a stronger sense of who I am—and regardless of what technically I end up doing—what I want to do with my life, and the person I want to be, has meant the world to me . . .
>
> You have to do one production to be a theatre major. And I did Romeo and Juliet, and I was the understudy and so I got my one performance as Juliet. And that was, that was nice. But I said to my mom . . . "I'm not going to do another one because I can't with choir, and I refuse to quit choir." Somewhere along the line, a decision got made and that was it.
>
> You know, I've gotten a lot of Bs. There's been a couple of C+s just be-cause . . . I didn't always put enough time into the work . . . And my mom said, "That's OK, because you . . . made the decision that your college ex-perience is not about your grades; or not about even necessarily the classes you've taken. It's about the people you've met, and it's about the things that you've learned just by being here."
>
> That's probably the most astute way anyone's ever summed up my college experience . . . (Judy, senior)

Most American students don't have that luxury. But in national higher ed-ucation debates, Judy's "outcomes" would not even be considered. In those discussions, college exists to produce a reliably skilled, readily available, low-cost workforce. Students, we hear, need identifiable skills, available on the day of graduation; colleges should be evaluated on how well they train their students in those skills and on how much students improve their skills during their college years. The assessment and accountability efforts of the past twenty years—driven by state legislatures, business groups, and the federal Department of Education, and enforced through the regional ac-crediting associations—focus almost entirely on standardized skills and mar-ketable knowledge, and to some extent on attitudes (teamwork, reliability) that employers are seeking. "Workforce development" is the operative phrase, prefaced by warnings of a coming tsunami of Chinese and Indian engineers as well as failures of international competitiveness. Fair enough: governments and businesses have their own agendas, and they're entitled to know whether they're getting their money's worth.

But marketable skills, we suggest, are not fundamentally what students themselves (and their parents) are looking for. Neither skills, nor knowledge, nor connections, nor degrees *per se* are really their final goal. Those are just steps along the road to a better life; and the steps, and the goals, are different for different students. All of them, though, want their own lives to be better for having gone to college, whatever that means: a better job, good friends, exposure to classic works of art, mastery of differential equations, the joy of singing in a choir, the thrill of no-holds-barred conversations in a dorm, or the lifetime satisfaction of rising out of poverty to a respected position in one's community and the world. So when one asks, "Is college too expensive for the result?" the answer is, "It depends on the individual student." For some, college is "worth it" if they get into medical school; for others, if they land a job with the local manufacturer; for others, if they find a good mate. For some, the experience itself—four years of hanging out on the quad all day and boogying down at dance parties all night—may be "worth it." It depends on the particular student.

Among assessment experts, "satisfaction" is routinely disparaged as an "indirect measure" of students' gains in college, since it doesn't directly tap the defined academic skills gained. We think, quite to the contrary, that genuine satisfaction might be one of the best measures of all. And—if colleges want to improve their students' lives—alumni satisfaction is better still. Once they are years (or decades) out of college, former students have some perspective. They've forgotten the minor ups and downs. They can then judge whether college was worth the cost; they can factor in the value of friendships, and job placements, and student debt; they know whether their major mattered, and if so, how. If you want to find out, two or ten or twenty years after graduation, whether the college experience was worth all the time and money, just ask the former students themselves. Who would know better?

The satisfaction of former students—ultimately, their happiness—is not, then, just another legitimate outcome of going to college. It's the whole point.

8

Lessons Learned

How does college work? How does a college produce whatever positive gains its students make? In this book, we have followed students through their college careers in order to understand, from their point of view, what makes a difference. We have been interested in the growth of the students themselves—in their skills, experiences, happiness, and so on—not in the extrinsic "outcomes" such as jobs or increased salaries that depend on other people. Along the way, we have tried to discern *how* an institution helps its students learn, in the broad sense. This is certainly not a comprehensive study, then, of college life; we have not, for instance, focused on the negative behaviors that are all too endemic at many undergraduate institutions, such as heavy drinking, drug use, problems of sexual assault or vandalism or hazing. We've said little about out-of-control partying or the deep, continuing inequalities of race and class that pervade many college campuses. These are important topics, but they are not ours, except as they impinge on the positive educational results we hope to protect and enhance. Our goals are pragmatic; we want to help college leaders (especially), professors and staff, parents, and even students themselves to understand how college produces its benefits. Yes, the college we studied is exceptionally well resourced and therefore not a typical undergraduate institution, but it does at least provide a nice laboratory for a close review of all of the possible positive outcomes available. If a variety of good things can happen to students in college, many of them, we think, probably occur on this campus.

In this closing chapter, we set out our general findings about "how college works" for students at the college. Then we suggest, based on those findings, some actions that might improve a range of positive college outcomes for undergraduates. We mention two standard approaches to improvement that don't actually work very well, and offer suggestions for how institutions can usefully assess their own work. We then close with a few final thoughts.

The key to improving education in a college, we think, is found less in the organization of *programs* than in the deployment of *people*. Leaders should help good students (those who want to learn) find other good students as early as possible in their college careers; help students find good teachers as early as possible; and design policies (and programs) with those ends in mind. It's all about helping the right people find each other at the right time.

How College Works: The Basic Principles

To improve students' education, leaders need to understand the fundamentals of how college works. From our research, we propose ten broad generalizations:

1. *Students face a chronological sequence of challenges in college*, the later ones building on the success (or failure) of the earlier ones. Our chapter titles designate these challenges: entering, choosing, belonging, learning, and finishing.

2. *Relationships are central to a successful college experience.* They are the necessary precondition, the daily motivator, and the most valuable outcome. Therefore, specific human beings matter. A student must have friends, needs good teachers, and benefits from mentors. A student must have friends, or she will drop out physically or withdraw mentally. When good teachers are encountered early, they legitimize academic involvement, while poor teachers destroy the reputation of departments and even entire institutions. Mentors, we found, can be invaluable and even life changing. Relationships shape in detail students' experience: what courses they take or majors they declare; whether they play a sport or join an extracurricular activity; whether they gain skills, grow ethically, or learn whatever is offered in various programs. Relationships are important because they raise or suppress the motivation to learn; a good college fosters the relationships that lead to motivation.

3. *Students enter, then follow, readily available pathways.* Some pathways are easier to find and follow: the fraternity one's father was in, the sports team

whose coach is actively recruiting, the "popular" majors with classes conveniently scheduled and registration open. Dormitories with long hallways and open doors are an invitation to friendship, and activity fairs in the dining halls make joining extracurriculars easy.

4. *Even crucial decisions are often made opportunistically.* What appear to be "big moments"—the declaration of a major, pledging of a society, picking of roommates or an advisor—are often shaped by minor contingencies of scheduling, availability, and happenstance. Sometimes students' formal decisions really just ratify smaller, "local" decisions already made. This holds true even though students themselves afterwards rationalize their choices, investing them with a purpose and clarity not in fact evident at the time.

5. *A college itself makes some pathways more easily available than others*, thereby providing "structured opportunities" for certain kinds of people to meet and organize—and then to have influence. Some groups are easier to find, some classes easier to enroll in, some professors easier to meet; some meetings are held at convenient times and places, others are not. Through these patterns, college implicitly favors some activities—and kinds of people—over others.

6. Due to the inescapable arithmetic of finite resources, *the best opportunities for engagement are limited.* Only some teachers are great in introductory courses; only some potential mentors are actually good mentors; only some classes can be scheduled at the most favorable times. A small proportion of faculty have vastly disproportionate influence on students, while a student only needs one or two great teachers, plus two or three friends, to have a fulfilling college experience. A single professor, if made available, can help thousands of students—even tens of thousands—during his or her career. The good news for leaders is that while such potentially influential faculty may be few in number, only a few are needed—if properly deployed.

7. *Belonging to larger groups and to the college itself motivates students* to explore new options, reinforces commitments, and even helps them establish identities. Some of these memberships can be positive, others not.

8. *Because path dependencies set in quickly, early events and choices in a student's career can be decisive.* On entering the college world, students are more

available—more open to possibilities—than they will ever be again before graduation. Good or bad experiences here have disproportionate impact; they open or close doors. Ironically, these crucial experiences are lived when the students have the least information and wisdom to make good decisions. So many of their choices, in effect, depend on luck or on the opportunities made most readily available.

9. *College can provide a wide variety of benefits.* Far more than disciplinary knowledge or technical skills are at stake; in fact, an overemphasis on them may even limit what students can gain. Knowledge and skills count, but so do relationships, attitudes, standards and habits of work and thinking, and membership in broader communities, all less easily acquired later in life. One invaluable potential outcome of college is the motivation to continue learning, supported by a remembered community of fellow students and teachers.

10. Finally, *isolated from the people who carry them out, programs, practices, and pedagogies seem to have little impact.* What matters instead is who meets whom, and when. Programs succeed only when they bring the right people together. If the right people are involved, a variety of curricula can serve colleges well. If they aren't, no curriculum will work.

What to Do

Given these findings, what should college leaders—presidents, deans, department chairs, anyone who wants to help students—do?

Below we offer our own suggestions, specific enough to be usable but broad enough to apply to a wide range of colleges and universities. We obviously can't know for sure whether our ideas will work in, for instance, large public land-grant institutions, private research universities, denominational colleges, military academies, or community colleges—all so different from the liberal arts college we studied. But the research literature on higher education suggests that the processes we describe may be very common, if not universal. At all institutions, for instance, students see college differently than do administrators, staff, and faculty. Students almost never know how tenure works, why publishing (instead of teaching) is sometimes important, whether advanced seminars will be more interesting than introductory lectures, or what deans actually do. What makes them students in the first place is their excusable ignorance of how college, disciplines, and professors work. For students, too, finding friends and "fitting in" is virtually always important, certainly at any residential school. Students are typically opportunistic, looking for the biggest rewards (grades? jobs? happiness?) for the least amount of work, and they make decisions based at least partly on the local and highly contingent situations they face when deciding. Their chances for real engagement are always limited by the available resources (teachers, activities); but even a very brief positive encounter (even a single conversation) can motivate a student for a surprisingly long time; those positive encounters can always be leveraged to maximize students' gains. Path dependency is universal in education systems: STEM disciplines notoriously filter students out at every stage, while freshman experiences have long been recognized as deeply consequential. Early experiences were important at the college; at institutions with more elaborate curricular requirements (that is, most institutions) the impact of the early years must be that much greater. Finally, every institution shapes the pathways by which people come together (or not), channeling students into Greek life, or extracurriculars, or appealing academic work, or not much at all. So we think our recommendations will work, basically, anywhere.

Foremost, our suggestions here are designed to be realistic. We won't suggest, as some authors seem to, that you reinstate a fullbore traditional curriculum, or get your entire faculty to adopt new teaching methods, or change the culture of your institution. We call for no grand strategies, or bold new visions for higher education. Those can be exciting, and they're definitely fun to read about, but they almost never actually happen. In comparison, our proposals may seem quite modest. But they will work. The actions we propose are, we think:

- *Clearly effective.* These interventions will reliably work. There may be no glory for you in what we propose, but they will almost always help students gain more from their undergraduate experience.
- *Highly leveraged.* Very small efforts will produce major results. For instance, a few hours of careful course scheduling by a department chair can significantly affect hundreds of students, giving them ready contact with better teachers. With our recommendations even a few efforts should produce noticeable gains.
- *Widely available.* Almost any leader—indeed, almost anyone involved with a college—will be able, on her own, to adopt some part of these

suggestions. Any individual, that is, can use our ideas; they neither require big institutional action nor simply call for "greater efforts" by lots of other people.

• *Resource-neutral.* No new budget expenditures will be required, or any significant political efforts, or even the cooperation of many colleagues. You won't even need to hire new or different people, although that is certainly a powerful way to improve a college.[1] You only need the resources your institution already has.

With those principles in mind, here's how we think leaders can most effectively help students:

1. *Deploy the best teachers for maximum impact.* Remember that if used properly, a small number of outstanding professors can produce huge results. Good lecturers should teach large classes where they can benefit the most students, especially at the introductory level, where professors can open new intellectual horizons and legitimize the academic enterprise. Potential mentors likewise need to meet sizable numbers of students early in the students' careers. Deans and department heads: Make sure your top teachers' classes are filled to capacity with the kind of students who will benefit from them; recognize too that different professors have very different strengths that can all be used to good purpose somewhere. (Then be sure to protect your high-enrollment professors from being buried in other, less useful work.) And—an important corollary—try to minimize students' contact with professors who do damage. For heaven's sake don't, in the name of fairness among faculty, put poor lecturers in front of a huge introductory class where they can discourage many students. We recognize that different teachers have different strengths; those strengths should be utilized. If some teachers do well in small classes but not large, have them teach small classes. Individual teachers: learn and use your students' names, and remember that even a tiny bit of personal contact goes a long way.

2. *Use space to help people meet.* Physical architecture as well as assignments of long-term spaces (student dorm rooms, faculty offices, department buildings) practically lock in all sorts of social relationships, so use them carefully. Dormitory design should be "high contact," helping new students to meet lots of people: long hallways, shared bathrooms and common rooms, and high-traffic

areas all benefit socially less adept students who may not quickly join clubs or be on sports teams. Don't isolate freshmen in apartment-style rooms or "singles," even if they want them. Better that they should live in four-person rooms and be guaranteed to know some peers. High-contact dorms can also increase the odds for your intellectuals to meet; the "nerdy" kids can more easily find each other, and all students gain from expanding the range of their social contacts. Faculty offices should be set in the flow of campus traffic so students can easily and naturally drop in. Try housing some willing faculty members in dormitory apartments, where they'll have a chance to meet students and will likely improve the atmosphere, if only a little.[2] It's certainly true, especially perhaps at large schools, that some students aren't looking for new friends, faculty conversations, or mentors, but in our research, at least, even those students often benefitted. Intellectually oriented clubs and activities should have favorable locations to encourage participation: just as a well-placed fitness center gets more business, a well-located student newspaper office can attract drop-ins who may then join the staff.

3. *Use strategic scheduling to improve the odds for learning.* Remember: lots of academic advising is really done by the course schedule. Put your best courses and teachers in favorable time slots, with minimized competition from other courses to make access easy. If you want more students to take science classes, put those classes at good times and locations (and with good teachers). Make it easy for students to find worthwhile classes and teachers. Try this: Pick one course that you think would be valuable to students, but is not fully enrolled. Can you as dean or department chair, or the professor herself, change when or where it's offered? Can you as a colleague talk to the professor and suggest she try to get a better time? Better scheduling is sometimes quite easy yet powerful: *a single good introductory class, scheduled at the right time, can change the academic lives of literally hundreds of students.* Get good courses out in front of motivated students; make sure you always have courses available to meet the demand of students who *want* to learn. Scheduling requires modest effort while producing huge gains. Finally, grab those occasional focal opportunities when students are already paying attention: convocations, major campus events, crises, or scandals. They really are "teachable moments." Don't waste them.

4. *Help motivated students find each other.* Dorm layouts and assignments are a start, of course. But there are many ways colleges help different kinds of students to get together: athletics and Greek-letter organizations are obvious

examples. Try to support music, debate, publications, writing centers, and maybe (if carefully done) theme housing—that is, more intellectually oriented activities. Foster "hot centers" of intellectual life, where motivated students meet each other.

Opportunities for helping eager students find each other abound. Invite a selection of bright freshmen over for dinner so they meet each other. If your institution has a "common reading" program for freshman orientation, it needs to be truly engaging and well run, with the support of your most able faculty. Field trips, too, can be dramatic events for students, simultaneously memorable, exciting, socially engaging, and educational. Honors colleges obviously can gather and support strong students, but remember that to help the broader campus community, an honors program should remain open to any student who starts meeting the standards, and not just be a prize for old high school achievements.

All of these suggestions tap into the "Collins dynamic" described in Chapter 5: when like-minded people get together regularly, they reinforce their values and become more motivated to continue the activities. If you help good students—that is, those who want to learn—find each other they may become mobilized and even begin to elevate the campus culture. Academic policies are too often designed to control unmotivated students rather than to benefit and mobilize learners. That's a mistake. Start designing policies and decisions around the preferences of willing students, and you'll soon find their numbers growing, drawn like roving cats to a saucer of cream.

5. *Focus especially on students' early careers.* Early actions have disproportionate impact, because they happen before students have committed to friends, activities, academic interests, and attitudes about college. Students' first weeks should feature intellectual excitement, fulfilling academic experiences, and interesting new friends. The easiest, most available pathways should guide students into activities and places where the college can, in fact, do the most good. If the first weeks and months go well, students avoid many problems later on.

6. *Use the arithmetic of engagement*—the probabilities of meeting good people—to leverage good teachers, courses, departments, and programs. Students won't see your entire institution, but only the parts they actually use. Therefore a few productive people and programs can do most of the educating and do it well. Students don't need all of their teachers or fellow students to

be helpful or even competent: they only need to find one or two great teachers, and two or three good friends—that's all.

Remember, too, that apparently small actions (using a student's name, for instance) can have surprisingly large results; what is small for you may in fact loom large in a student's experience (a visit to a faculty home, a private meeting about writing). Small actions can make a big difference. Some years ago, hospitals discovered that patients waiting for surgery wanted their feet to be warm, so nurses started providing warmed blankets to patients as they lay on gurneys. Patients loved it, baffling some nurses: a patient might be facing coronary bypass surgery, and he seemed genuinely pleased just to have warm feet! The gesture was comforting, and you only need to be a patient once to understand it. Similarly, even a tiny gesture from a respected (to the student) person can mean a lot. At Fordham University's commencement dinner in 2008, President Father Joseph McShane moved throughout the huge tents when families were eating, stopping briefly at each group—or even just saying a word or two ("How's the food?" "Having fun?"), leaving in his wake tables full of beaming faces. A small gesture—but more than expected, and clearly memorable.

Knowing how different so many institutions are from our own, we can't pretend to offer much detailed advice. But if you need more action ideas, just ask a few good students (again, those who want to learn). You'll probably be surprised. Their suggestions may sometimes be quite easy to implement, so easy in fact you might think they don't matter. Our students and alums told us they didn't really care about academic prizes (the college gives out many); they were sometimes actually embarrassed by the generous facilities; and they didn't even know about most of our president's big policy initiatives. On the other hand, they liked the idea of some selective-enrollment "honors" classes, some tougher grading, and even a few required evening lectures—if many students must attend a lecture, still other students may attend then as well, seeing a potential social opportunity. And they told us that being a guest in a faculty home had a huge impact on their college experience. So easy! At first we didn't believe it, but it was true. "Warm blankets" make a difference.

For any students who might read this (or their parents), we also have some simple practical advice: spend your time with good people. That's the most important thing.

People, far more than programs, majors, or classes, are decisive in students' experiences of college. Without the motivating presence of friends, teachers, and mentors even the best-designed, potentially most valuable academic programs will fail. So students who want to both enjoy college and get the most from it in the long run must find at least a few good friends, and a couple of great teachers. A great mentor—a trusted adult advisor—if one can be found, adds a tremendous advantage.

Now admittedly, one of our main arguments has been that students often don't control the processes by which they make friends and meet mentors, especially in the crucial early years. Administrators and faculty have the primary responsibility for creating environments to generate interaction. But students can consciously improve their chances of success and happiness, simply by encountering and repeatedly spending time with people who can significantly improve their college experience. There are five steps students can take to improve their odds of fully engaging with opportunities on the campus: (1) start early, (2) choose teachers over topics, (3) seek out physical locations full of other people, (4) participate in regular activities with others, and (5) don't have all your eggs (friends, activities, academic efforts) in one basket.

1. *Start meeting people right away.* We have shown in several places the importance of early advantages; they tend to magnify later on in a student's college career, producing significant benefits. Nowhere is this truer than in making friends.

Students who make friends early have a significant network advantage, because early birds have a greater number of "weak ties" (friends of friends) whom they can then meet. The logic is mathematical and multiplicative: if I as a typical student have, say, five friends, then each friend I make can potentially connect me to still five more people. In the first few weeks of college, having five (somewhat unrelated) friends connects me to a fairly wide pool of potential friends and acquaintances. But if I cling to just one person, this seriously limits my network's ability to expand. Making a variety of friends early gives one a head start in natural network growth. This wouldn't be a huge advantage if students' networks continued to rapidly expand throughout all four years of college, but they don't. (They can, of course, but it often requires real effort: to join new extracurriculars, to quit old ones, to study a new discipline, etc.) After a few months, cliques start to form and settle, students find their place (or don't), and the pace of friend making slows dramatically.[3] The "mad rush" is over. While students' social circles may shift some in the remaining years, by far the most important changes happen in these first few weeks and months. Students, then, benefit tremendously by fully participating in the chaos of early friend making.

2. *Choose teachers over topics.* Find out who the good teachers are—those who excite and inspire, who care about their students, who can show you the joy of learning. Good teachers will motivate you to learn in all sorts of disciplines, not just the ones you initially like. When you work with good teachers, they can help you make other academic and personal decisions wisely.

3. *Pick your places.* We have also described how physical space—the layout of campuses and dorms, the availability of common spaces, the features of dorm rooms, the location of faculty offices and other resources—matters for student outcomes. To benefit from social ties, a student must first make those ties and then be able to maintain them. Both depend on how physically convenient it is to interact with peers and mentors. So seek out spaces that increase your probability of meeting, and repeatedly seeing, people. Having roommates is better than living alone; a dormitory where you'll regularly see forty to eighty people is ideal. It's much better to live, work, and play on-campus, right in the middle of things, in spots where people pass by often, than to live off-campus, especially alone, and have to make major efforts to see other people.

4. *Join high-contact activities.* Extracurriculars put students in contact with one another, and potentially with adult advisors. Routine activities repeatedly focus the attention of their participants on a shared object—a performance, a game, a political issue, a newspaper—which quickly fosters solidarity, teamwork, and ultimately friendship. Meeting and really getting to know people is much easier when you share a passion, and friendship and community can quickly follow. Classes led by engaging professors matter for the same reasons: they put students and professors together, in a shared setting, focused on particular material. They provide a legitimate and frequently repeated context for student-faculty interaction, as well as (some) student-student interaction.

5. *Keep some options open, socially and academically.* Throughout this book, we have argued that having good friends is vital to one's success at college. But we have also seen that isolation in a tight-knit, exclusive group can be detrimental.

Fraternity members who live, eat, study, and then practice and play for a team together certainly develop close relationships, but we found (at least in this small college) they tend to be less satisfied and happy with their social lives than students who spend time with a variety of people. For the same reasons, romantic attachments, while undeniably appealing and valuable, can become somewhat limiting. Be sure to vary your social life: don't do only the things your friends do; try other things as well, or occasionally visit some places your friends don't go. True, students with a few good friends typically do fine in college, but those with friends across multiple groups really thrive. Similarly, committing too early to a major or area of study may well cut you off from valuable alternatives. Don't put all your eggs in one basket.

Overall, our best advice for students is to seek out a mix of places and situations where you will meet other people, early as well as throughout college, and to avoid closing yourself off to further opportunities for social engagement, either with students or faculty. Remember, happiness and success are most likely to depend on the people you spend time with.

If things aren't going well, you might reconsider whom you are hanging out with.

What Doesn't Work Well

The most efficient method for dramatically improving college education is basically to help the right students and teachers get together. Other popular approaches have their virtues, but often fail to meet our criteria for a realistic chance of success. Two examples may suffice to illustrate their weaknesses:

1. *Strategic planning.* Strategic planning[4] seems to be perennially popular with governing boards, and is typically mandated by accreditors; they evidently believe it's a good idea. Colleges and universities write plans, all the time. With its language of strategy, mission, task forces, and such, planning evokes images of World War II naval deployments, with carrier battle fleets steaming out into the Pacific to assault an enemy empire. In practice, though, planning entails lots of committee meetings and both in-person and online discussions, eventually culminating in a stack of reports in leatherette binders distributed all around, which end up—the result is so conventional as to be a

cliché—sitting on a shelf gathering dust. Then a few years pass, a new administration arrives (or reaccreditation approaches), and another round begins: planning marches on. When Dan Chambliss served on an accrediting commission for six years, he read (or at least skimmed) hundreds of these things, many from institutions which appeared to have benefitted not at all. Some planning, obviously, is necessary. But too often, the whole enterprise, or at least the greater part of it, appears to be a huge waste of time.

The waste comes from trying to microengineer human behavior. Most plans assume that an organization's "mission" (as if there's only one) can and should be spelled out in public; that meaningful goals can be stated, broadly accepted, and then actually worked towards; and that employees will gladly set aside their own preferences, now and many years into the future, to faithfully carry out the assignments ("action items") detailed in some paragraph buried deep within that binder. Such plans envision a rationalist's utopia of clear goals, detailed means of getting there, and a rational division of labor. If only everyone would just do what they're supposed to, great things should happen.

But they almost never do (certainly not in universities), and therein lies the problem. Strategic planning too often ignores the actual, real people who must do the acting. Planning succeeds—indeed, is necessary—for projects like putting up new science buildings, but buildings can't decide they don't want to be built. No steel girder got bored and walked away, or had its own agenda, or simply stopped attending meetings. People, though, do exactly that; people are famously recalcitrant materials. Hence strategic plans in practice require lots of oversight, monitoring, updates, and enforcement, all quite costly both to associate deans and to those they monitor. Everybody has to write more reports for the higher-ups, since (reasonably enough) no one can be counted on to carry out, on their own, what the plan calls for.

So most strategic plans are, in a word, unrealistic. They work well in the manufacturing of defined physical products, but not in the management of living human beings with their own goals and motivations. Sometimes—yes—they can be helpful to top leadership in setting priorities. But don't start believing, for instance, that you can overcome personnel problems by going through a "strategic planning process."

Then why is planning so popular? In a sense, too many planning initiatives are praised not for their ease but for their very difficulty; huge tasks are so much more inspiring, judged by their long-term ambition rather than by their short-term results. Leaders, for their part, love these big ambitions. The careers of presidents and deans rely on launching splashy programs that promise to "bring us into the twenty-first century" with fundraising titles like "The Campaign for Creativity" or "Exceeding All Expectations" or "A Destiny Worth Defending." Such programs make great fodder for alumni speeches, addresses to the Board of Trustees, and articles in the college magazine, not to mention the regional and even national press. Nothing says *New York Times* coverage like a "bold initiative" to eliminate distribution requirements, or to reinstate severe ones, or build a sprawling new bioengineering complex. It's heady stuff. In 1999, one president of a top-tier national liberal arts college told us that his institution was launching, with great fanfare, a new curriculum, building a variety of "state-of-the-art" new facilities, and funding the entire business with yet another record-breaking capital campaign. None of it, he confided to us, would really improve the education offered at the school. Why, then, do it? "That's easy," he replied. "It's the year 2000, and the trustees want something millennial."

We aren't calling for an end to such projects. After all, presidents and deans need to make a living too, and trustees, regents, and legislators need to be motivated and inspired, since their enthusiasm is crucial. But our research, at least, suggests that education itself really happens in a much simpler way: when two or more thinking people get together.

2. *Pedagogical innovation.* If strategic planning represents institution-wide approaches to improvement, we might label as "pedagogical innovation" a host of microtechniques, applicable in the classroom. We include here new teaching methods, the incorporation of "new knowledge about how students learn," lessons from neuroscience, the expansion of "learning technologies," use of "smart classrooms," active/collaborative/hands-on education, and an entire range of what are called "best practices." As with strategic planning there's no harm in doing these; it can be enjoyable for faculty, can sometimes (not always) improve their teaching, keep them motivated, etc. Many no doubt work, when enthusiastically adopted. But for leaders trying to improve results, efforts both to change such practices as well as to improve individual professors' teaching will often prove frustrating. Lots of time and money can be spent with little to show.

Consider Professor George Kuh's concise, well-researched list of "high impact educational practices," perhaps the best-validated and most popular such list in higher education. The list includes ten practices: freshman seminars and experiences; common intellectual experiences; learning communities; writing-intensive courses; collaborative assignments and projects; undergraduate research; diversity/global learning; service learning/community-based learning; internships; and capstone courses and projects.[5] (Note, by the way, that many of these work by bringing students and teachers closer together around their academic work, which we see as fundamental.) Well-controlled research, based on *ceteris paribus* assumptions, shows that students who participate in these practices clearly benefit. But in the real world, *ceteris* aren't *paribus*—other things are not equal. Many of these high-impact practices, for instance, are in fact quite costly. To have freshman seminars, writing-intensive courses, undergraduate research, a good internship program, and senior projects for all students in an institution—which a handful of elite colleges do in fact offer—requires an enormous budget. They are good ideas all, but for the most part expensive, and therefore not widely adoptable. ("Common intellectual experiences" and "learning communities" may be important exceptions that require little additional funding over the long run.)

What about helping individual teachers? After all, as the saying goes, you can't separate pedagogy from the pedagogue—the actual human being who is leading the class and using the pedagogy. So maybe the best approach is retrain professors into using new methods. Unfortunately, that's hard to do. It's often quite difficult to change the daily working habits, not to say the personality, of an adult, especially one who has succeeded in landing a nice tenured position at a respected institution.[6] And the more prestigious the institution, the tougher it will be to change how your professors do things, precisely because what they've done so far has succeeded so well. They've already been rewarded, by the sheer fact of being hired and promoted. In his superb book *Our Underachieving Colleges*, Derek Bok, for twenty years president of Harvard University, complains that college professors spend too little time thinking about their teaching, reevaluating their courses, and keeping up with the latest cognitive science on teaching and learning. Maybe he's right, but if he includes his own institution in this critique, he's serving up a palpable irony: Harvard, which could hire almost anyone in the world, may have hired people Bok now considers a bit wrong for the job. Asking them at this point to reconsider their career strategies would seem quixotic, at least.

In sum, to dramatically change programs and personalities is hard; our method—moving people around a little—by comparison is much easier. So if you have some grouchy old misogynist who isn't up to date in his discipline and doesn't like young people, yes, you could send him off to some workshops, propose he introduce more collaborative learning, and see what happens. Or—our suggestion—you could just minimize the damage: schedule his class at 8:00 A.M. and hope that no one shows up.

Assessment

Under legal requirements of the federal and state governments, and enforced more or less vigorously by accrediting agencies, virtually all colleges and universities in America must now have in place some kind of program for the assessment of student learning. Our own research, the Mellon Foundation Assessment Project at Hamilton College, was intended as a demonstration project in the development of assessment strategies, in particular for the liberal arts. Over an eleven year period, we used different methods and popular instruments (including, for instance, the National Survey of Student Engagement), evaluated others that the college decided not to use (the Collegiate Learning Assessment), and attended perhaps twenty or so assessment conferences around the country. We learned a lot about assessment.

Honestly, after a decade of work, we came away skeptical of the entire assessment enterprise. We know, without doubt, that assessment as conventionally practiced is routinely derided by conscientious professors, including those at evidently excellent schools; that it frequently demands significant amounts of new work for both faculties and administrations; and that the evidence for its efficacy is, at best, mixed.

Even the simplest cause-and-effect connections between intensive assessment and educational improvement seem weak. Ask yourself these questions:

1. Is your own institution, now that a (mandated) assessment program is in place, producing better-educated graduates than it did before?
2. In general, are institutions with aggressive assessment programs better at educating students than those without such programs?
3. After roughly twenty years of a growing and increasingly powerful "assessment movement," is higher education in the United States better than it was before?

We've asked these questions to colleagues across the country, and the answers seem to be (1) maybe, (2) no, and (3) no—typically delivered after some slightly embarrassed chuckles.

Nevertheless, higher education has to live with assessment, and in theory at least it might work. We can offer a few suggestions on how, perhaps, to do institution-wide assessment that can actually help your students.

First, *use individual students as your unit of analysis.* This is a critical step. "Units of analysis" is social science jargon for the things you are studying. This dictum means you should *not* use stand-alone assessments of courses, or teachers, or individual programs, or academic departments. They aren't what you ultimately need to measure or want to know about. All of these units can be manipulated to mislead you, for instance, by off-loading weaker students. Unfortunately, they are convenient units of analysis because they are the ones that educators see every day, but evaluating them won't tell you what you need to know. It's fine, for instance, if you have lots of great teachers, as evaluated individually; but that tells you nothing about what students have gained in total from college. Similarly, it's quite possible for most academic departments to be excellent (taken on their own) while most students still graduate with poor educations (for instance, by enrolling predominantly in the few weak departments).

You also need to understand how students experience your institution. Try to see things from their point of view. Listen to them; you'll almost certainly be surprised. What may seem to you a minor problem—long lines at registration, poor heating in a dormitory, a professor who surprisingly changes deadlines for a term paper—may for students be an enormous problem. What may seem like minor niceties—learning and using students' names in class, or faculty inviting students to their homes—may prove to be truly invaluable aids in student motivation, with effects far outweighing the effort of observing them. Simply asking students and former students what was important, for good or ill, in their college experience can help you focus on what works. Don't assume that you know what matters.

Second, *be open to all good outcomes.* Your institution probably produces a variety of results, good and bad. Your assessment, based on students, should be sensitive to all of them, expected or not. There's nothing wrong with unanticipated benefits, so don't limit yourself to "goals" established before you start. Some of your most valuable results may be completely unplanned and unannounced. Few colleges, for instance, wish to publicly declare that they are "the world's best dating and mating service," but it's probably true, and it's immensely valuable to students.[7] Skills, knowledge, jobs, relationships, happiness, and values all can be enhanced by college, and probably other things can as well. Remember, too, that good outcomes extend far beyond graduation day, so don't let your assessment—and efforts—be stuck at what some test or survey shows about students' skills in their final semester. That's dangerously shortsighted.

Finally, *keep assessment simple.* Too many people think that more assessment is better assessment—"every student, every course, every department, every year" is the mantra from some assessment mavens. This "comprehensive" approach is often mandated by accreditors. But it's a huge waste of time and effort, makes assessment a burden, and is just pulling up flowers to see how the roots are growing. It's detrimental.

What you should aim for ideally, in fact, is the *least* assessment work for the most information gained. Education service vendors love selling surveys with 120 items (they look impressive and cost lots), but ten or twelve carefully targeted questions could probably elicit more carefully considered responses, with a higher response rate from happier students who have completed the survey. Try not, in your assessment efforts, to interfere with your faculty doing their real work, and don't "change the culture" of the entire institution in order to do assessment, unless your college is a failure overall.

That said, here's a simple but powerful technique; we think it's the single best assessment method for an undergraduate college. Ten years after a cohort of freshmen enter your institution, draw a random (in the scientific sense) sample of them.[8] Some will be six years past graduation, others will be nine years past dropping out, others may still be inching along trying to finish. All will be adults, with a little distance from adolescence and enough experience in the world to know, more or less, what worked and what didn't. Call them up (a committee of faculty and staff can do this, each taking three or four names) and ask: Overall, What did you think of our college? What were the best things? What were the worst? How could we do better?

They will tell you what, in the long run, really mattered. Don't just talk to degree-completing graduates. That would be cheating, since it leaves out some of your biggest failures. (Social scientists call this error "sampling on the dependent variable.") If certain skills are important to their lives, the former students will tell you. This method will take into account career success, personal happiness, skill sets, financial burdens, the role of faculty, the role of extracurriculars, even the importance of dining halls and dormitories. It lets the students themselves, with just enough time to have forgotten the trivial aggravations, tell you what really helps their lives.

Which is, in the end, what you should care about.

A Final Note

In recent years higher education in the United States has come under attack from many quarters. As state support has eroded, and as more students attend college in an increasingly desperate attempt to find viable jobs, the price to students of attending an institution of higher education has gone up, especially at more selective institutions. Rising costs; increasing pressures on access; the (apparently) diminishing value—at least in terms of immediate employment—of the bachelor's degree; and a growing belief, whether justified or not, that a college education no longer delivers the skills necessary to succeed—all of these and more have prompted a wide range of critics to propose a host of solutions to the perceived problems of higher education.

We aren't dealing in this book with policy-level answers to the declared "crises" of higher education, nor do we wish to offer detailed critiques of the various proposed solutions offered, such as the whole "assessment and accountability" movement. But one recently popular category of proposed solutions—online education—exemplifies what is wrong with almost all of the others: it ignores the central importance of student motivation.

Some recent reformers suggest that online education, especially in the form of "MOOCs"—massive open online courses—might solve some of the problems of higher education. Such offerings promise to bring down the price of college, provide access for millions more students, and reduce the dependence of institutions on highly paid professors. Why can't colleges and universities just find the few very best lecturers in the country, put them in front of video cameras, and record top-quality instruction—which could then, very cheaply indeed, be made available across an entire university, or even around the world? Wouldn't that work? Wouldn't that provide quality education to millions of students at a low price? The answer is Yes—for highly motivated students whose location or circumstances prevent their physically getting together with other students and teachers. Compared to getting no exposure to higher education, online learning is a huge gain; but compared to actually being at Princeton or Stanford or MIT, or in a good seminar anywhere, almost certainly not. That's because there's more to education than (even very good) information; the availability of quality content, in other words, isn't the big problem that most American college students face.

The "massive-access" approach has been tried before. In fact, it's been tried for about six hundred years, and in important ways it has worked marvelously.

For several thousand years, the world's greatest thinkers worked out their best ideas and wrote them down in exquisite detail. Then, starting in the mid-1400s, with the development of the printing press, many of those ideas, lectures, research findings, treatises, and such, including the Bible itself, were mass produced in a form—printed books—which eventually became so cheap and so widely available that basically anyone in the developed world who wanted to find one could. By the mid-nineteenth century, in fact, almost the entire range of human knowledge became readily accessible to the literate population of the West, with revolutionary implications for mass education. Books were the online courses of their day.

By the middle of the twentieth century in America, then, vast numbers of middle-class homes were well equipped with the latest "information technology" needed to educate their children, in the form of excellent multivolume encyclopedias, sometimes including the great Britannica.

All too frequently, though, these incredible books sat completely unused on the shelf for years. And there's the rub. Simply having information easily available—even right in front of the potential student—doesn't educate anyone. Today, for under $10, any eighteen-year-old can buy a good used calculus textbook from an online seller and—in theory—work their way through it, learning what Isaac Newton worked so hard to develop. But real eighteen-year-olds won't do that. Similarly, online video lectures, even excellent ones, will too often go unwatched, or if watched will not be studied. That's because the fundamental problem in American higher education is no longer the *availability of content*, but rather the *availability of motivation*. Information is amazingly easy to come by these days, and no doubt has benefited lots of people. Certainly for most higher education in America, at least, there is no shortage of books, or knowledgeable professors, or even good online courses. None matter, though, unless students first and most importantly *want* to learn, and wanting—even at elite institutions—is highly variable. It goes up and down, as we've said, sometimes even on a daily basis, depending mainly (we think) on which people students are spending their time with.

The good news, as we have argued in this book, is that even a tiny bit of high-quality human contact, applied at the right moment in a student's career, can noticeably raise motivation. A helpful resident advisor in the first few weeks, an engaging teacher in a single introductory class, a writing instructor who sits with a student one-on-one to go over a paper, one field trip with a congenial group—with a regular smattering of such lucky breaks, a willing student can have a very satisfying and educationally productive college career. The trick is, as we said in our introduction, that somehow the right people must find each other at the right times so they can support and energize the right kind of work. That's where leaders, at all levels, can have their quickest and most reliable impact. And best of all, the process can then be self-sustaining: when thinking people meet each other and engage, they become energized to do more thinking, with more people. It takes a little initial effort to get them together, but once they do the process creates more energy.

There is, however, one inescapable cost to leaders. Anyone who wants to improve collegiate education using our approach must accept the responsibility of deciding who "the right people" are. Which professors can do the most good? For which students? And when? Which students do you want to bring to your campus, and which ones not? Who are the students you most want to support? Around which groups and activities do you want to build your institution's culture? These are value questions; at root, they are moral questions about what you—the leader who takes up this challenge—are trying to accomplish. There's no avoiding such judgments; there's no technocratic or financial solution that transcends them. What you do with money or technology or facilities remains a value question, a question of how you regard human beings. In the end, it's about the people.

Good colleges have always been fundamentally human institutions. Pardon the facile example, but Socrates and his followers didn't have a fitness center. They didn't have much of a campus, or dorms, or "smart" classrooms with Smart Boards, clickers and docu-cams, and video capability. So far as we know, they didn't do strategic plans. They didn't even have books, printed or electronic or online.

What they did have, though, was each other. To make college work, that's all you need, too. *is it though?*

1 college provides different types of benifits
2 being apart of groups can provide students with belonging
3 the challenges of college help students success in the end
4 relationships are essential to a successful college experiance
5 having an good professor is important to successful college.
6 students are in a place were they can & should make mistakes
7 living on campus is important for making comunity
8
9
10

Appendix

Notes

Acknowledgments

Index

Appendix

Methods

In this appendix we describe some details of our research methods that are not presented elsewhere in the text or notes.

Our research began in 1999. From the outset, we aspired to carry out a comprehensive, multimethod, longitudinal study of student-learning outcomes. The Mellon Assessment Project at Hamilton College has used both subjective (self-report) and objective measures, and both quantitative and qualitative approaches. After receiving full Institutional Review Board approval, validated by other administrative safeguards and numerous consent procedures along the way, we employed everything from written student work and videotapes of class presentations, to focus groups discussing specific topics, to a comparison of Hamilton College GRE scores against national standards, to quantitative analyses of academic transcripts for an entire student body, to standardized questionnaire surveys, to overtime series of interviews with scientifically selected students over their entire college careers and beyond.

This multimethod approach had several advantages. First, it allowed us to objectively verify a range of students' self-reported information. For example, students may overestimate how much their writing or public speaking has improved over time, or they might forget what classes they took, what their professors' names were, or what grades they received. Objective measures of validity such as academic transcripts, writing samples, and videotaped public presentations provided us with ways of determining student growth and development outside of students' own opinions.

Second, using different methods allowed us to ask and answer different questions. For example, determining the particular key moments in students' academic careers, and how these moments unfolded, is most easily done through in-depth interviews, where the interviewee can provide a full description of events. Determining the proportion of students at the college from different backgrounds, on the other hand, can easily be accomplished through a survey.

Third, the multimethod approach helped us verify that our panel of closely tracked students accurately represented the student body as a whole. Survey data from the entire student body verified that what students were telling us in the interviews was likely also true of the students we didn't interview. With both sources of data—a qualitative, in-depth study of a sample of the students, and a broader, though less in-depth, survey of every student—we felt more confident in making claims about the entire student body in general.

Finally, by identifying the same students across multiple datasets, we gained a fuller picture of the lives of each student. By the end of the research we had collected from some of the students in our panel six in-depth interviews covering an eight-year period; a complete academic transcript including courses taken and grades received; five writing samples spanning a period of five years; and a set of survey responses covering a wide range of topics. No single data source could offer so complete a picture.

Our methods were also, notably, longitudinal. For each of the students in our sample, data were collected yearly throughout college, some of it reaching back even before college entrance and extending well past graduation. Longitudinal information allowed us to determine how the students' lives changed over time, and often why. Instead of a snapshot of students at a particular time in college, we had a moving film, and could determine at what moments and for what reasons decisive things happened (or didn't happen).

The remainder of this appendix will detail some of the methods of data collection and analysis we used in the study. The Writing and Oral Communications Studies have already been explained in Chapter 6 ("Learning").

Panel Interviews

Our interview study consisted of a longitudinal set of in-depth, tape-recorded interviews with a panel of one hundred (initially) students who enrolled in the college in 2001. The students were selected at random from the college's enrollment list. Panelists were then contacted by an interviewer and invited to participate; all but five agreed. Random sampling yielded a panel of students broadly representative of the student body in general, as verified by cross-referencing their sample's demographics with those reported in student surveys, which covered the entire class.

Interviews were conducted by several professionals as well as trained student interviewers; transcripts from new interviewers were reviewed to ensure a standard application of the interview guide.

The interview guide consisted of twenty to thirty open-ended questions, as well as a set of basic demographic questions. Year to year, interview guides were modified to explore different areas of student experience, especially key events that had occurred during that year (declaring a major, studying abroad, graduating, etc). Some questions were repeated annually, such as what classes the students were taking. The open-ended nature of the interviews often allowed the students to direct the topic of conversation away from the question, which frequently led to interesting discussions of topics not explicitly in the interview guide. Interviewers were, however, instructed to return to each question to make sure it had been satisfactorily answered before moving on.

While there was some variation in the quality of the interviews, and in how well the interview guide was used, the vast majority of interviews were satisfactory and useful.

Students in the panel were contacted yearly, throughout their years in college, and once every other year after graduation. Each interview lasted on average around forty-five minutes, and was recorded using a small handheld recorder. Whenever possible, interviews were conducted in person at a quiet location on campus. During the summer months, and following graduation, interviews were conducted via telephone. Panelists were also asked each year to provide a sample of written work completed for a class.

All the interviewees were asked to sign a consent form before the interview began, approving the use of the tape recorder and agreeing that their interviews could be used in published work. Each panelist was assigned a pseudonym.

After graduation, interviews were changed considerably to accommodate the wide variety of lives and careers (some had good jobs and were living independently, some were unemployed and living with their parents).

Most interviews were fully recorded, but on occasion recordings were interrupted, either intentionally because the interviewee felt uncomfortable speaking on record, or because of a malfunctioning tape recorder, loud background noise, or another such unplanned event. Interviewers were instructed to write notes during or after the interview on responses that would not have been picked up by the recording (nonverbal cues, reasons for the interruption of the recording, general "tone" of responses, etc). Following each interview, interviewers submitted a one-page summary of the interview, as well as the tape. All interviews were then transcribed verbatim by Marcia Wilkinson, the Project administrative assistant.

The response rate, overall, was very good for a panel study of this kind. Of the one hundred students initially selected, eighty-four remained in our sample nine years after the study began. The rest either declined to participate in the study or had dropped out of the college. In any given year, interviews were typically completed with sixty to seventy students, with a quarter of the sample participating in every one of their eligible years. In the end, the study had collected 394 interviews, totaling well over ten thousand transcribed pages of text.

Transcribed interviews were analyzed using a variety of traditional methods. In addition to simply reading each interview from start to finish, transcripts were also organized as "all responses to a single question." Towards the end of the study, when the data collection was nearly complete, a "book" was compiled for each of the nearly one hundred panelists with all of their interviews in order plus additional information (for example, course transcripts), so that we could read through them and, effectively, get as close to the "whole picture" of the student as possible. Reading longitudinally was especially helpful in seeing the key moments in their college histories, and what shaped those moments. Finally, qualitative data analysis software was employed to search for key terms and particular issues students raised across different questions, and to better determine students' perspectives on issues not explicitly addressed in the interview guide.

Academic Transcript Analyses

Academic transcripts, which are kept highly confidential, display information about the classes students have taken as well as their grades, professors, major(s), minor(s), and advisor. Through arrangement with the college Registrar, and under policies presented in our Institutional Review Board (IRB) confidentiality procedures, we used student transcripts in three ways. First, Brian Cody and Bijan Warner, sociology graduate students at the University of Chicago, conducted an analysis tracing the pathways of students towards their respective majors. They determined the probabilities of students declaring particular majors based on their enrollment in classes in that major during their first year; this research contributed directly to our discussion of pathways to academic majors. Second, transcripts were used in the aforementioned longitudinal "readings" of student stories, as supplemental information when reading interviews. On occasion academic transcripts were used to verify student accounts of their own academic histories. Finally, a simple "flip-through" of transcripts proved invaluable in revealing the clustering of students in particular majors, how broadly or narrowly students focused their own coursework, and how students tended to "follow the grades" in building their academic careers. It was a simple but very useful method.

The Higher Education Data Sharing Consortium Survey (HEDS)

During the years our study was being conducted, the college, as a member of the Higher Education Data Sharing Consortium, administered an annual survey to all of its seniors. This survey covered a wide variety of topics including students' backgrounds, experiences in college, satisfaction with college, learning outcomes, college activities, and plans for the future. We compiled an integrated database of these surveys from 2000 to 2006, including 2,251 respondents. In many of those years, the response rate was close to 100 percent, as survey completion was virtually required for participation in commencement. In other years, with different delivery methods, response rates dropped dramatically. Having trend data (cross-section, over time) allowed us to see the impact of curricular shifts, while the 100 percent years provided a check against selection biases that may have affected results in the off-years. This integrated survey database, with thousands of respondents answering scores of questions, allowed us to carry out multiple regression statistical analyses on questions such as students' self-reported perception of improvement in various academic areas, shifts in intended majors, and—as described in Chapter 3—the impact of being a guest in a faculty member's home, all while statistically controlling for a wide range of variables.

Network Analysis

Data on students' participation in extracurricular activities, athletics, majors, and Greek-letter societies were collected during the panel interviews and compiled into a single database of student "activities." From this, network "edgelists" were created, containing the affiliations (ties) between activities. These were the basis for the diagram in Chapter 5. In the activity-tie edgelist, activities (the nodes) were treated as being affiliated if they shared students. For example, if Hank participates in both French Club and in lacrosse, then these activities will have a tie between them. Ties were also weighted, by the number of overlapping students participating in activities. For example, if the football team had five people on it who also worked at the radio station, football would have a tie weighted 5 with radio, and hence, it would appear thicker.

This dataset was analyzed using Ucinet, and visualized using NetDraw. Cluster analysis, which attempts to mathematically determine what nodes "best fit" together according to the patterns of network ties and the weights of these ties, was used to determine which activities were more closely associated to each other. Once completed, the six clusters were represented visually in the network diagram.

Notes

1. The Search for a Solution

1. We here join a growing body of scholars who try not to assume that anything we (college employees) do actually matters, and instead, start from the ground up to determine, based on students' experience, what actually *does* matter to them and to their educations. See Anthony Lising Antonio, "The Influence of Friendship Groups on Intellectual Self-Confidence and Educational Aspirations in College," *Journal of Higher Education* 75, no. 4 (2004): 446–471; Alexander W. Astin, *What Matters in College: Four Critical Years Revisited* (San Francisco: Jossey-Bass, 1993); Kenneth A. Feldman and Theodore M. Newcomb, *The Impact of College on Students* (San Francisco: Jossey-Bass, 1969); George D. Kuh, "The Other Curriculum: Out-of-Class Experiences Associated with Student Learning and Personal Development," *Journal of Higher Education* 66, no. 2 (1995): 123–155; Richard J. Light, *Getting the Most out of College* (Cambridge: Harvard University Press, 2001); Ernest T. Pascarella and Patrick T. Terenzini, *How College Affects Students: A Third Decade of Research* (San Francisco: Jossey-Bass, 1991); Paul D. Umbach and Matthew R. Wawrznski, "Faculty Do Matter: The Role of College Faculty in Student Learning and Engagement," *Research in Higher Education* 46, no. 2 (2005): 153–185.

2. The importance of personal relationships in the college experience has been noted by numerous authors, but rarely studied directly: "Much is made of the influence of peer culture on college students, but the processes by which peers influence learning and development remain largely opaque to higher education researchers and administrators." Kristen A. Renn and Karen D. Arnold, "Reconceptualizing Research on College Student Peer Culture," *Journal of Higher Education* 74, no. 3 (2003): 261–291. See also Ana M. Martinez Aleman, "Understanding and Investigating Female Friendship's Educative Value," *Journal of Higher Education* 68, no. 2 (1997): 119–159; Astin, *What Matters in College*; Antonio, "The Influence of Friendship Groups"; Kuh, "The Other Curriculum";

Michael Moffatt, *Coming of Age in New Jersey* (New Brunswick, NJ: Rutgers University Press, 1989); Cathy Small, *My Freshman Year* (Ithaca: Cornell University Press, 2005); Scott L. Thomas, "Ties That Bind: A Social Network Approach to Understanding Student Integration and Persistence," *Journal of Higher Education* 71, no. 5 (2000): 591–615; Vincent Tinto, *Leaving College: Rethinking the Causes and Cures of Student Attrition* (Chicago: University of Chicago Press, 1987).

3. Tinto, *Leaving College*, 136.

4. Ken Bain, *What the Best College Teachers Do* (Cambridge: Harvard University Press, 2004).

5. See Astin, *What Matters in College*; Pascarella and Terenzini, *How College Affects Students*; Tinto, *Leaving College*; Tricia A. Seifert, Kathleen M. Goodman, Nathan Lindsay, James D. Jorgensen, Gregory C. Wolniak, Ernest T. Pascarella, and Charles Blaich, "The Effects of Liberal Arts Experiences on Liberal Arts Outcomes," *Research in Higher Education* 49, no. 2 (2008): 107–125; Umbach and Wawrznski, "Faculty Do Matter."

6. Cristin Bates, Lee Cuba, Nancy Jennings, Heather Lindkrist, and Suzanne Lovett, "How Did It Go? Students' Perceptions of Success in the First Year of College" (paper presented at the meetings of the American Educational Research Association, April 16, 2009).

7. Alan Reifman, Grace M. Barnes, Barbara A. Dintcheff, Michael P. Farrell, and Lois Uhteg, "Parental and Peer Influences on the Onset of Heavier Drinking among Adolescents," *Journal of Studies on Alcohol* 59, no. 3 (1998): 311–317.

8. Richard Arum and Josipa Roksa, *Academically Adrift: Limited Learning on College Campuses* (Chicago: University of Chicago Press, 2011).

9. Richard Arum, Michelle Budig, and Josipa Roksa, "The Romance of College Attendance: Higher Education Stratification and Mate Selection," *Research in Social Stratification and Mobility* 26, no. 2 (2008) 107–122. See also forthcoming research from Richard Arum and Karly Sarita Ford.

10. Mitchell Stevens, *Creating a Class* (Cambridge: Harvard University Press, 2007) details how admission works at such colleges.

11. Arum and Roksa, *Academically Adrift*.

12. What we have sacrificed in terms of the generalizability of our findings, we have gained in depth and richness of data—almost a decade's worth of students' lives and stories recorded on hundreds of hours of tape and transcribed to thousands of pages. Researchers seeking generalizable findings are often forced to sacrifice such depth in their data in exchange for having a larger number of cases—a representative sample. While such samples are incredibly valuable, discovering social processes, and the mechanisms through which particular variables relate to one another, is a goal more easily accomplished through case-study research—ethnography, interviews, and so on—in which the researcher can directly observe, ask about, and investigate social processes, often as they happen. We agree with a body of social science methodologists who firmly believe that there is a place in the social sciences for both types of data, and for the methods that yield them, so long as the methods employed can meaningfully and logically answer the researcher's research question. It is our hope that this book can be fruitfully used

by future researchers using representative datasets to test our findings across multiple institutions, in the same way that we have used existing research to help suggest the ways in which our own findings may apply elsewhere. The institution we studied is in many ways unlike "most" institutions. But so too, in all likelihood, is the reader's own. It is also our hope and expectation that college leaders will approach our prescriptions with an eye towards whether and how they will work at their own particular institutions. For more on the case study methods we employ in this book, see Charles C. Ragin and Howard S. Becker, *What Is a Case? Exploring the Foundations of Social Inquiry* (Cambridge: Harvard University Press, 1992); Mario Luis Small, "How Many Cases Do I Need?" *Ethnography* 10, no. 1 (2009): 5–38; Robert Yin, *Case Study Research* (Thousand Oaks, CA: Sage, 2002).

13. Notably, many of the core processes we describe here persist throughout society. Homophily, the tendency of people to associate with those like themselves, and the consequences of propinquity that lead to people near each other to interact and become friends, are two examples of social dynamics that are central not just to college life, but social life in general. For research on homophily, see Miller McPherson, Lynn Smith-Loving, and James M. Cook, "Birds of a Feather: Homophily in Social Networks," *Annual Review of Sociology* 27 (2001): 415–444; on propinquity, see Lazarsfeld and Robert K. Merton, "Friendship as Social Process: A Substantive and Methodological Analysis," in *Freedom and Control in Modern Society*, ed. Morroe Berger, Theodore Abel, and Charles Page (New York: Van Nostrand, 1954) 18–66.

14. See Kuh, "The Other Curriculum."

15. Our project was approved by the college's Institutional Review Board, in keeping with federal guidelines especially with regard to respecting the confidentiality of students studied; guidelines are also enforced by the Office of the Registrar and the Admission Office.

16. Additional details can be found in the Methodological Appendix.

17. Mary Grigsby, *College Life through the Eyes of Students* (Albany: State University of New York Press, 2009); Moffatt, *Coming of Age in New Jersey*; Small, *My Freshman Year*.

18. Arum and Roksa, *Academically Adrift*; Derek Bok, *Our Underachieving Colleges* (Cambridge: Harvard University Press, 2005); Barrett Seaman, *Binge: Campus Life in an Age of Disconnection and Excess* (Hoboken, NJ: John Wiley & Sons, 2005).

2. Entering

1. This phase of life is described by developmental psychologist Jeffrey Arnett as "emerging adulthood"—a "period from the late teens through the twenties" consisting of "a time of life when many different directions remain possible, when little about the future has been decided for certain, when the scope of independent exploration of life's possibilities is greater for most people than it will be at any other period of the life course." Jeffrey Jensen Arnett, "Emerging Adulthood: A Theory of Development from the Late Teens through the Twenties," *American Psychologist* 55, no. 6 (1997): 469–480.

See also Arnett, *Emerging Adulthood: The Winding Road from Late Teens through the Twenties* (New York: Oxford University Press, 2004).

2. The extensive literature on nationwide student attrition and persistence shows this effect precisely. For research on how social integration is a strong and significant predictor of graduation, see John P. Bean, "Dropouts and Turnover: A Synthesis and Test of a Causal Model of Student Attrition," *Research in Higher Education* 12, no. 2 (1980): 155–187; Bean, "Interaction Effects Based on Class Level in an Explanatory Model of College Student Dropout Syndrome," *American Educational Research Journal* 22, no. 1 (1985): 35–64; John M. Braxton, A. S. Sullivan, and R. M. Johnson, "Appraising Tinto's Theory of College Student Departure," in *Higher Education: Handbook of Theory and Research*, ed. John C. Smart (New York: Agathon, 1997): vol. 12, 107–164; Ernest T. Pascarella and Patrick T. Terenzini, "Interaction Effects in Spady and Tinto's Conceptual Models of College Attrition," *Sociology of Education* 52, no. 4 (1979): 197–210; Pascarella and Terenzini, *How College Affects Students*; Vincent Tinto, "Dropout from Higher Education: A Theoretical Synthesis of Recent Research," *Journal of Higher Education* 45, no. 1 (1975): 89–125; Tinto, *Leaving College*. For research showing that too little or too much engagement with peers is negatively related to graduation, see Norman D. Aitken, "College Student Performance, Satisfaction, and Retention: Specification and Estimation of a Structural Model," *Journal of Higher Education* 53, no. 1 (1982): 32–50. Ernest Pascarella and his colleagues have also found that in four-year residential colleges, social integration is more important to retention than academic integration, though the latter is still important. See Ernest T. Pascarella and David W. Chapman, "A Multiinstitutional, Path Analytic Validation of Tinto's Model of College Withdrawal," *American Educational Research* Journal 20, no. 1 (1983): 87–102; Ernest T. Pascarella, Paul B. Duby, and Barbara K. Iverson, "A Test and Reconceptualization of a Theoretical Model of College Withdrawal in a Commuter Institution Setting," *Sociology of Education* 56, no. 2 (1983): 88–100.

3. See forthcoming research from the Wabash National Study of Liberal Arts Education by Charles F. Blaich and Kathleen S. Wise.

4. Students are referred to by their pseudonym and their class standing at the time of the quoted interview.

5. Moffatt, *Coming of Age in New Jersey*, 29.

6. Research on the association between the amount of time students spend with their friends and their academic success has suggested that students benefit (in terms of college satisfaction, primarily) from the amount of time they spend with their peers, but only to a certain point, after which students' grades begin to suffer. Several studies have examined the effects of students' inability to balance work and play (social life). Aitken (1982) finds that, while "the development of peer relationships is essential for students' satisfaction with their campus residential experience . . . on the other hand, the more time spent on social relations the less available for study, which tends to lower both the students' grades and academic satisfaction." Aitken, "College Student Performance." See also Arthur J. O'Shea, "Peer Relationships and Male Academic Achievement: A Review and Suggested Clarification," *Personnel and Guidance Journal* 47 (1969): 417–423.

Similarly, it is clear that not all kinds of peer interaction contribute to students' success. For example, activities such as drinking or watching television with peers are not associated with academic success. See Astin, *What Matters in College*; Kuh, "The Other Curriculum." Further, romantic relationships in college have been found to be negatively related to (particularly female) students' academic success and social life outside of the relationship. See Shannon K. Gilmartin, "The Centrality and Costs of Heterosexual Romantic Love among First-Year College Women," *Journal of Higher Education* 76, no. 6 (2005): 609–633; Dorothy C. Holland and Margaret A. Eisenhart, *Educated in Romance: Women, Achievement, and College Culture* (Chicago: University of Chicago Press, 1990). The delicate balance between work and play has also been explored by Susan Blum in *My Word! Plagiarism and College Culture* (Ithaca: Cornell University Press, 2009).

7. Elizabeth A. Armstrong and Laura T. Hamilton, *Paying for the Party: How College Maintains Inequality* (Cambridge: Harvard University Press, 2013).

8. Forming social ties depends on whether actors interact at all—that is, on the availability of opportunities to interact with strangers. See Mario Luis Small, *Unanticipated Gains: Origins of Network Inequality in Everyday Life* (New York: Oxford University Press, 2009).

9. Such programs are increasingly common at institutions nationwide. See Small, *My Freshman Year.* We have given ours a deliberately generic pseudonym.

10. Participating in college orientation has a significant effect on social integration during college, which in turn has a significant effect on freshman-year persistence. See Ernest T. Pascarella, Patrick T. Terenzini, and Lee M. Wolfe, "Orientation to College and Freshman Year Persistence/Withdrawal Decisions," *Journal of Higher Education* 57, no. 2 (1986): 155–175.

11. The importance of dormitories as a source of friends has been established by other researchers: Mary Grigsby, *College Life through the Eyes of Students* (Albany: State University of New York Press, 2009); Moffatt, *Coming of Age in New Jersey*; Pascarella and Terenzini, *How College Affects Students.* At the college we studied, living in dorms was mandatory for students early on, the cost was a flat rate, and only a small portion of seniors were allowed to and opted to live off-campus. As a consequence, freshman dorms at the college typically housed a range of students representative of the campus body as a whole. As Grigsby has pointed out, though, at colleges that offer housing at a variety of costs, and at colleges where many students live off-campus, students' economic background will affect where they live and with whom, which can lead to the clustering of students according to their financial background.

12. See Leon Festinger, Stanley Schachter, and Kurt W. Back, "The Spatial Ecology of Group Formation," in *Social Pressure in Informal Groups*, ed. Leon Festinger, Stanley Schachter, and Kurt W. Back (Oxford: Harper, 1950) 33–59.

13. Moffatt observed that freshmen bonded with each other quite well precisely because the conditions they lived in during their first few months were, in many ways, rather miserable—solidarity through suffering, such as in military boot camp. He observed freshmen taking a test in a room "well over a hundred degrees in the late summer heat. I theorized to myself that the long lines and other procedural ordeals

of orientation at Rutgers were the modern functional equivalents of older, suppressed practices of student hazing and inadvertent ways in which the bureaucracy, rather than the upperclassmen, now bonded us together in mild solidarity as common fellow sufferers" (Moffatt, *Coming of Age in New Jersey*, 12).

14. This point was made years ago by Theodore Newcomb, who described the importance of "propinquity" (the proximity of people to each other) in the growth of college peer groups. Newcomb noted that chance meetings "are likely to be found wherever local arrangements—of living, dining, studying, engaging in student activities—result in very frequent associations among a given group of students." Theodore Newcomb, "The General Nature of Peer Group Influence," in *College Peer Groups*, ed. Theodore M. Newcomb and E. K. Wilson (Chicago: Aldine-National Opinion Research Center, 1966), 8. This point was also made by Festinger, Schachter, and Back, and more recently, examined by Mario Small. See Festinger, Stanley Schachter, and Kurt W. Back, "The Spatial Ecology of Group Formation"; Mario Luis Small, *Unanticipated Gains*.

15. For further research on the institutional and social power of sports teams on college campuses, see Stevens, *Creating a Class*. For a historical discussion of the role of athletes on college campuses, see Helen Lefkowitz Horowitz, *Campus Life: Undergraduate Cultures from the End of the Eighteenth Century to the Present* (Chicago: University of Chicago Press, 1987); James L. Schulman and William G. Bowen, *The Game of Life: College Sports and Educational Values* (Princeton: Princeton University Press, 2001); William G. Bowen and Sarah A. Levin, *Reclaiming the Game: College Sports and Educational Values* (Princeton: Princeton University Press, 2003).

16. Both Cathy Small and Mary Grigsby also found that students rarely became friends with classmates. Small, *My Freshman Year*; Mary Grigsby, *College Life*.

17. Each of the factors that we find leads to social-tie formation has been found by other researchers in a wide variety of settings. Several authors have emphasized the importance of propinquity and proximity in developing ties: Leon Festinger, Stanley Schachter, and Kurt W. Back, "The Spatial Ecology of Group Formation"; Maureen T. Hallinan, "Structural Effects on Children's Friendships and Cliques," *Social Psychology Quarterly* 42, no. 1 (1979):43–54; Lazarsfeld and Merton, "Friendship as Social Process"; Newcomb, "The General Nature of Peer Group Influence"; Ray Oldenburg, *The Great Good Place: Cafes, Coffee Shops, Community Centers, Beauty Parlors, General Stores, Bars, Hangouts and How They Got You through the Day* (New York: Paragon House, 1989); Mario Luis Small, *Unanticipated Gains*. Authors who have argued for the importance of the frequency and repetition of interaction in developing ties include: Randall Collins, *Interaction Ritual Chains* (Princeton: Princeton University Press, 2004); George C. Homans, *The Human Group* (New York: Harcourt, Brace, 1950). Researchers have also suggested that social ties often develop accidentally, as a by-product of other activities: Newcomb, "The General Nature of Peer Group Influence"; Small, *Unanticipated Gains*. Scott Feld has argued that the focus of mutual activities, and individuals' mutual coordination towards such activities, also influences the formation of ties. See Scott L. Feld, "The Focused Organization of Social Ties," *American Journal of Sociology* 86, no. 5 (1981): 1015–1035; Feld, "The Structural Determinants of Similarity among

Associates," *American Sociological Review* 47, no. 6 (1982): 797–801; Feld, "The Structured Use of Personal Associates," *Social Forces* 62, no. 3 (1984): 640–652.

18. The effects of crime, and particularly assault, on college campuses have been examined by several authors. See Elizabeth A. Armstrong, Laura Hamilton, and Brian Sweeney, "Sexual Assault on Campuses: A Multilevel, Integrative Approach to Party Rape," *Social Problems* 53, no. 4 2006: 483–499; Bonnie S. Fischer, John J. Sloan, Francis Cullen, and Lu Chunmeng, "Crime in the Ivory Tower: The Level and Sources of Student Victimization," *Criminology* 36 (2000): 671–710; Martin Schwartz and Walter DeKeseredy, *Sexual Assault on College Campus: The Role of Male Peer Support* (Thousand Oaks, CA: Sage, 1997); John J. Sloan and Bonnie S. Fischer, *The Dark Side of the Ivory Tower: Campus Crime as a Social Problem* (New York: Cambridge University Press, 2011).

19. According to Helen Lefkowitz Horowitz, in the early life of the American college, "Classes and books existed as the price one had to pay for college life." Certainly for many students, the same still holds today. Horowitz, *Campus Life*, 12.

20. Students' preconceptions of college as well as their initial attitudes towards college and the academic work that is required of them are strongly related to the degree to which the student becomes academically integrated. See John P. Bean, "Nine Themes of College Student Retention," in *College Student Retention: Formula for Student Success*, ed. Alan Seidman (Westport: Praeger Publishers, 2005) 215–244; Tinto, *Leaving College*. We found that students who did not consider the college their first choice expressed greater dissatisfaction with their college experience than their peers, throughout their four years.

21. Several authors have maligned students' tailoring of their work to their professors, suggesting that it amounts to manipulation and the avoidance of actual academic work and learning. For discussions of such behavior, see Arum and Roksa, *Academically Adrift*; Blum, *My Word!*; Mullen, *Degrees of Inequality* (Baltimore: Johns Hopkins University Press, 2010); Small, *My Freshman Year*. While we agree that students often do this to avoid having to work hard, we found some benefits to this behavior: students learn how to write for multiple, different audiences, and develop a sense of how to change and edit their work to meet the demands of their superiors, skills that will no doubt be useful to many of them in their future careers.

22. Researchers of higher education have studied whether it is, as the phrase goes, better to be a big fish in a small pond, or a small fish in a big pond. See Antonio, "The Influence of Friendship Groups"; James A. Davis, "The Campus as a Frog Pond: An Application of the Theory of Relative Deprivation to Career Decisions of College Men," *American Journal of Sociology* 72, no. 1 (1966):17–31; Thomas J. Espenshade, Lauren E. Hale, and Chang Y. Chung, "The Frog Pond Revisited: High School Academic Context, Class Rank, and Elite College Admission," *Sociology of Education* 78, no. 4 (2005): 269–293; Donald L. Thistlewaite and Norman Wheeler, "Effects of Teacher and Peer Subcultures on Student Aspirations," *Journal of Educational Psychology* 57, no. 1 (1966): 35–47.

23. Less prepared students may struggle academically, at first. But the benefits of attending a selective college where the academic expectations and difficulties are highest

are significant: social scientists have repeatedly found that attending a more selective institution actually increases one's chances of graduating, controlling for a range of background factors. These less prepared students may receive lower grades than their peers, but are considerably more likely to graduate college than they would have been had they attended a less selective institution. See William G. Bowen and Derek Bok, *The Shape of the River: Long-Term Consequences of Considering Race in College and University Admissions* (Princeton: Princeton University Press, 1998); Thomas Kane, "Racial and Ethnic Preferences in College Admission," in *The Black-White Test Score Gap*, ed. C. Jencks and M. Phillips (Washington, D.C.: Brookings Institution, 1998) 431–456.

24. For research on romantic relationships on college campuses, see Kathleen A. Bogle, *Hooking Up: Sex, Dating, and Relationships on Campus* (New York: New York University Press, 2008); Laura Hamilton and Elizabeth A. Armstrong, "Gendered Sexuality in Young Adulthood: Double Binds and Flawed Options," *Gender & Society* 23, no. 5 (2009): 589–616; Gilmartin, "The Centrality and Costs"; Holland and Eisenhart, *Educated in Romance*.

25. See Claudia Buchmann and Thomas DiPrete, "The Growing Female Advantage in College Completion: The Role of Family Background and Academic Achievement," *American Sociological Review* 71 (2006): 515–541; Grigsby, *College Life*; Laura Walter Perna and Marvin A. Titus, "The Relationship Between Parental Involvement as Social Capital and College Enrollment: An Examination of Racial/Ethnic Group Differences," *Journal of Higher Education* 76, no. 5 (2005): 485–518.

26. Alberto F. Cabrera, Amaury Nora, Patrick T. Terenzini, Ernest T. Pascarella, and Linda Serra Hagedorn, "Campus Racial Climate and the Adjustments of Students to College: A Comparison between White Students and African American Students," *Journal of Higher Education* 70, no. 2 (1999): 134–160; Scott V. Solberg, Keum-Hyeong Choi, Samira Ritsma, and Ann Jolly, "Asian-American College Students: It Is Time to Reach Out," *Journal of College Student Development* 35 (1994): 294–301.

27. The "social mismatch" theory of minority-student attrition argues "that elite colleges present socio-cultural environments alien to and insufficiently supportive of black students, since the latter are more likely than whites to have come from non-elite and non-white environments." Mario Luis Small and Christopher Winship, "Black Students' Graduation from Elite Colleges: Institutional Characteristics and Between-Institution Differences," *Social Science Research* 36, no. 3 (2007): 1257–1275. See also Camille Z. Charles, Mary J. Fischer, Margarita A. Mooney, and Douglas S. Massey, *Taming the River: Negotiating the Academic, Financial, and Social Currents in Selective Colleges and Universities* (Princeton: Princeton University Press, 2009); Douglas S. Massey, Camille Z. Charles, Garvey F. Lundy, and Mary J. Fischer, *The Source of the River: The Social Origins of Freshmen at America's Selective Colleges and Universities* (Princeton: Princeton University Press, 2003).

28. Armstrong and Hamilton, *Paying for the Party*. In recent years, research on stratification within institutions of higher education has increasingly focused on class differences. See Elizabeth Aries, *Race and Class Matters at an Elite College* (Philadelphia: Temple University Press, 2008); Charles, Fischer, Mooney, and Massey, *Taming*

the River; Sara Goldrick-Rab, "Following Their Every Move: An Investigation of So-cial-Class Differences in College Pathways," *Sociology of Education* 79, no. 1 (2006): 61–79; Grigsby, *College Life*; Massey, Charles, Lundy, and Fischer, *The Source of the River*; Mullen, *Degrees of Inequality*; Stevens, *Creating a Class*.

29. Bruce Sacerdote found that randomly assigned roommates at Dartmouth af-fected each other's GPA. See his article "Peer Effects with Random Assignment: Results for Dartmouth Roommates," *Quarterly Journal of Economics* 116, no. 2 (2001): 681–704.

30. Moffatt, *Coming of Age in New Jersey*, 28. Social scientists have repeatedly called for an increased focus on student experiences outside the classroom: Kenneth A. Feld-man and Theodore M. Newcomb, *The Impact of College on Students* (San Francisco: Jossey-Bass, 1969); Kuh, "The Other Curriculum"; Pascarella and Terenzini, *How Col-lege Affects Students*. Despite this, remarkably few sociological studies, outside of the few ethnographies of student life, have paid much attention to student learning in extracur-ricular and social settings.

3. Choosing

1. That students often select courses with short-term goals in mind has been widely recognized, though the consequences of this kind of behavior for their majors and fu-ture careers have usually been ignored. Students' "decisions are indeed based on personal preferences, but student perspectives are often exceedingly myopic and focused on short-term gains, understood as increased freedom from strenuous academic effort" (Arum and Roksa, *Academically Adrift*, 76). "Around registration time, there is a spate of information exchanges concerning professors and courses and centering on workload . . . A definite theme that emerged in these student-to-student recommendations was an affirmation of 'easy' courses" (Small, *My Freshman Year*, 114). See also Blum, *My Word!*

2. For research on self-assessed ability in academic fields, and particularly how this pertains to gender, see Shelley J. Correll, "Gender and the Career Choice Process: The Role of Biased Self-Assessments," *American Journal of Sociology* 106, no. 6 (2001): 1691–1730; Correll, "Constraints into Preferences: Gender, Status, and Emerging Career As-pirations," *American Sociological Review* 69, no. 1 (2004): 93–113.

3. We have chosen not to use the acronym "STEM" (science, technology, engineer-ing, and mathematics) here, as STEM traditionally includes fields of study not offered at the college. The college lacks engineering classes and an engineering major, and also offers no technology major aside from computer science. Further, the college includes psychology among its sciences, which is not the case in many other institutions. Instead of STEM, we here simply refer to the "sciences," and separately, mathematics. However, many of our findings regarding the sciences and mathematics are directly related to national discussions of STEM fields.

4. We did find evidence of the gender segregation in the sciences that has been widely reported in research on higher education: Maria Charles and Karen Bradley, "Equal But Separate? A Cross-National Study of Sex Segregation in Higher Edu-cation," *American Sociological Review* 67 (2002): 573–599; Maria Charles and Karen

Bradley, "Indulging Our Gendered Selves? Sex Segregation by Field of Study in 44 Countries," *American Journal of Sociology* 114 (2009): 924–976; Jerry A. Jacobs, "The Sex Segregation of Fields of Study: Trends during the College Years," *Journal of Higher Education* 67 (1986): 134–154; Jacobs, "Gender and Academic Specialties: Trends among Recipients of College Degrees in the 1980s," *Sociology of Education* 68 (1995): 81–89; Jacobs, "Gender Inequality in Higher Education," *Annual Review of Sociology* 22 (1986): 153–185; Karen Bradley, "The Incorporation of Women into Higher Education: Paradoxical Outcomes?" *Sociology of Education* 80 (2000): 1–18. At the college, female students were generally as likely to major in the sciences as male students (a trend that does not persist at the national level), but for non–science majors, females were far less likely than men to take nonmajor elective classes in the sciences. Research on gender segregation by field of study has almost entirely focused on students' majors. Little attention has been paid to differences in whether male and female students who don't major in the sciences take science classes as nonmajor electives.

5. In *How College Affects Students*, Pascarella and Terenzini provide an excellent overview of the literature that generally supports the existence of a relationship between high levels of student-faculty interaction and positive student outcomes.

6. For an excellent book on the topic of college teaching, see Ken Bain, *What the Best College Teachers Do* (Cambridge: Harvard University Press, 2004).

7. The importance of the first quarter/semester experience, especially for retention, has been stressed throughout the literature. We would add simply that students can mentally drop out while remaining physically in attendance. See especially Astin, *What Matters in College*; Tinto, *Leaving College*.

8. Katherine Kroleski, "The Creation of Meaningful Relationships between Students and Professors" (Senior thesis, Hamilton College, 2009).

9. The same logic that applies to the process of making friends, discussed in Chapter 2, applies to finding a mentor—to develop the relationship, the people involved must meet in the first place. See Hallinan, "Structural Effects on Children's Friendships and Cliques"; Lazarsfeld and Merton, "Friendship as Social Process"; Newcomb, "The General Nature of Peer Group Influence"; Oldenburg, *The Great Good Place*; Small, *Unanticipated Gains*. Furthermore, the intensity of the activity (such as in labs, classroom discussions, office hours, and collaborative research) and the repetition of interaction (weekly classes, office hours) affect the development of the mentoring relationship. See Collins, *Interaction Ritual Chains*; Feld, "The Focused Organization of Social Ties."

10. Most literature on students' choice of major focuses on correlations between student background (for example, gender or social class) and their major. Our approach is, instead, to examine not just *who* picks a major, but *how*. In *Degrees of Inequality*, Mullen takes a similar approach.

11. Choice of major has generally been found to affect post-college careers and income, but the degree to which it matters may vary according to institution type. Mark C. Berger, "Predicted Future Earnings and Choice of College Major," *Industrial and Labor Relations Review* 41, no. 3 (1988): 418–429; Donna Bobbit-Zeher, "The Gender

Income Gap and the Role of Education," *Sociology of Education* 80 (2007): 1–22; Anthony P. Carnevale, Jeff Srtohl, and Michelle Melton, *What's It Worth? The Economic Value of College Majors* (Washington, D.C.: Georgetown University Center on Education and the Workforce, 2011); John Robst, "Education and Job Match: The Relatedness of College Major and Work," *Economics of Education Review* 26 (2007): 397–407; Josipa Roksa, "Double Disadvantage or Blessing in Disguise? Understanding the Relationship between College Major and Employment Sector," *Sociology of Education* 78 (2005): 207–232; Russell W. Rumberger and Scott L. Thomas, "The Economic Returns to College Major, Quality, and Performance: A Multilevel Analysis of Recent Graduates," *Economics of Education Review* 12, no. 1 (1993): 1–19; Scott L. Thomas and Liang Zhang, "Post-Baccalaureate Wage Growth Within 4 Years of Graduation: The Effects of College Quality and College Major," *Research in Higher Education* 46, no. 4 (2005): 437–459.

12. The literature on how students select their majors has ignored the consequences of students' course selection on their choice of major, despite the obvious fact that majors are, essentially, collections and sequences of courses. Christopher G. Takacs and Daniel F. Chambliss, "Local Decision Making in College Students' Selection of Major" (paper presented at the American Sociological Association Annual Meeting, Denver, Colorado, August 20, 2012).

13. Nearly a quarter of male students at the college were "committed before college" to a certain major, often a career-driven "preprofessional" major such as economics, government, or biology. These students fit the model, laid out in some of the literature, of students selecting their major as an investment. Peter Arcidiacono, V. Joseph Hotz, and Songman Kang, "Modeling College Major Choices Using Elicited Measures of Expectations and Counterfactuals," *Journal of Econometrics* 116 no. 1: 3–16 (2012); Richard K. Celuba and Jerry Lopes, "Determinants of Student Choice of Undergraduate Major Field," *American Educational Research Journal* 19, no. 2 (1982): 303–312; Henry Sauerman, "Vocational Choice: A Decision Making Perspective," *Journal of Vocational Behavior* 66 (2005): 273–303; Michael B. Tannen, "The Investment Motive for Attending College," *Industrial and Labor Relations Review* 31, no. 4 (1978): 489–497. Most of the rest of the students—the remaining males, and most of the females—didn't fit the investor mold whatsoever, and instead followed the much more contingent, localized path of decision making that we describe here. Notably, if similar gendered patterns are found elsewhere, they may help explain gender differences in major selection. Maria Charles and Karen Bradley, "Equal But Separate? A Cross-National Study of Sex Segregation in Higher Education," *American Sociological Review* 67 (2002): 573–599; Jerry A. Jacobs, "The Sex Segregation of Fields of Study."

14. See Herbert A. Simon, "Rational Choice and the Structure of the Environment," *Psychological Review* 63 (1956): 129–138; James G. March and Herbert A. Simon, *Organizations* (New York: John Wiley and Sons, 1958).

15. See Howard S. Becker, "Notes on the Concept of Commitment," *American Journal of Sociology* 66 (1960): 32–44.

4. The Arithmetic of Engagement

1. In the worst cases, students and faculty form what George Kuh has called a "disengagement compact," where each effectively agrees not to give the other too much work. See George Kuh, "What We're Learning about Student Engagement," *Change* 35, no. 2 (2003): 24–32. Also see Arum and Roksa, *Academically Adrift*, for an excellent discussion of this problem.

2. For a summary of this literature see Pascarella and Terenzini, *How College Affects Students*, 94–95.

3. Here lies the appeal of online courses.

4. Blum observed that a general precondition for student intellectualism and intellectual exchange is shared knowledge of a given topic. See Blum, *My Word!*

5. Notably, a core curriculum can serve the same purpose, though at considerable cost.

6. See Hallinan, "Structural Effects on Children's Friendships and Cliques."

5. Belonging

1. For more on the types of students and student cultures that typically populate college campuses, see Grigsby, *College Life*; Horowitz, *Campus Life*; Burton R. Clark and Martin Trow, "The Organizational Context," in *College Peer Groups*, ed. Theodore Newcomb and Everett K. Wilson (Chicago: Aldine, 1966) 17–70.

2. Astin, *What Matters in College*; Mary J. Fischer, "Settling into Campus Life: Differences by Race/Ethnicity in College Involvement and Outcomes," *Journal of Higher Education* 78, no. 2 (2007): 125–160; Tinto, *Leaving College*.

3. Blum, *My Word!*; Horowitz, *Campus Life*; Moffatt, *Coming of Age in New Jersey*.

4. Horowitz, *Campus Life*; John R. Thelin, *A History of American Higher Education* (Baltimore: Johns Hopkins University Press, 2004).

5. See Chapter 6 in this volume, as well as Pascarella and Terenzini, *How College Affects Students*.

6. Emile Durkheim, *The Elementary Forms of Religious Life*, trans. Karen E. Fields (New York: The Free Press, 1995 [1912]).

7. Collins, *Interaction Ritual Chains*. See also, for discussion of how this influences intellectualism, Collins, *The Sociology of Philosophies: A Global Theory of Intellectual Change* (Cambridge: Belknap, 1998).

8. See also the work of Scott Feld for more on the importance of focus. Feld, "The Focused Organization of Social Ties"; Feld, "The Structural Determinants of Similarity among Associates"; Feld, "The Structured Use of Personal Associates."

9. See Umbach and Wawrznski, "Faculty Do Matter."

10. Newcomb, "The General Nature of Peer Group Influence," 7.

11. Ibid., 8; emphasis added.

12. As Susan Blum puts it, the residentiality of college life encourages a "collaboration ethic" in which "working around others is the norm." Blum, *My Word!*, 68. See also Small, *My Freshman Year*, 57.

13. Amy J. Binder and Kate Wood, *Becoming Right: How Campuses Shape Young Conservatives* (Princeton: Princeton University Press, 2013).

14. For an excellent description of the college "bubble" see Blum, *My Word!* For discussion of how this influences students' political views and expression, see Binder and Wood, *Becoming Right.*

15. Armstrong and Hamilton, *Partying and Privilege.*

16. Sociologist Erving Goffman wrote about "total institutions," in which the entire life of "inmates" was controlled and encompassed by the institution—prisons, mental institutions, boarding schools—but for Goffman, these were typically coercive, involuntary settings. The residential college is a kind of voluntary total institution. See Erving Goffmann, *Asylums: Essays on the Social Situation of Mental Patients and Other Inmates* (New York: Anchor Books, 1961). Blum also characterizes residential colleges as total institutions: Blum, *My Word!* 105–107.

17. Students' friendship networks are quite individualized; Cathy Small has called them "ego-centric." Unlike the typical clique structure of high school, where two friends share the same friends, in college, "one student's network, although it may overlap with those of others, is essentially personal"—a unique set of multiple organizations and classes, each peculiar to an individual. Small, *My Freshman Year,* 56.

18. Mark Granovetter, "The Strength of Weak Ties," *American Journal of Sociology* 78 (1973): 1360–1380; Mark Granovetter, *Getting a Job: A Study of Contacts and Careers* (Cambridge: Harvard University Press, 1974).

19. See Mario Small's book *Unanticipated Gains* for a discussion of how organizations broker networks.

20. A technical description of the methods used to create this figure from our data follows here. In Figure 5.1, each activity (the nodes) is treated as being affiliated (tied to each other) if they share one or more students who participate in both activities. Ties were weighted according to the number of overlapping students participating in activities. For example, if five students participated in both football and the college radio station, football would have a tie weighted 5 with radio. This weight would then be visualized on the figure as a thicker line. We collected data on students' participation in extracurricular activities, athletics, majors, and Greek-letter societies during the panel study interviews, and compiled them into a single database of student activities. From this, we created an "edgelist"—a matrix of associations between extracurriculars—that can then be used by network analysis software. We then used cluster analysis, which attempts to mathematically determine what groups "best fit" together according to the patterns of network ties. We ran several different kinds of cluster analysis, but consistently found one large, highly interconnected cluster and several peripheral clusters. Keep in mind that visualizations such as these are meant merely as ways of presenting data to enable us to better see associations that might otherwise be hidden in other kinds of data (in our case, thousands of pages of interview transcripts). The figure itself is not the analysis. The *interpretation of* the figure is the analysis. As such, it is appropriate to describe how to (and how not to) interpret the figure. The particular location of any one node in relation to any other particular node in its

cluster, and any one of the peripheral clusters in relation to any other peripheral cluster, is effectively arbitrary. What matters far more is which activities are clustered with which other activities, and which activities they are not grouped with. For example, it is not important that crew is located closer to the core than swimming (lower right peripheral cluster)—their location in this particular cluster is effectively arbitrary. What *is* important is that both crew and public policy are located in the same cluster, that this cluster is not the core cluster, and that the peripheral cluster to which they belong does not include a host of other activities in it. For our purposes here, what is most important is that the figure confirmed several of the suspicions we developed through reading interview transcripts about some activities being peripheral and somewhat isolated from the "cultural core" of campus. Further, it demonstrated to us what activities, in particular, were peripheral, and which belonged to the core, which helped us to better determine the reasons *why* some activities were core and some peripheral. These two datasets were analyzed using Ucinet (S. P. Borgatti, M. G. Everett, and L. C. Freeman, *UCINET For Windows: Software For Social Network Analysis* [Lexington, KY: Analytic Technologies, 2002]) and visualized using NetDraw (S. P. Borgatti, *Net-Draw: Graph Visualization Software* [Lexington, KY: Analytic Technologies, 2002]). More information on core and periphery structures in network analysis can be found in Stephen P. Borgatti and Martin G. Everett, "Models of Core/Periphery Structures" (*Social Networks* 23 (1999): 375–395).

21. See Armstrong, Hamilton, and Sweeney, "Sexual Assault on Campus."

22. As Erving Goffman would say in this context.

23. Though Smelser didn't describe parties in his book on social odysseys, some of what we discuss here fits his description. See Neil J. Smelser, *The Odyssey Experience: Physical, Social, Psychological, and Spiritual Journeys* (Berkeley, CA: University of California Press, 2009).

24. David Grazian beautifully described at length the "pregaming" scene at a large university in his ethnography of urban college nightlife. David Grazian, *On the Make* (Chicago: University of Chicago Press, 2008).

25. Ibid.

26. Admittedly, for some, consuming alcohol, and getting drunk, is the end goal of parties, and even of social activity in general in college. See Seaman, *Binge.*

27. For a description of ritual dance and eroticism, see Collins, *Interaction Ritual Chains.*

28. Georg Simmel, "The Sociology of Sociability," trans. Everett C. Hughes, *American Journal of Sociology* 55, no. 3 (1949): 254–261.

29. Reflecting a different dynamic, many minority students and international students reported not feeling as much a part of the college community as they perceived their white American peers to be. For more on the consequences of this, see Charles, Fischer, Mooney, and Massey, *Taming the River*; Massey, Charles, Lundy, and Fischer, *The Source of the River*; Small and Winship, "Black Students' Graduation from Elite Colleges."

30. For research on the costs of romantic relationships in college, see Bogle, *Hooking Up*; Gilmartin, "The Centrality and Costs of Heterosexual Romantic Love"; Holland and Eisenhart, *Educated in Romance*; Laura Hamilton and Elizabeth A. Armstrong, "Gendered Sexuality in Young Adulthood: Double Binds and Flawed Options," *Gender & Society* 2 (2009): 589–616.

31. Horowitz, *Campus Life*.

32. Benedict Anderson, *Imagined Communities: Reflections on the Origin and Spread of Nationalism* (London: Verso, 1983).

33. Armstrong and Hamilton, *Paying for the Party*.

6. Learning

1. At the institutional level, sociologists have debated for at least forty years whether higher education as an industry is primarily a reproducer of social class (as Bourdieu argues), a setting for building networks, a site for fostering personal development and human capital, an incubator for a power elite, a sieve for sorting people into stratified layers, a temple for legitimating knowledge, a hub where various institutional sectors come together, or a combination of some or all of these. See Pierre Bourdieu, "Cultural Reproduction and Social Reproduction," in *Knowledge, Education, and Cultural Change: Papers in the Sociology of Education*, ed. Richard K. Brown (London: Tavistock, 1973) 56–68; Pierre Bourdieu and J. P. Passerson, *Reproduction in Education, Society and Culture*, 2nd ed. (Beverly Hills: Sage Publications, 1990); Mitchell L. Stevens, Elizabeth A. Armstrong, and Richard Arum, "Sieve, Incubator, Temple, Hub: Empirical Advances in the Sociology of Higher Education," *Annual Review of Sociology* 34 (2008); 127–151.

2. Though Armstrong and Hamilton show that in important cases—sheer time for school work vs. sorority obligations—they can indeed be mutually exclusive. See Armstrong and Hamilton, *Partying and Privilege*.

3. Astin, *What Matters in College*; Tinto, *Leaving College*.

4. See Arum and Roksa, *Academically Adrift*; Pascarella and Terenzini, *How College Affects Students*.

5. See the work of K. Anders Ericsson and his colleagues on deliberate practice. K. Anders Ericsson, Ralf Th. Krampe, and Clemens Tesch-Romer, "The Role of Deliberate Practice in the Acquisition of Expert Performance," *Psychological Review* 100, no. 3 (1993): 363–406.

6. Daniel F. Chambliss, "The Mundanity of Excellence: An Ethnographic Report on Stratification and Olympic Swimmers," *Sociological Theory* 7, no. 1 (1989): 70–86.

7. See forthcoming research from the Wabash National Study of Liberal Arts Education by Charles F. Blaich and Kathleen S. Wise.

8. Robert K. Merton, "The Matthew Effect in Science: The Reward and Communication Systems of Science Are Considered," *Science* 159 (1968): 55–63.

9. Arum and Roksa, *Academically Adrift*, 36.

10. See George Farkas, review of *Academically Adrift: Limited Learning on College Campuses*, by Richard Arum and Josipa Roksa, *American Journal of Sociology* 117, no. 3 (2011): 1000–1002.

11. Arum and Roksa, *Academically Adrift*, 56.

12. See forthcoming research from the Wabash National Study of Liberal Arts Education by Charles F. Blaich and Kathleen S. Wise. For further discussion of values, see Pascarella and Terenzini, *How College Affects Students*.

13. Psychology is an arguable case, regarded by students at least as more of a social science.

14. See Shelley J. Correll, "Gender and the Career Choice Process"; Correll, "Constraints into Preferences."

15. Mullen also found that students' status evaluations of majors mattered, and that it matters more to men than to women. See Mullen, *Degrees of Inequality*.

16. We would also note that women, more flexible in their responses to academics, were also generally more satisfied with their overall experience at the college.

17. Researchers have also found that the support departments provide to students matters, and may help explain why women tend to avoid the sciences. See James C. Hearn and Susan Olzak, "The Role of College Major Departments in the Reproduction of Sexual Inequality," *Sociology of Education* 54 (1981): 195–205.

18. James Downey, *The Study Abroad Program at Hamilton College: A Report for the Mellon Assessment Project*, 2004.

19. See Smelser, *The Odyssey Experience*.

20. Downey, *The Study Abroad Program at Hamilton College*.

7. Finishing

1. Pascarella and Terenzini, *How College Affects Students*, 211.

2. See John Mirowsky and Catherine E. Ross, *Education, Social Status, and Health* (New York: Aldine de Gruyter, 2003).

3. See Pascarella and Terenzini, *How College Affects Students*, 2005, 263.

4. The research literature is quite clear that peer effects can be positive or negative, depending on how students relate. Having academically successful friends can be demotivational for students who are not themselves successful, but having a group of ambitious and hopeful friends can be motivating and helpful. Notably, the influence of peers may differ depending on how "peers" are defined—whether friends and close ties are studied, or whether the entire student body is considered. Antonio, "The Influence of Friendship Groups"; Thomas, "Ties That Bind."

5. Mitchell Stevens describes how this occurs at a similar institution. Mitchell Stevens, *Creating a Class*.

6. Blum, *My Word!*

7. Arum, Budig, and Roksa, "The Romance of College Attendance."

8. Bowen and Bok, *The Shape of the River*; Pascarella and Terenzini, *How College Affects Students*.

8. Lessons Learned

1. See Daniel F. Chambliss, "Hiring Departmental Faculty," American Sociological Association, http://www.asanet.org/teaching/white_papers_and_web_links.cfm.

2. When Dan Chambliss's stepdaughter moved into her freshman dorm at Fordham University, she and her three roommates were welcomed first by a priest who lived in the dorm, and then later by a youngish man carrying a baby. "My wife's a professor," he said. "We live downstairs." When he left the room, the young women exchanged sheepish, silent grins. Dorm life, we heard, was rather sedate.

3. Small, *My Freshman Year.*

4. And its strictly academic little brother, curriculum reform.

5. George D. Kuh, *High Impact Educational Practices* (Washington, D.C.: Association of American Colleges and Universities, 2008).

6. This is not to say that teachers can't improve; they can. See Daniel F. Chambliss, "Doing What Works: On The Mundanity of Excellence in Teaching," in *The Social Worlds of Higher Education*, ed. Bernice A. Pescosolido and Ronald Amizade (Thousand Oaks, CA: Sage, 1999) 419–434.

7. Arum, Budig, and Roksa, "The Romance of College Attendance."

8. Notably, the sample need not be huge. Though we sampled one hundred students for our study, in our relatively homogenous institution fewer might have been sufficient to achieve the "saturation" of findings suitable for a case study. For more on saturation sampling, see Small, *How Many Cases Do I Need?*

Acknowledgments

The Mellon Assessment Project at Hamilton College began in 1999 and continued until the completion of this book in 2013. It actively involved scores of researchers. Here we thank some of the many people who have helped along the way.

First, institutional support. This project was initiated and generously supported, for ten years, through four separate grants to Hamilton College from the Andrew W. Mellon Foundation. The Foundation made this project happen. They bear no responsibility for our conclusions—indeed, they actively encouraged our independence—but if there's anything of value here, the Foundation and its then Vice President Mary Pat McPherson, who oversaw the grants, deserve great credit.

At Hamilton College, then President Eugene M. Tobin and Dean of Faculty David Paris approached Dan Chambliss in 1999 and asked him to undertake this project. Their strong and ongoing support, over many years, has been truly extraordinary. Their commitment to the well-being of college students and courageous insistence on intellectual honesty in research on higher education has been an inspiration for our work.

In more recent years, Deans Joseph Urgo and Patrick Reynolds, and President Joan Hinde Stewart, have continued Hamilton's commitment to thoughtful and scientifically sound assessment. Without such support, needless to say, the project would not have been possible. In addition, Hamilton College has provided funding through a series of endowed professorships held by Dan Chambliss. Dan's colleagues in the Sociology Department, as well as Alfred Kelly in History, have provided a wonderful daily working environment and constant stimulation. Robin Vanderwall, the Sociology Department administrative assistant at Hamilton College, deserves special thanks for creatively managing many of Dan's professional responsibilities so that he could devote time to this project.

Our closest colleague over all the years has been Marcia Wilkinson, the project's administrative assistant. Marcia set up and ran project offices in three different locations; oversaw the work of dozens of student assistants; managed huge paper and electronic files of data, presentation graphics, and written reports; almost single-handedly organized and ran eight annual miniconferences for assessment researchers and practitioners; managed the financial affairs of the project, including payments to consultants and vendors; transcribed all 394 interviews of student panelists (whom she also kept track of); and—finally—handled all of the secretarial work for this book, including a half-dozen rough drafts, as well as a full two-hundred-page rough draft of a different (now defunct) book also based on the research. She managed all of this with uncompromising integrity and thoroughgoing attention to detail, while keeping the entire project on track through generous applications of firm, wise counsel, delivered with her trademark candor. ("I'm working on Chapter 3," Dan would say; "You'd better be," Marcia would reply.) Marcia's intelligence lies behind much of the work you see here. She did not actually write the words of this book, so no blame can be attached to her for its failings. But she deserves tremendous credit that it exists at all.

Next, the research itself. We are immensely indebted to the many students (especially panelists) and alumni of Hamilton College who consented to talk with us about their experiences, share with us papers they had written, and in many cases open their collegiate lives to our sometimes rather close scrutiny. Their generosity, repaid only by the occasional thank-you letter and $10 gift certificate for the campus coffee shop, made all of our work possible. We are grateful.

Much of our research in various forms—transcript analyses, study of videotapes, statistical analyses of survey databases, network graphings, focus-group meetings, compilation of course catalogs, etc.—was carried out as discrete projects by colleagues who deserve special mention: Leann Atkinson, Jennifer Borton, Matt Carr, Brian Cody, Sarah Damaske, Gene Domack, James Downey, Ted Eismeier, Tim Elgren, Ann Frechette, Kevin Grant, Katey Healy-Wurzburg, Jim Helmer, Gordon Hewitt, Tim Kelly, Phil Klinkner, Tara McKee, Ann Owen, Dan Ryan, Jr., Kaylene Stevens, Shauna Sweet, Kim Torres (multiple projects), Bijan Warner, and especially Sharon Williams, who oversaw the Writing Study (detailed in Chapter 6).

Most of the panel interviews were conducted by student research assistants, either in person or via telephone (for alumni interviews): Axtell Arnold, Leann Atkinson, Elizabeth Barrett, Dan Bleeker, Ryan Burke, Becky Conrey, Ciere Cornelius, Jenny Davis, Sarah Doane, James Downey, Joanna DuFour, Sarah Entenmann, Keith Foster, Jeremy Gleason, Kristen Hague, Lorena Hernandez, Paige Kaneb, Evan Klondar, Dale Ledbetter, Alexandra London, Cassandra Magesis, Chris Marcal, Tim Nelson, Katherine Northway, Lauren Perkins, Doreet Preiss, Jill Pugach, Samantha Rabin, Emma Racine, Kathryn Steck, Nate Stell, Kaylene Stevens, Shauna Sweet, Eliza Timpson, Erin Voyik, William Wieczorek. Four student assistants in particular were outstanding in obtaining high-quality interviews: Emma Leeds, Mallory Reed, Amy Schloerb, and Katie Yates.

A series of Faculty Working Groups formulated the operating principles of this project, conducted its first Alumni Interview Study, and shaped the course of our research. In addition to those already mentioned above, we thank Sally Cockburn, Todd

Franklin, Stuart Hirshfield, Betsy Jensen, Rob Kolb, and Edith Toegel. On numerous occasions, Andrea Habbel and, later, Gordon Hewitt saved us with their mastery of Institutional Research questions.

Colleagues around the country have been invaluable, some by providing detailed comments on written drafts, others by their generous flow of ideas and support over the years. Some of them certainly disagree with our approach and conclusions, but all have contributed to whatever useful may be found in these pages: Elizabeth A. Armstrong, Vige Barrie (a true mentor), Charles Blaich, Lee Cuba, George Farkas, Jerry Jacobs, Katherine McClelland, Richard O'Connor, Diane Pike, Josipa Roksa, Jim Rosenbaum, Dan Ryan, Jr., Dave Smallen, Mitchell Stevens, Carol Trosset, Steve Weisler, Robert Zussman, and six anonymous reviewers from Harvard University Press.

For the past five years, our work has benefitted considerably from Chris's colleagues and mentors at the University of Chicago. Kristen Schilt provided comprehensive and extremely helpful comments at a critical moment in the writing process. Discussions with Andrew Abbott, Mario Small, and Ryon Lancaster provided insights into areas ripe for sociological explanation, while Jim Leitzel provided helpful comments on several sections of the book. Research and writing also benefitted from discussions with Emily Art, Michael Corey, Jan Doering, Laura Doering, Monica Lee, Katherine Lewandowski, John Levi Martin, Abi Ocobock, John Padgett, Phil Redman, and from several of Chris's undergraduate peers: Dan Bleeker, Alan Clark, Daniel Klag, Alexandra Sear, Benjamin Turner, and Dan Walker.

An enjoyable conversation with the Polytechnic Institute of New York University President Jerry Hultin provided insight into the feasibility of many of our book's suggestions.

We would also like to thank the faculty and students of the various colleges and universities where portions of this research have been presented.

Our colleague and friend Mitchell Stevens has a special place in these acknowledgments for having introduced our work to Elizabeth Knoll, executive editor-at-large for Harvard University Press. Elizabeth has been a gift to our work: supportive from the beginning, incisively intelligent on the key issues, understanding of our delays—but stern enough, when needed, for us to get the job done. This was the press and the editor we wanted.

Chris especially thanks his parents, William and Donna Takacs, for their unwavering support, guidance, and encouragement. Chris would also like to thank his friends and family for their continued love and support, without which he never would have continued to follow his dreams. Dan thanks his family, especially his brother Thom, who loves books in general and has nurtured this one in particular. Lawton Harper remains a steadfast ally through thick and thin. Most importantly, Susan Morgan has lived with this work from the beginning, as sometimes a blessing and often a shared burden. Her love and support are priceless.

Finally, the cliché bears repeating: none of these people are responsible for what we say here; indeed, many openly disagree with us. For the good parts, they deserve much credit. For everything else, we deserve all the blame.

Index